Praise for *Life-Changing* V

"The best teachers somehow magically inspire you from the inside. This wonderful guide shows you how the magic is performed."

—Jonathan Foust
Senior teacher and former president of Kripalu Center for Yoga & Health. Author of *Energy Awareness Meditations*, and *Body-Centered Inquiry*

"As I've experienced directly myself, good workshops are powerful ways to heal and grow, but until this ground-breaking book, there was no comprehensive guide to creating and leading them. What a masterful, thorough, encouraging, and *useful* book! With specific tips, heartfelt support, respect for the diversity of teachers and participants, and practical troubleshooting for any issues that arise, this book is full of value for both beginner and experienced workshop teachers. What a gem!"

—Rick Hanson, PhD
Author of *Buddha's Brain, Hardwiring Happiness*, and other books—and has been leading workshops for 45 years

"*Designing & Leading Life-Changing Workshops is* a beautifully written and masterful guidebook that eloquently shows how to *embody* the skills we so wish to impart—a challenge for even the most seasoned leader. Profound and practical, this seminal work reveals the road all leaders must travel to create inspiring, stimulating, and life-changing learning environments. A must-read for all leaders."

—Richard Miller, PhD
Founder of iRest Institute and author of *iRest Meditation: Restorative Practices for Health, Resiliency, and Well-Being* and *Yoga Nidra: A Meditative Practice for Deep Relaxation and Healing*

"An inspiring and practical guide to creating transformational group experiences that enable us to connect, grow, and heal. A valuable addition to the field."

—Lisa Nelson, MD
Family physician and Director of Medical Education for Kripalu Center for Yoga & Health

"This evergreen 'manual' offers potent practices to help you hone your craft, create transformational space, and produce powerful learning experiences that change lives. Whether you are a new or seasoned leader, you'll garner practical tools and techniques to share your knowledge, experience, wisdom, and story in service of the development of others. I've been leading workshops for over 25 years, and I will surely return to this book for inspiration for years to come."

—Jillian Pransky
Author of *Deep Listening: A Healing Practice to Calm Your Body, Clear Your Mind, and Open Your Heart*

"With a wonderful blend of real-life stories, hard-won wisdom, and soulful science, *Life-Changing Workshops* weaves a gift to the world. If you care about transformation—for yourself, for others, or for our world—read this book. Allow its gentle message to wash over you; it will energize your spirit, enliven your mind, and enhance your life."

—David Fessell, MD
Author, coach, speaker, and professor of radiology, University of Michigan, Ann Arbor

# DESIGNING & LEADING

# Life-Changing Workshops

Creating the Conditions for Transformation
in Your Groups, Trainings, and Retreats

Ken Nelson, David Ronka, Lesli Lang
with Liz Korabek-Emerson and Jim White

**CLIFFHOUSE PRESS**

Kittery Point, Maine

Cover and interior design by Carole Allen Design Studio
Graphics by David Ronka and Lesli Lang with appreciation to Sonia P. and Amir S.
Body text in Adobe Garamond Pro
v1.0


ISBN-13: 978-1-7320033-0-9

*This book is dedicated to the
participants, guests, staff, and teachers
at Kripalu Center for Yoga & Health,
a leader in holistic workshops
for nearly 50 years.*

# Table of Contents

# Foreword

*H*igh on a promontory in the Berkshire Hills of western Massachusetts sits a massive red-brick building that dominates the landscape for miles around. "What in the world *is* that building?" one wonders upon first driving by it. It is simply impossible to ignore.

Look twice, and you will most likely guess that this 1950s brick fortress must be a Catholic monastery. It just must be. It screams, "I'm here—deal with it," and bears the mark of Catholic triumphalism. We've seen this architect's work all over the country, haven't we?

But don't be fooled. Yes, the building originally housed Catholic Jesuit novitiates, but that was many years ago. Now it's Kripalu Center for Yoga & Health—the largest yoga-based retreat center in the United States. 40,000 people a year come to this retreat center on the hill—looking for health, healing, wholeness, salvation. For nearly five decades, Kripalu has been a pilgrimage site for hundreds of thousands of contemporary pilgrims of all spiritual and religious stripes. They come searching for their souls, their bodies, their personalities, their most sublime aspirations. They come with questions. Who am I, really? What am I called to in this life? How can I connect with the deepest sources of human wisdom? How can I be a fully alive human being?

Here in our mountaintop retreat—in our now-wonderfully-converted Jesuit monastery—these modern-day pilgrims engage in two-, three-, or five-day workshops or month-long retreats with some of the world's top teachers in meditation, yoga, personal growth, and integrative health.

Each of these pilgrims is on a quest. Each of them has left the safety of their "normal" lives and routines—the so-called known world—and entered into a period of searching. The great Jungian psychologist Carol Pearson calls these seekers Wanderers.

But who are these people?

The Wanderer, says Pearson, is in search of her highest self. She intentionally sets out to confront the unknown, taking a journey that, as Pearson says, "marks the beginning of life lived at a new level." During their travels, "Wanderers find a treasure that symbolically represents the gift of their true selves."[1] And to find this gift, the Wanderer will suffer a deep reorganization of her life. Indeed, she will go to any lengths to find the Holy Grail that is a full life. The Wanderer sets off—usually alone—on the "road of trials." This road will offer her initiation into a kind of modern-day heroism.

The Wanderer archetype is embodied in the lives of saints and mystics throughout the ages—from the wandering shamans of ancient India to more contemporary Wanderers like Henry David Thoreau or Jack Kerouac.

These Wanderers—both ancient and modern—seek situations that provide the conditions for transformation. They are drawn toward situations that provide some auspicious combination of safety and challenge, freedom and discipline, known and unknown, security and adversity. They are drawn toward what I like to call Transformational Space.

And this is precisely what we provide at Kripalu—Transformational Space.

What is the character of this Transformational Space?

Well, it has a number of predictable qualities that I've written about at length in my books.

1. Transformational Space provides *refuge* for the seeker.

2. It encourages *creativity, experimentation*, and the acknowledgement that the self is plastic—*mutable*.

3. Transformational Space is organized around relationships and structures that are *constant* and *reliable*, but not dogmatic or doctrinaire.

4. It provides us with *techniques* to master our own transformation.

5. Transformational Space does not rigidly prescribe these techniques but is open to a wide array of them. It is quite *pluralistic*.

6. Transitional Space offers models—*exemplars of transformation*—who are flesh-and-blood human beings with whom we can interact directly.

It turns out that there is an art to creating Transformational Space, and the teachers and workshop leaders at Kripalu have been refining this art for nearly five decades.

*Life-Changing Workshops* captures the fruits of these four decades of experiential knowledge on paper for the first time. Ken Nelson and his team have brilliantly mined the wisdom of this art form and made it accessible to anyone who wishes to try his or her hand at recreating it in their own community.

The book you hold in your hands is a great gift. For many years, this wisdom tradition—Kripalu's tradition of experiential training—has been available only through a kind of apprentice system.

I myself participated in this apprentice system. When I arrived at Kripalu more than 30 years ago, I eagerly observed a generation of young men and women who had become masters in this art of creating Transformational Space and truly effective workshop experiences. I observed them at work. I observed them in their interactions with our contemporary pilgrims. And I watched the magic that ensued.

In those days, we had a kind of apprentice system, as I have said. We—the younger aspirants, the teachers-in-training—learned from the masters. We stuck our toes in the water of transformation. We tried our hands at offering our own workshops. We fell short of the mark. We got feedback. We tried again.

We began this process because we were inspired. Our inspiration moved us to imitate our teachers. Eventually, we introjected the lessons of the masters, and soon enough, these lessons became our own. We individuated our teachings. We found our own voice. We hit our own unique stride.

If you have picked up this book, it is likely that you have some inner longing to learn more about transformational teaching. Perhaps you are inspired, as I was. I am glad for you, because in my own experience, there is nothing more fulfilling than this work of creating Transformational Space.

Let me tell you one of the many important lessons that I have learned: There is something exhilarating about being a teacher and finding the willing student. The hungry student's longing—and even their desperation—draws forth your best instincts. You want to help. You learn that you *can* help. And so you *do* help. This is miraculous.

After apprenticing, I myself became a senior teacher in this Kripalu guild system. Early in my years of service at Kripalu, I had the privilege of encountering Ken Nelson, who arrived just as most others had: broken. But Ken was broken in the most auspicious way—he was ready to learn. His story is beautifully told at the beginning of this book.

Since then, Ken has himself become a master teacher and has gathered others to join in this work and in the creation of this book—Lesli Lang, David Ronka, Jim White, and Liz Korabek-Emerson. All of them bring decades of experience in creating Transformational Space within the fields of education, holistic health, government, the arts, and business. The world will be blessed to see the culmination of their collective journeys—a systematic map for others to follow into this wonderful, magical world of Transformational Space. In this exquisitely designed book, Ken and his team have captured lightning in a bottle. Please listen and learn!

> Stephen Cope
> Scholar Emeritus
> Kripalu Center for Yoga & Health
> January 2020

# Ken's Story

## Remember Who You Are!

**What has formed you? What difference do you want to make in the world? Ken's story shows how suffering can lead to greater self-awareness and a call to serve others. His story invites us to reflect on our own journeys of transformation and how they have shaped who we are as well as our purposes in life.**

*I* was in my early forties and had been a teacher, teacher educator, and director of a small international school. But despite outer success—winning teaching awards and grants to study and teach abroad—I was dying on the inside. I was missing a big chunk of myself, yet I didn't see myself as unhappy. My routine was comfortable, and I had no plans to change.

But life had other plans. My mother died suddenly in a car accident, triggering deep grief, a loss of faith in what I had been doing in the world, and an intense hunger for meaning. Each morning, I struggled to get up and drag myself to work. Then one day, I gave my notice. The job wasn't serving me, so I let it go. Then, expecting my wife to support me in my transition to a new, healthier career as I had for her, I got blindsided. Like every relationship, ours had flaws, but I didn't expect her to give me notice, leaving me for another man—a friend of ours. It felt like an earthquake under my feet. My familiar landscape loosened around me and crumbled. It was a dark, uncertain, messy, and terrifying time.

Before this, I didn't want change. Now, change wanted me. Home from my mother's funeral, my lower back hurt. A fog descended. I found no joy in music, swimming, books, tennis, gardening, golf, sailing, friends, and the things of my former life. Even the spiritual side of me that once drew me to yoga, qigong, meditation, and mystical traditions had dried up, leaving me empty and cold. While I had been a spiritual seeker in my younger days, what I had studied did not offer basic life skills for dealing with loss and transition. I had few coping strategies or psychological tools to manage the sudden and unbidden chaos of my world.

They say people change because they see the light or feel the pain. I wasn't seeing the light, but pain got my attention. My body rejected me. I felt like a complete stranger in my own skin. I was ambushed by colds, an achy lower back, sleepless nights, and fatigue. When I thought it couldn't get worse, I broke out in hives. The pain disarmed me. I came unglued. All I had was loss, grief, and defeat. I had come to the end of one way of being. But I hadn't found a new way forward. I had to listen to what life seemed to be saying.

It's hard to ask for help. But when everything—my wife, my career, my health—had turned away from me, I surrendered totally. Humbled, I turned to family to take me in. I went to live with my sister, her husband and their five girls, in their big house in Maryland. Their home, like the one we grew up in, was both loving and chaotic. There was a dog, guinea pigs, a stream of neighbor kids, carpools, ballet, violin, soccer, swimming lessons, giggling, bare feet running up the stairs, puking, and doo-doo. But sometimes a little one would fall asleep in my arms.

That cold winter, I slept in the family den, a dark and lonely cave at night. What I wanted most was to hibernate or disappear. But each morning, my two-year-old niece Jen Jen would bounce in, jump on my pullout bed, and wake me with her gap-toothed, happy-without-a-reason smile. When she tried to say my name, it came out "Bum Bum." So I became known as Uncle Bum Bum. No job. No home. Not a single bum. A double bum.

Each morning, Jen Jen greeted Bum Bum with, "Wanna wa Simba!" So, every morning we watched The Lion King and encountered the mystifying question of identity that challenged Simba: Who are you? The counsel he received? "Remember who you are!" Take your place "in the circle of life."

But my circle had collapsed, and I was a complete stranger to myself. From this place of emptiness and surrender, I set out alone, wandering like a pilgrim and visiting spiritual retreat centers, looking for a new home. But as the poet Rumi says, "What you seek is seeking you." As I was looking far and wide for a new beginning, a new beginning was looking for me. It showed up at my local studio where I practiced bodywork, yoga, qigong, and meditation. A new yoga teacher, Rakesh, arrived, and his yoga caught me by surprise. He began each practice by quoting the Buddha, "Oh Noble Ones, remember who you are!"

Just as I didn't know much about myself at that time, I didn't know one yoga style from another. I just followed the teacher as best I could—sweating and barely breathing until I was glad to be done. But Rakesh changed all that. "Breathe," he said, and I took the deepest breath I had taken in years. "Relax what you don't need. Let go of striving. No forcing. No holding back. Be steady and comfortable. Muscles relax when they feel safe. Being a C student is enough. Notice when you judge yourself, your body, your ability. Witness sensations arise and flow through you. Watch your own experience as it happens. Allow everything to be just as it is. Let it be!"

I was shocked. Isn't he going to criticize me and adjust my posture? Tell me to move my foot? What happened to the rules? What's going on? Am I still doing yoga?

But he was right! When I focused on form and technique, I obsessed about doing the posture correctly, seeking approval, fearing rejection. When I stopped imposing my will on my body, and exchanged thinking for feeling, my body was suddenly alive with sensation.

In the following months, Rakesh taught me a meditative practice with five steps—breathe, relax, feel, watch, allow. It allowed me to enter the present moment, without judgment or expectation. I began to appreciate how body and breath work together. Feelings awakened that I had not felt for a long time. Like being in a greenhouse, I could grow my connection to my mind-body in a protected place.

In my personal practice, I began to enter meditation-in-motion—the experience of posture flow and moving spontaneously by following my inner guide and riding the wave of experience. I would let myself feel the rising tide of sensation, stay on it, and surf the waves of my experience, not jumping off when the experience became too intense. After the postures, sitting in stillness, reconnecting, and paying attention to the moment became my new way of being.

Over time, I noticed the breath softening my heart. Deeper rhythms emerged that led to me accepting more of myself with less praise or blame, leading to more opening, greater ease, and more peace in my life.

Winter turned into the spring of 1996, and I'd realized I wanted to be a yoga teacher and help guide others on a journey of transformation. By grace, I was led to Rakesh's yoga teacher training community, Kripalu Center for Yoga & Health in the Berkshire Hills of western Massachusetts.

But when I arrived, Kripalu was in turmoil. The guru's misconduct had been uncovered, and he was forced to resign. The community was reeling. Kripalu's upheaval matched my own. With almost perfect symmetry, I found myself in a place shaken to the core, just as I was! I felt right at home in the chaos of this apparently dysfunctional family.

Yet the community had something I didn't have: skills and tools to cope with their own shattered lives. The residents were able to observe their anger, fear, and grief with compassion. This ability to compassionately witness guided them to bear the reality of betrayal and gain perspective—not by judging or overriding feelings, but by exploring them. They understood that when we're judging our experiences, we can't be fully in them. I found strength in how they met their own test. The results were not always pretty—sometimes messy—but they struggled on. And it gave me hope.

Kripalu survived the guru-paradigm meltdown. The patriarchal model was crumbling, and the residents were building a new intentional community based on integrity, presence, compassion, self-inquiry, service, and practice. It seemed to be just the fit for me. But I had another big surprise in store.

One day, after a deep breath-work experience in a workshop, my body felt tingly. I was shaken and must have looked as vulnerable as I felt. The leader came over to me and said, smiling, "You look just like a kid with a baseball cap." His words hit me in the chest and knocked me to my knees. In that moment, I relived the shock of being a 10-year-old boy who'd just lost his father. The words baseball cap triggered a huge release of grief. After my father died, my mother—overwhelmed with her own loss, and with five kids to care for—gave me a baseball glove, as if to say, "Go out and play." She did the best she could to comfort us by carrying on, trying to live a "normal" life, and hiding her sorrow. In that world, I never got a chance to grieve openly and mourn the loss of my dad.

Decades later, that intuitive leader and the accepting community around me helped me realize how much repressed grief had been trapped in my body. My mother's sudden death had triggered a deeper grief that set me on the path to healing. Incomplete mourning had waited 30 years for resolution, wanting to be seen, felt, and released—but only under the right conditions. I had to feel safe enough to experience my feelings in a community that could reflect the best in me and accept me as I was.

In the new Kripalu, I stepped into a new life, and my apprenticeship began in the spring of 1996. I found a community, a set of practices, and a view of life that drew me in and welcomed me to the center of it. I found embodied, flesh-and-blood leaders who were imperfect people but authentic models of compassion, skillfulness, and devotion, inspiring me to step into the role of leader myself. And it was this confluence of events that led me to discover my passion: helping others to lead workshops and retreats that are truly transformational.

You can read more about Ken Nelson in the About the Authors section of this book.

# Introduction

*If you want to help the world,
teach people how to live in it.*

—Joseph Campbell

ho has not felt alone and overwhelmed, tangled in a knot of suffering? How do we satisfy the need for belonging and fulfillment? How can we use our collective creative potential to relieve suffering and promote well-being? A student asked the Buddha, "Who can untangle this tangle?"[2] The answer in this book is to become more mindful and self-aware, and to create workshops where we can be conscious and kind together.

It took your whole life to get you here, so now what? What's calling you? When you're clear about your calling and have the right tools, you're in a powerful position to serve others. If you have an idea for a workshop, a passion that cannot be contained, or a sense that you have more to contribute on a larger stage, then this book is for you.

Our promise to you is that, no matter your profession or passion, this book will help you bring what you really love into the world in a way that invites people to learn, heal, grow, and awaken. This book is designed to help you understand yourself—that is, enhance self-awareness—while giving you a step-by-step guide to designing and leading life-changing workshops.

In our opening story, Ken finds a community, a view of life, and a set of practices that lead him to discover his passion and gifts. He learns how to help others craft workshops and retreats that are transformational. We'll return to Ken's story in Chapter 1.

How about you? What difference do you want to make in the world? Have you experienced your own transformation and want to share it with others?

As a workshop leader, we know you can move and inspire people by:

- Sharing your knowledge, experience, wisdom, and story to touch others.
- Expanding your reach from one-to-one interactions to group work.
- Bringing transformational mind-body experiences into your workshops.
- Being a more present, confident, and effective workshop leader.

We've trained thousands of people who wanted to make a difference by leading workshops, each person compelled by a vision they just couldn't ignore any longer. It doesn't matter what your line of work is. Leaders have come to our trainings from a wide range of fields. They've been therapists, professors, managers, health care professionals, civil servants, clergy, artists, yoga instructors, life coaches, lawyers, schoolteachers, and more. This book gives you the resources to weave life-changing workshops into your journey.

## ORIGIN OF THE BOOK

Our book began with the living connections we've made with thousands of workshop participants. We've seen what works and what doesn't by leading workshops, retreats, and trainings, and by coaching workshop leaders.[i]

For decades, our work has been crafted and tested in retreat centers, yoga studios, nonprofits, schools, businesses, government offices, universities, and other creative settings worldwide.

From this real-world experience, we know how to design and lead workshops that create the conditions for transformation.

The seed of our work grew from an in-house training for Kripalu workshop leaders in the 1990s called The Secrets of Powerful Experiential Workshops.[ii] We expanded

---

[i] Throughout the book, we use the term *workshop* to refer to any kind of group learning experience, including retreats, trainings, and seminars. We use *participants* as the general term to describe the individuals who participate in whatever group you serve.

[ii] Kripalu Center for Yoga & Health has been a field leader in yoga- and mindfulness-based education for more than 40 years. Located 2.5 hours north of New York City and west of Boston, in the Berkshires of

that program into a three-part training-the-trainer curriculum that became the basis for this book:

1. Creating Transformational Workshops: An Introduction to Mind-Body Learning

2. Designing and Leading Transformational Workshops: The Craft of Mind-Body Teaching

3. Facilitating Transformation Workshops: Group Dynamics and the Power of Presence

## THE NATURE OF THE WORK

This book is an open inquiry into our true nature, our relationship with others, and our life's mission. Our guiding principles are informed by ancient wisdom traditions, direct experience, and modern mind-body science. Perennial wisdom teaches that a deep sense of freedom is possible. Yoga, mindfulness meditation, and other forms of self-inquiry are practices that help us to see clearly and act kindly. Science has shown that change is possible at the biological, psychological, and neurological levels.

We've been inspired by great teachers, practitioners, and researchers in many traditions, including: Tara Brach, Brené Brown, Pema Chödrön, Stephen Cope, the 14th Dalai Lama, Jonathan Foust, Joseph Goldstein, Dan Goleman, Thich Nhat Hanh, Rick Hanson, John Heron, Jean Houston, Dale Hunter, Roger Jahnke, Sam Kaner, Byron Katie, Thomas Keating, Robert Kegan, Jack Kornfield, Swami Kripalu, Joanna Macy, Kelly McGonigal, Richard Miller, Thomas Merton, Parker Palmer, Stephen Porges, Richard Rohr, Dan Siegel, David Whyte, Ken Wilber, Marion Woodman, and others. A common theme in their teachings is that humans can grow and transform, and

> *" Understanding my identity is the first and crucial step in finding new ways to teach: nothing I do differently as a teacher will make any difference to anyone if it is not rooted in my nature. "*
>
> —Parker Palmer

---

western Massachusetts, Kripalu is the largest retreat center in North America, offering hundreds of programs and workshops with world-class teachers and presenters on topics that cover mind, body, and spiritual health. For information about Kripalu, please visit www.kripalu.org.

that we can know ourselves as complete and wakeful beings through a variety of disciplines and practices.

Our primary method is self-inquiry. It is not a creed. People from all backgrounds report profound experiences and remarkable breakthroughs in mind and body through a nonsectarian approach that relies on self-acceptance and self-awareness. As Teilhard de Chardin said, "We need to have more specialists in spirit who will lead people into self-discovery." Offering workshops is a powerful way to do this.

## HOW THE BOOK IS ORGANIZED

Our book is divided into three parts and includes a conclusion and appendices. Below are the questions that we explore in each section.

## Part I: Transformation

- What is transformation, and how do people learn, heal, grow, and awaken?
- Why are self-awareness and presence so important in transformation?
- What makes a workshop life changing?
- How do wisdom traditions and mind-body science inform this work?

## Part II: Designing Your Workshop

- How does your life experience help you design a workshop that is an authentic expression of who you are?
- How do you create powerful learning experiences that change lives?
- How can you make sure your workshop is inclusive of all learners?
- How can you be sensitive to the stages of group formation?

## Part III: Leading Your Workshop

- How is being present the most important skill you can develop for leading transformational workshops?
- How do you deliver your content while still managing the group dynamics?
- How do you co-create a safe environment that invites full participation?
- How can you learn to respond skillfully to challenges, upsets, and obstacles?

## Conclusions

- How can you support yourself to be a better leader and sustain your work over time?

- How can offering transformational workshops help you make a bigger impact in the world?
- How do you get people to come to your workshops? What resources and tools can you use right away?

Additionally, there are three appendices to help you explore further:

- Appendix A is a brief overview of the research and theory behind mind-body learning.
- Appendix B offers a view toward trauma-informed workshops.
- Appendix C includes practical resources, such as checklists and worksheets.

Notes that provide additional or clarifying information are included as footnotes throughout the book and are numbered as Roman numerals (e.g., i, ii, iii, iv). Citations are included as endnotes so as not to interrupt the flow, with the exception of Appendix A and Appendix B, where they are included as footnotes.

## HOW TO GET THE MOST FROM THIS BOOK

This book offers guidelines and practices. It's not prescriptive or comprehensive. Rules and models will only take you so far—you have to make it your own. This work is deeply personal, and it invites you to do your own transformative work, because *who you are* is more important than *what you teach*.

We'll engage you experientially with:

- real-life stories from workshop leaders
- exercises, self-assessments, and guided meditations to hone your workshop design and leadership skills
- journal prompts for reflection on how to apply it to your own work
- graphics and illustrations to make concepts come alive
- tools you can use right away in your workshops

*Life-Changing Workshops* is a guide and a go-to reference for the transformational workshop leader. Parts II and III can be read in either order. For free downloads of the Appendix C resources, visit: www.life-changingworkshops.com.

Offering workshops is a path of self-discovery that unfolds out of your own sincerity and openness. We hope this book is a useful companion on your quest to serve others.

# Part I

# Transformation

*My boat struck something deep.*
*Nothing happened.*
*Sound, silence, waves,*
*Nothing happened.*
*Or perhaps everything happened*
*and I'm sitting in the middle of my new life.*

—Juan Ramón Jiménez

# Erica's Story

## Letting Go of Striving

In Part I, we'll explore transformation as a path to freedom through self-inquiry—not as a self-improvement project, but as a creative and integrative process of transcending and including what came before. In Erica's story, an internal voice challenges her worldview, and an encouraging workshop leader helps her pay attention, soften self-judgment, and begin—finally—to accept herself as she is.

*I*n 2007, I received the message. I awoke one August morning and looked around my room. Everything appeared to be different, but nothing had visibly changed in any way. I heard a voice inside my head. It said, quite clearly, *Your life will never be the same.* I had no idea what that meant. Nothing changed in the ensuing weeks, but I couldn't forget that moment. I was 35 years old. I had three small children. I lived in the suburbs of New Jersey. And I desperately needed to start living life.

Until that point, I had lived a life of earnest striving. I had learned from family, school, and American culture that life was about achieving success. The word on the street was that *success* meant getting into an Ivy League college (check), getting a job in business, law, or medicine (check), getting married to the "right" type of person (check), and having children and a house and the right "stuff" (check).

Deep inside, I had a desire to be the best person I could be and to make the most out of this life. But what I felt most of the time was a nagging sense of failure and an inability to find peace. Despite all my academic and work-related achievements, I lived in a low-grade panic that I wasn't living up to the very high standard that I had created for myself. Every mistake or bump in the road felt like utter failure. An internal voice took hold and berated me on a daily basis. If I tripped on a curb, I would hear, *You idiot! Watch where you're going!* When I couldn't get my son to eat vegetables, I felt like I'd failed as a mother. I thought that if I could just get everything right, I would find peace and be happy.

But underneath it all, there was a quiet voice, always whispering, *This isn't your life. This isn't your path.* I was too afraid to really listen; that is, until that warm August morning in 2007. Two months after "the message" (*Your life will never be the same*), I attended a workshop with teacher Frank Jude Boccio. It was there that I first heard the concept of being present and aware.

I had been practicing yoga for nine years, but these ideas were foreign to me. My yoga practice had been guided by a school of thought that was right up my alley—focusing on precision, intense effort, and aiming for the ideal pose. I had heard intermittent admonitions from teachers throughout the years, babbling something about "practicing my own yoga" or "honoring where my body was at that moment." Yada, yada, yada. That soft approach did not compute with my just-do-it, no-pain-no-gain, no-excuses mindset. I had always operated at 150 percent, and I had gotten excellent results. You know, except for the whole inner-peace thing.

I first noticed the difference as we were practicing yoga that weekend. Frank was leading us in a seated forward bend—the bane of my existence. How was it that I managed to get straight As throughout high school, graduate from an Ivy League college, and yet I still couldn't touch my toes after nine years of yoga practice? Frank encouraged us to listen to our bodies with compassion and respect—to be present and pay attention. I saw in that moment that I had been reaching for my toes just as I reached for everything else in my life. My body was telling me to let go of the striving, and it was time to listen to it. It was time to fully inhabit this body that had been given to me and to stop trying to be someone I wasn't.

This idea of being present to *what is* radically changed the way I went about doing life. But the changes were small at first. Frank taught us one particular practice—"the bell of mindfulness"—that brought the *concept* of being present into the *actual practice* of being present. Whenever I heard a bell, I was to remind myself to be present. A ringing phone, an incoming text message, and the chime of the doorbell could all be reminders to come back to my breath and stay in the present. Over time, my children joined me as well. They would hear the bell of mindfulness at times when I was too caught up in the details of life to be present, and their joy and glee at hearing the bell when I didn't was all I needed to come back to the here and now.

Later, my friend Christina helped make this a daily part of my routine and bought me a tiny bell to hang from my rearview mirror. Each time my suburban New Jersey driving caused the bell to ring, I would stop fretting about where I was going or what the person in front of me was doing. Instead, I would take three deep, slow breaths. My life as a mother of three toddlers didn't have room for hour-long meditations three times a day, and this sort of "micro-practice" was perfect for me.

In time, I expanded my awareness practice by following Thich Nhat Hanh's advice of being present to whatever I was doing— folding laundry while I was folding laundry and walking up steps while I was walking up steps. After practicing laundry-, walking-, and driving-mindfulness for a while, I noticed that mindfulness could help when I was upset.

Unfortunately, I always seemed to notice this super helpful truth *right after* I was all done being upset. Remembering to be compassionate, I would congratulate myself for being aware that it was an option. I would then go over the situation in my head to see how mindfulness could have helped it play out differently. In time, I caught some challenges midway through and was able to divert my reactivity to a healthier response. Eventually, I found myself becoming aware of when an upsetting situation was starting, and I would notice my unhappy, knee-jerk reaction in time to adjust my outward response to one that would be kind, compassionate, and helpful.

I've continued to grow and transform since the day the message came in 2007 that my life would never be the same. I'm beginning to see more clearly the big results of taking thousands of tiny, mindful steps. Last fall, I fell off my front steps while walking my son to school. I knew immediately that I had broken a bone. As a busy single mother of three children, I didn't have time for a broken nail, much less a broken foot. The "old me" would have lost her mind. I saw the concerned look on my son's face and just smiled. I remembered reading somewhere that "your response to a situation literally has the power to change the situation itself." This time, my response needed no filtering. With a genuine smile on my face, I simply and calmly said to him, "And now this."

A few months later, an appliance repairman was fixing my refrigerator. Since the water was turned off, I decided to fix a leak in my sink. I dismantled the faucet while we chatted about his new baby. He called me over to help him with the fridge, and a few minutes later he had it fixed. He asked me to turn the water back on so he could test the ice maker. I ran down to the basement and turned the handle, listening to the happy gush of the water starting back up. Immediately, I heard not-so-happy yelling from upstairs. I turned the water back off and ran up to the kitchen. I had forgotten that the faucet was dismantled, and water had sprayed up like a geyser all over the kitchen. There was water on every surface, including the ceiling, and it went into the dining room and family room as well. The repairman was aghast. I took one look and burst out laughing—a true and profound transformation in just 10 short years. "And now this."

Through this process of becoming more present and aware, I have come to know myself in new ways. I now listen to the incredibly peaceful voice inside me. It knows equanimity. It knows my true path. Today, I know the peace that comes from knowing for sure that I am living an authentic life.

This story was written by Erica Conway and edited by the authors. She is a coach and workshop leader helping people bring mindfulness to their homes and spaces. Erica makes her home in Ho-Ho-Kus, New Jersey. You can see more of her work at www.ericaconway.net.

# Chapter 1

## Exploring Transformation

*Disguised since childhood,*
*haphazardly assembled*
*from voices and fears and little pleasures,*
*we come of age as masks.*
*Our true face never speaks.*
*Somewhere there must be storehouses*
*where all these lives are laid away*
*like suits of armor or old carriages*
*or clothes hanging limply on the walls.*
*Maybe all the paths lead there,*
*to the repository of unlived things.*

—Rainer Maria Rilke

What is transformation, and how do people learn, heal, grow, and awaken? In this chapter, we'll explore the conditions for transformation, discuss compelling questions about identity, meaning, and self-awareness, and reveal how to become fully alive and creative by living out our true nature. Understanding your personal journey is essential to stepping into the role of leader, and to co-creating the conditions for transformation in your workshops.

## WHO ARE YOU?

Both Ken and Erica started out with the trappings of conventional success, but they felt an underlying deficit, a craving or striving for what seemed to be missing. They were lost in the forest of their lives, feeling alienated by not living authentically. They had to restore a connection to themselves and others and recover a sense of belonging.

We all want to be at home again, at ease internally—mind, body, heart, and spirit—and externally. Poets, mystics, and yogis tell tales of this longing for homecoming, as in Rumi's poem, "The Reed Flute's Song":

> Listen to the story told by the reed, of being separated. "Since I was cut from the reed bed, I have made this crying sound. Anyone apart from someone he loves understands what I say. Anyone pulled from a source longs to go back."

Wisdom traditions and modern-day science teach us that our belief systems motivate and direct human behavior and impact what we get out of life. In other words, you can be miserable in places of privilege and happy in dire ones because of your mindset, or worldview. For better or worse, conditioned attitudes set in motion our thinking, being, and doing. They color the meaning we assign to the daily events of our lives—and meaning is everything! When we interpret our experience through the lens of negative conditioning, we form a limited identity and a default story.

*Human beings are afflicted. . . . Our true affliction is not our inability to get what we want, or our inability to get rid of what we don't want—mostly sickness, old age, death. The true nature of our affliction is that we are unable and unwilling to come into our inheritance as fully alive human beings.*

—Stephen Cope

We all tell ourselves stories. Some are helpful; some are not. Negative self-talk can catastrophize an event, turning disappointment into rejection and separation into abandonment. Before you know it, you've collapsed the whole house of cards. In Erica's case, every bump in the road triggered a harsh internal reaction: *You idiot! Watch where you're going!*

When we feel something is missing or something is wrong, we spend our time wishing things were different or trying to improve the situation. How does this play out in our workshops?

People come to workshops for a variety of reasons. They want to be happier and healthier.

They want to learn a skill or experience something new. It's normal to aspire to become something better, but often there is a deeper, hidden drive to rearrange life—to "fix" what is broken or add whatever appears to be missing. Feeling disintegrated, we sometimes try to get it together and force change from a place of self-judgment, inner criticism, shame, guilt, or self-hatred: *If people really knew me, they wouldn't like me. I need to fix the way I am. If only I could do* _____. *Then I would be* _____.

---

**Pause for Practice:
Your Thoughts Matter**

Take a moment to quiet down and settle. Say these words to yourself: "Something's missing. Something's wrong. Something's wrong with *me*." Repeat this a couple of times, and feel it in your body. Notice the sensations. Notice your breathing. Notice your mood or emotions.

Now repeat these new words a couple of times: "Everything I really need, I already have." Again, notice your sensations, mood, and your breathing.

How did you react to those two different messages?

---

Figure 1.1 Pause for Practice: Your Thoughts Matter

"Any attempt to change yourself is rooted in self-hatred," says Richard Miller. When we watch these movements of the mind, we can see that the thought, *something's wrong*, arises from a feeling of separation or alienation. If we can catch the mind in the act of judging, we can see how the mind is constructed. The next movement of the mind is often *something's wrong with me*. This is the ego's reaction to the feeling of loneliness and isolation—it claims the experience for itself. *There must be something wrong with me* is a common negative thought, perhaps the most familiar of unwelcome guests in the mind.[3]

How do we find our way home and restore overall well-being? Feeling complete and whole—in our bodies, our relationships, and with all of nature—is to feel integrated, flexible, and free.[4] This is what is meant by the word *yoga*: "to yoke," "to join," "to unify." Mind-body integration and relational integration is a way of understanding how we can bring the parts of ourselves and our entire being into harmony.

Erica was suffering from low-grade panic, believing that she was not living up to her own high standards. Then, in a workshop, guided by an encouraging teacher, she was able to soften self-judgment and listen to her body with compassion and respect.

She began to let go of striving for how things should be and focus only on how things were. Erica was able to accept herself when she learned to pay attention to her own lived experience. Through the mindful steps of her micro-practice (three slow, deep breaths), she became more responsive and less hurtful and reactive. "In just ten short years," she said, she had experienced "true and profound transformation."

## WHAT IS TRANSFORMATION?

Transformation is organic, natural, and inevitable. We see it everywhere in the birth and rebirth of life, constantly forming and reforming. A classic example is the metamorphosis of the butterfly, who, guided by nature, struggles to emerge at the right time from the protective container of the chrysalis.

Life is an unfolding process of moving from one stage to another, with each stage incorporated into the next. The human brain evolved from the reptilian hindbrain, to the mammalian midbrain, and finally to our neocortex. The evolution of life from atom to molecule to cell to organism is nested, each level containing the old but progressively more complex. In this sense, transformation is a continual process of moving to a new stage that transcends and includes the old.[5]

The transformation of human consciousness is a process of change in our beliefs, attitudes, responses to situations, and in the meaning we make from our perception of experience. Transformation is not a one-and-done project achieved all at once, nor is it the endless road toward self-improvement. It's not about denying the painful realities of loss, illness, and death, or about avoiding conflict or escaping responsibilities. It's not about magical thinking, supernormal powers, dogmatic beliefs, or peak experiences like ecstasy or bliss. All states of consciousness are temporary. While liberating insight can happen in a flash, for most of us, transformation is a process of integrating moments of awareness over time.

We tend to believe our temporary thoughts and identify with things that don't last, and so we suffer unnecessarily. We become dis-integrated. When we're not integrated, it's often because we've defined ourselves by our body, mind, or personality, or by what we have or don't have. Whenever we identify with or cling to words of ownership—*I, my,* or *mine*—there is a grasping, an attachment, a painful contraction, a limitation.

Transformation is the process of getting to know your default story and loosening your grip. Getting some distance from it, you begin to see the limitations of any story and find the courage to step out of habitual ways of interpreting experience. Your sense of identity gets bigger, broader, and more inclusive. You become less identified with pleasant or unpleasant reactions, less caught up in the past or future, or needing to make something happen.

There is an underlying joy and peace that can be known and that doesn't end. When you can practice being yourself and going beyond a limiting story, you create the conditions for transformation and begin walking a path of freedom.

## SHIFT HAPPENS: THE CONDITIONS FOR TRANSFORMATION

Life has a way of getting our attention. Sometimes an event like divorce, death, illness, financial loss, or unemployment can wake us up or challenge us to take the next step on our path. Ken's setback brought him face-to-face with despair and shattered his beliefs about *me* and *mine*. In Erica's case, the catalyst was a quiet but compelling internal voice that challenged her worldview.

Whatever the circumstances, something shifts. Something inside awakens. It's a mystery. Wordsworth called it a "dark invisible workmanship." We are invited to look through a new lens, to experience our inner world and our unexamined belief systems. We may realize that the goals of a conventional life—to acquire possessions, success, power, and relationships—are no longer dependable or satisfying.

Ken and Erica got curious about their own journey. They took responsibility and began to move toward something more satisfying. They both turned to the supportive chrysalis of community, where they could be fully seen and heard. They got a sense of "feeling felt," and they were mirrored in the welcoming presence of wise teachers. They learned self-reflective practices like mindfulness, self-compassion, and emotional awareness, lighting the path home to their hidden wholeness.

*Mindfulness* is paying attention on purpose, in the present moment, nonjudgmentally.[6] It's seeing things as they are, not as we prefer them to be. It's not taking sides in the pushing and pulling of the mind—wanting this and not wanting that. Mindfulness enhances attention, emotional self-regulation, and self-compassion. It decreases rumination, emotional reactivity, and mind wandering.[7] The practice of mindfulness develops self-awareness, or meta-awareness, which is both internal and external awareness.

Self-awareness is the key to transformation. With self-awareness comes *self-regulation*—an ability to effectively monitor and manage one's behavior, emotions, and thoughts. Erica began to notice how and where she was directing her attention. As she did, she became aware that despite her outward achievements, she was driven by a nagging sense of failure and an inability to find peace. Her unconscious thoughts conditioned her way of being in the world. When she was able to stop and self-assess, it gave her breathing space. It led her to see the bigger picture, to see how striving was not serving her.

## THE FOUNDATION FOR EXPERIENCE

The pyramid in Figure 1.2 shows the foundation for experience. It reminds us to welcome and explore the aliveness of the body, starting at the bottom with physical sensations. A practical way to unpack your default story is to go within and feel what is happening in the body. Like a hero's journey, this task requires the courage to look deeply and feel—to notice nonjudgmentally the layers of your mind-body experience and, most importantly, to investigate the processes governing your experiences.

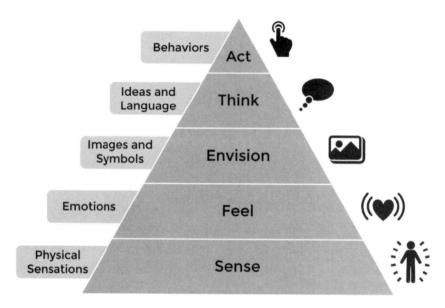

Figure 1.2 The Foundation for Experience: A Mindful Journey

What we (and others) can see is the tip of the pyramid—our behavior. But most of our experience occurs internally, and much of it is unconscious—what we think, what we imagine, what emotions we feel, and what we physically sense. These sensations, emotions, and thoughts are messengers, and monitoring them with nonjudgmental observation leads to self-understanding. It begins with *embodiment*—noticing your somatic experience. Becoming aware of urges and impulses as they arise will allow you to respond to life directly and free yourself from regrets about the past and worries about the future.

When we mindfully attend to the everyday world of family, community, and work, we begin to loosen attachment to the default story and become more interested in other people and relationships. We begin to trust that there's nothing wrong, that we're okay just the way we are.

## YOU ALREADY HAVE EVERYTHING YOU *REALLY* NEED TO LIVE FULLY

In our trainings, we clearly state that everyone already has everything they *really* need—the capacity for insight and empathy. Insight comes from an intuitive understanding of ourselves and the ability to see clearly the inner nature of things. Insight helps us to overcome a sense of alienation from self and to discover our innate wholeness. Empathy is our natural ability to see ourselves in others and connect with and understand one another. This understanding arises because we can recognize and feel what others feel—the pain and the joy.

In the end, what we all need is in every one of us. When you strip it all away, insight and empathy are already on board guiding us. We already have everything we need. By simply acting out of our true nature, we nudge ourselves along the path we are already on.

Over time, wisdom flows from insight, and compassion flows from empathy. These two qualities reinforce each other—compassion helps us break through narrow, self-centered views, enabling wisdom. This wisdom reminds us that nothing is really separate, enabling compassion. The interplay of compassion and wisdom becomes self-reinforcing. By igniting this force in ourselves and others, it multiplies exponentially. Knowing that you already have insight and empathy within you is an inner resource for leading life-changing workshops. This knowing develops with practice.

> *Just as ripples spread out when a single pebble is dropped into water, the actions of individuals can have far-reaching effects.*
>
> —The 14th Dalai Lama

## THE RIPPLE EFFECT

The transformation of one human being has unlimited potential to touch others' lives. When we deepen our insight and empathy, we show up in the world differently. Waking up from narrow self-interest, we invest ourselves in positive relationships and have a more profound social impact.

"When you know who you are, you will know how to act" is the ancient wisdom resurrected in Stephen Cope's book, *The Great Work of Your Life*. Our decisions about our actions flow from our understanding of who we are. When we are fully alive, our true calling lives in us as divine guidance and moves us to serve our purpose in the world.

What is *your* purpose? Are you called to nurture the creative potential in others? As a leader, you can connect workshop participants with their innate insight and empathy, ultimately co-creating a world where wisdom and compassion ripple out from individuals to groups and communities.

## IN SUMMARY

Wisdom and compassion are hard-earned by anyone who is willing to suit up and undertake the hero's journey. This means meeting life as it is, inevitably through pain and ultimately to great joy. Becoming fully alive—being present—is the greatest gift you can give to yourself and others.

In this chapter, we set out to investigate the mystery of transformation and living a life of purpose. In the next chapter, we'll explore how workshops—given the right transformational conditions—can create opportunities for insight and empathy so that wisdom and compassion can mature in your participants.

By fully owning and embodying your ability to influence, you have the power to effect positive personal and social change.

**Putting it into Practice:**
**Journal Prompts**

- Think back on your life. Have you experienced a shift in your self-understanding? Was it caused by a sudden event, an internal voice, or something else?
- Does the story you tell yourself feel limiting or freeing? In what way?
- How could you become more self-aware in your daily life?

Figure 1.3 Putting it into Practice: Journal Prompts

# Melanie's Story

# Finding my Voice in the Group

In Chapter 2, we'll look into what makes a workshop life changing. In this story, Melanie undertakes a journey to find her voice and struggles to overcome feelings of separation. In the safety of the group, she connects deeply with herself. Through mind-body experiences, she begins to believe that she really does have everything she needs.

*I* love to express myself in words—written words. I came to the Designing and Leading Transformational Workshops training hoping to make my writing workshops more experiential. But I also wanted to stop stifling my voice in a group.

I felt conflicted. My writing voice feels natural, but my speaking voice is not my own. What's easy for me to say on paper is hard for me to say out loud. In my family of origin, speaking from the heart was met with violence, denial, or indifference. Whenever I spoke up, I was rejected. They weren't "bad" people; they were doing the best they could. But now, I can see how deeply wounded I was.

As I sat down on opening night of the five-day workshop, I glanced around the circle, aware that I was avoiding eye contact. *Who are these people?* I thought to myself. There were men and women of all ages. They seemed confident—so darn comfortable engaging in quiet, easy conversations with each other. *Did they all meet before the workshop began?*

I put the voice in my head aside as the workshop started. The leaders welcomed us and led a quiet reflection, inviting us to make an intention for the week. They encouraged us to be "present, not perfect" and to have a "don't-know mind." We didn't have to be experts. We just had to show up without putting on a face or pretending—to be open to possibilities, without judging ourselves or others.

These all sounded like reasonable requests, but I wondered if I truly could break my habit of hiding and staying small. I was already noticing that familiar constriction and aversion to "showing up" in a group.

I didn't have much time to mull it over, because the leaders asked us to stand up and do some simple movements. *Where is this going?* And then we were asked to pair up with another person and do "partner yoga"—holding the other's arms while doing some simple yoga poses. *They want me to do what?* Now I was nervous. But I was surprised—the partner yoga actually made me feel calmer! Despite that slight shift, I still felt myself cringe as we shared our intention for the week with our partners. (I'd have to speak!) With no choice but to swallow my fear, I spoke my intention and was met with warm, accepting eyes.

As we returned to the group, the leaders then invited us to all speak our intentions to the whole group. *I'm going to die.* My hands got sweaty and my mouth dried up as the microphone made its way around the circle. Then it was suddenly in my hand, and to my surprise, the words left my lips automatically. "My intention is to learn how to make my writing workshops more impactful and to overcome my fear of speaking up in a group." A feeling of deep relief and something bordering on pride washed over me as the microphone slipped out of my sweaty palm and into the hand of the person next to me.

As opening night came to a close, I felt both hopeful and skeptical. The group included men and women, which gave me pause. My experience with the men in my family made me wonder if I'd be able to own my voice and speak up.

My radar was already active and had identified one man in particular who seemed to trigger my insecurities. John came across as somewhat open and friendly, but I also noticed how he cut somebody off when they were speaking.

The next day, we were divided into groups of three. These small tribes, or pods, provided each of us with two others to connect with more deeply, share in our experiences, and support us on a more intimate level than the large group of 25. As fate would have it, I was put into a group with John and another woman, Connie.

As we introduced ourselves, Connie courageously spoke about her feelings of not being enough. I saw what she couldn't see. I saw her strength, integrity, and depth. I saw her ability to give. I decided to follow her lead, and I shared a little more about my fear of speaking from the heart while in a group. Before I was able to finish my story, John interrupted me: "I don't see why you'd have a problem—you seem confident enough to me." The words themselves didn't seem so bad, but his comment triggered something very deep in me. I felt unheard and invalidated, and I began to shut down.

Everything in me wanted to retreat to my room. Maybe I could claim I wasn't feeling well and just not return to the group. As these thoughts swirled in my head, I felt the familiar feelings of self-judgement and unworthiness. Then I recalled the invitation to be present, not perfect—to practice being vulnerable. I had gone through a lot to attend this retreat, and I felt renewed resolve not to give in or give up.

That afternoon, we were taught conscious dialogue—a tool for bringing awareness to feelings and needs, and having the courage to face difficult conversations in a safe and authentic way. I decided to use it to share my feelings with John. I first practiced with Connie, and she helped me clarify what I was feeling and what I wanted out of the conversation. But my first attempt with John got me nowhere good. He seemed to listen but then said, "Thank you for sharing, but I don't really see that there is a problem." I said nothing, but I was furious. He hadn't seen me or heard me.

I pulled Connie aside as we passed each other in the dining hall and shared what happened. I lamented that I blew my chance, and she said, "Well, you can do it differently next time." Next time. Yes, there could be a next time. This thought opened up space in my heart. Maybe I could try again.

I felt an emerging sense of hope. The leaders had created a safe space that was reliable and constant. They facilitated activities that supported us in witnessing each other's process. I saw others becoming more real and in the moment.

The exercises in mindfulness and somatic awareness—through body sensing and breath sensing—made me more aware of how much tension I held in my neck and shoulders. I began to notice the subtle sensations and the not-so-subtle thoughts that showed up whenever I had to speak up in the group.

I was becoming more and more aware of my immediate reactions of fear and caution. I grew in my resolve to show up more fully and authentically rather than default to blaming or isolating myself.

I decided to have another go at an honest conversation with John. Practicing first with Connie and then with Jane, another woman in the group, I tried again. I invited John for a walk down to the lake, and as we walked, I used conscious dialogue—observation, feeling, need, request.

Observation: "I noticed that I was in the middle of a sentence, and you began to talk."

Feeling: "When that happened, I felt frustrated and upset."

Need: "My need is for self-expression and respect."

Request: "Would you be willing to let me finish my thought before you start speaking?"

John responded off-handedly, "I think you're being too sensitive here, but okay, if that's what you need."

I was fuming! Nothing had changed, and I felt deeply hurt, not heard.

When I reported all this to Connie, she helped me to soften toward John—to see him as a symptom and not as the problem. He was only a reflection of what had been inside me all this time—this anger, this pain.

That night, I had an amazing dream. In the dream, I was enough. Just me, the way I am. I woke up feeling different. More peaceful. That peace lingered throughout the day.

Then I noticed something. John's behavior didn't change. He was still the same. But it didn't bother me so much. I was more willing to put myself out there—to speak my truth—regardless of his response. Something deep was happening inside, and I was experiencing a freedom and courage that I'd never felt before. I liked this new way of being, and I resolved to treat my not-good-enough voices with more kindness and to not indulge the urge to criticize myself. As the workshop progressed, I saw that I could take risks and speak, even on topics that had been taboo for me—such as power, sexual dynamics, and trauma.

On the second-to-last day of the workshop, the leader invited everyone to share their feelings with the group. Connie encouraged me to speak directly to John, in the circle. I felt very vulnerable and didn't know if I could do it. Just then, I had the thought, No! Go ahead! Speak to him from your heart! And I did.

What happened next broke a pattern I had experienced all my life. He did not respond harshly. His words were soft. Clearly, he'd been on his own journey during our five days together—dealing with his own shadows—and our sharing was deeply moving to both of us and to the group. I felt the glow of having spoken from my heart, and it gave me what I needed.

That night, alone in my room, I let myself feel the overwhelming elation of having a voice—of speaking my needs and being fully seen and heard. I wept and I sobbed. A huge wave of emotion washed over me as I let go of old wounds and fears. How many times had I colored my conversations by projecting my own insecurities? How many of my relationships had been impacted this way? Could I have been having real conversations as one adult to another?

I felt so light and open afterward. I discovered that "heart speaking" does not require a response. It's not about right and wrong, but about offering myself. This was a revelation and a relief. I also saw for the first time how my words, coming from my own truth, could deeply affect another human being.

This experience was a pivotal point in my life. I could see how each person in the group was a catalyst for my own growth. They helped me dial down my self-judging and performance anxiety. The group showed me what I was blind to—my own beauty and worthiness. They told me how I touched them and made a difference, which surprised and delighted me.

It became clear to me that one of the functions of the group is to give people a lasting memory of feeling okay together. I had been trying to process my pain and isolation on my own. Experiencing the acceptance of community taught me that I am not alone. I see this as my responsibility. I will come out of isolation and put myself in places where I can connect with people and reach out to others.

I left that workshop with faith in myself and a deep conviction that I was enough. I felt grateful and affirmed. I was ready to start over. If I could create workshops that do that for other people, it would be a joy and a privilege.

Melanie prefers to remain anonymous.

# Chapter 2

# Creating the Conditions for Transformation in Workshops

*When our hearts are small . . .*
*We can't accept or tolerate others*
*and their shortcomings,*
*and we demand that they change.*
*But when our hearts expand . . .*
*We accept others as they are,*
*and then they have a chance to transform.*

—Thich Nhat Hanh

hat makes a workshop life changing? More than 20 years of leading workshops and training leaders have shown us that intentional groups have a unique power to transform individuals. As a leader, you can influence people by how you show up and by the skills and tools you use to shape learning environments, above and beyond the subject or content of the workshop. In this chapter, you'll see how a transformational workshop differs from conventional and experiential workshops, and we'll explore the essential conditions for transformation that can empower individuals and ignite group wisdom in your workshops.

## WHAT IS A TRANSFORMATIONAL WORKSHOP?

Transformation is more than just changing our ideas about ourselves; it's a shift in identity that affects how we perceive ourselves and how we show up in the world.

But how does this happen? In Melanie's story, the workshop provided a safe place to try new ways of interacting and showing up. She made an intention to find her voice in a group. Remember the base of the pyramid in Chapter 1? Somatic awareness activities—attention to body sensations—helped her notice underlying thoughts and feelings: "My hands got sweaty and my mouth dried up."

With an attitude of curiosity, not of suppression, she was able to recognize old patterns: "I felt the familiar feelings of self-judgement and unworthiness." She recalled the invitation to be present, not perfect—to practice being okay the way she was: "I felt renewed resolve not to give in or give up." The conscious dialogue tool offered her a way to reframe a pattern of not speaking up by reflecting on her needs and practicing authentic expression.

Mind-body experiences, such as conscious dialogue and somatic awareness activities, are the *vehicles* of transformational learning. They move us toward greater insight and empathy and induce liminal states where new possibilities can emerge. On the one hand, mind-body experiences can bring awareness to and dispel identification with unhelpful mind states, such as Melanie's default pattern of shutting down and engaging in negative self-talk.

On the other hand, mind-body experiences reinforce positive mind states. For example, Melanie was learning to stay present to her discomfort, summoning compassion for herself, and owning the feeling of fear. She was moving from reactivity to receptivity. By learning to self-regulate, Melanie came to grips with her need for self-expression. She was mobilizing herself to break free. Melanie's identity was shifting, and she was more fluid and able to adapt to the conditions of the moment.

What is the role of the leader in all of this? Leaders facilitate (i.e., "make easy") the process of self-inquiry. They also have faith in new possibilities. Brain-based studies show that just having positive experiences is not enough to bring about lasting change. We need to engage actively and participate consciously in weaving them into our emotional memory in order to reshape old, unhelpful behavior and to free the mind and heart.[8] By doing this, positive states will become lasting traits.

In designing your workshops, you're co-creating the conditions for self-discovery in a supportive community using liberating practices. You're offering a safe space for individuals like Melanie to practice becoming choosers and deciders, and to realize that they have freedom in how to relate to themselves, others, and the world.

We have seen these shifts—great and small—in hundreds of workshops. But not all workshops are alike. We'll bring more clarity to *transformational* workshops in this chapter by comparing and contrasting different types of workshops. We'll explore how to design mind-body experiences in Chapters 4 and 5.

## CONVENTIONAL, EXPERIENTIAL, AND TRANSFORMATIONAL WORKSHOPS

Think back to the last workshop or training you attended. Were the chairs set up in a circle or in rows? Did you feel more like part of an audience or part of a community? Was the leader more of a lecturer or a facilitator? Did you actively participate, or did you mostly listen? Did you come away with new information, skills, or perspectives? These are all factors in the look and feel of a workshop.

Transformational workshops differ from both conventional and experiential workshops in important ways. *Conventional workshops* are about what you know. *Experiential workshops* are about what you can do. *Transformational workshops* are about who you are and who you are becoming. These differences are shown in Figure 2.1 and Figure 2.2. When you compare the models in these figures, it's clear how one builds upon the next—the transformational model *includes and transcends* the other two.

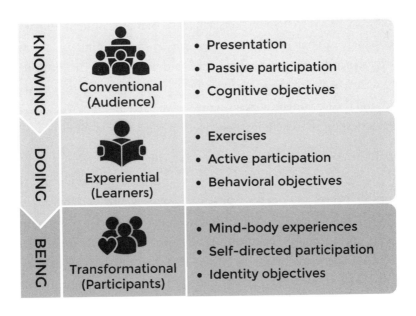

Figure 2.1 Three Kinds of Workshops

## The Conventional Model: Knowing

In the conventional model, objectives are mostly cognitive or knowledge based (i.e., what will the audience *know* as a result of the presentation?). The leader is considered to be the expert and relies on presentation, lecture, or didactic instruction. Audience members are mostly passive, looking to the leader to tell them what they need to know.

What is the layout of the room in a conventional setting? Usually, people sit in rows, all facing the front. The leader is at the head of the room and might rely on digital slides to deliver information. Most of the talking is done by the leader, with the audience sometimes responding to questions. There's very little interaction. In general, the conventional model is what's used in many schools and universities, at conferences, and in trainings.

The conventional model is good for conveying information quickly and efficiently, but your ability to engage the group, nurture creativity, and bring about lasting changes in perception and behavior can be limited.

## The Experiential Model: Doing

Can you really learn something without doing it? The experiential model is about *doing* something and is becoming more widely used today. Here, the leader coordinates exercises designed to help learners acquire a skill or skill set in line with behavioral objectives (i.e., what will learners be able to *do* differently as a result of the learning experience?). Learners are presented with a challenge that requires them to respond to or interact with their fellow learners. The point is the experience does the "teaching," and the learning occurs with the active participation of each learner. The leader uses her expertise to help learners develop their own abilities.

Experiential learning is often used for team building. Ropes courses or other challenge-based activities develop communication and teamwork skills and strengthen relationships between members. Apprenticeship—where the master craftsman guides the apprentice through a rigorous and extended process of watching, doing, failing, fixing, and eventually mastering a craft—is another example of the experiential model. The experiential model is powerful in that it *actively engages* learners and thereby helps them transfer their newfound skills and abilities from the learning environment to the real world.

| | CONVENTIONAL MODEL | EXPERIENTIAL MODEL | TRANSFORMATIONAL MODEL |
|---|---|---|---|
| **LEADER-SHIP** | **Hierarchical leadership.** A "sage on the stage." Learners may be inspired by the leader but may not necessarily experience self-directed learning. | **Guiding leadership.** An expert in the field who has the proper experience to direct and guide learners to known skill sets. | **Embodied leadership.** A designated driver (not a guru) who is dynamic and fluid, from director to negotiator to delegator. A steward of the common good—a "guide on the side." |
| **LEADER'S INTENTION** | Teaching is **knowing**. Transfer of knowledge and information is primary. Leader is the expert. | Teaching is **training** that supports acquisition of skills and provides access to knowledge and guidance toward mastering competencies. | Teaching is **being** personally aligned with the content, modeling being "present, not perfect," and embracing human imperfections with kindness. |
| **MEANS OF TEACHING** | **Teacher centered.** Relies primarily on presentation, lecture, and didactic instruction to convey information and ideas. | **Experience centered.** Relies on the experiential activity or environment to impart knowledge and skills. Often top-down, from trainer to individual. | **Participant centered.** Relies primarily on experience. Aimed at empowering self-directed individuals and sparking group creativity through direct experience and cooperative inquiry. |
| **CONTENT/ PROCESS** | **Content over process.** Focus is on information and delivery tends to be one way—not needing active involvement from participants. | **Process is part of content.** Learning takes place by doing, so it is dynamic and active. Can be reflective at the individual and group level. Learning is mostly personal and relational. | **Content and process are balanced.** Richly textured with real-life content. Processes are dynamic, active, and reflective. Learning is transpersonal. |
| **RELATION-SHIP** | **One to many** (instructor to students). Creates a collection of individuals who may or may not be in relationship with each other. | **One to many with many-to-many aspects**. As participants master skills and knowledge, they gain access to wider circles of cultures, personal relationships, or occupations. | **Many to Many.** Fosters emotional and personal connection. Creates a community of truth. Promotes group bonding through interactivity. |
| **OUTCOMES** | **Intellectual and conceptual.** Pursuing knowledge acquisition. The mind is the primary vehicle for learning. Objectives are primarily cognitive. | **Skill based.** Pursuing proficiency and competency that will move the participant toward a stated goal. Learning has specific behavioral objectives that can be affective as well as cognitive. | **Holistic and identity related.** Pursuing self-discovery, wisdom, and compassion. Knowing incorporates the mind, body, heart, senses, and beyond. |
| **TRANSFER TO REAL WORLD** | Supports **recall of information** for cognitive tasks and provides **mental frameworks** for dealing with real-world problems. | Supports **practical application** of the skills mastered. Relies on the repetition of skill use. Does not necessarily carry over to apply to all areas of life. | Supports **long-term application** through intentional and sustainable practices beyond the learning experience. Aimed at inclusive solutions and sustainable results through a living-systems approach. |

Figure 2.2 Comparison of Conventional, Experiential, and Transformational Models

## The Transformational Model: Being

What if you want to tap into the deepest level of human potential? If you want the greatest impact, why not weave together the best of the conventional and the experiential, and go beyond *knowing* and *doing* into transformational space? Now, your objectives are more about *identity* (i.e., how will each participant *be* different as a result of their participation?). In a transformational workshop, the participants come to perceive themselves, each other, and their world differently. The goal of coming together is to create the conditions for these perceptions to shift through insight and empathy, both in the individual and in the group.

The transformational model aims to embolden, support, uplift, and empower self-directed individuals and ignite group creativity through self-inquiry and cooperative inquiry. It's needs based and participant centered. You as the leader are the guardian of the common good. You cannot predict individual outcomes, but you can direct participants' attention to their own needs. How could anyone have known, for instance, what Melanie needed for her growth? Through self-awareness, she became an agent for her own learning.

The leader encourages curiosity and openness to explore the program content through information and direct experience, using activities crafted to engage the whole person—mind, body, heart, and spirit—in what we call mind-body experiences. Time for reflection and processing, both at the individual and group level, is integral to the learning process. Fostering self-awareness provides opportunities to make new meaning from experience.

How does the room layout support this model? Most of the time, sitting in a circle is optimal. Each person's contribution carries equal weight. It might be difficult at first glance to identify the leader because, in addition to teaching the content or guiding the agenda, the leader also moves among the participants and acts as a facilitator of the group process.

Each model can be used effectively depending on your intention. The question is this: What outcomes do you want? If you want to invite deep and lasting change in individuals and groups, then use the transformational model.

## THE CONDITIONS FOR TRANSFORMATION IN WORKSHOPS

The essential conditions for transformation in workshops are co-created by the leader and the participants. As an embodied leader, you form an intentional community where people can meet, join, and belong. Your holistic view honors the inherent worth of each person, and you believe that everyone already has what they need to live a purposeful life. You aim to engage the whole person, using mind-body experiences to cultivate self-awareness—the key to transformation. What emerges is group wisdom, giving rise to creativity, inclusive solutions, and sustainable results.

Figure 2.3 shows this interplay of these conditions. We'll describe each part of the model in the pages that follow.

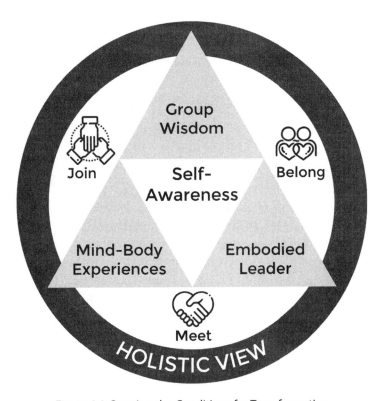

Figure 2.3 Creating the Conditions for Transformation

## Holistic View: See for Yourself

A worldview, or mindset, is a way of interpreting the world. It's an already-established set of attitudes that affects all areas of your life and often goes unquestioned. How you see and process things depends on your belief system, who you think you are, and what you think life is about. A holistic view begins with the good news that mindsets are not static. They can be changed. And changes in attitude lead to changes in behavior. People *can* change, heal, grow, and awaken by enhancing inner resources that are already on board.[9]

We often start a workshop by asking our participants, "What did it take to get you here?" We encourage them to reflect on their unique purpose and path, and to realize that each person has the inner resources to find their own way to the truth thanks to their own experiences. After all, it took them a lifetime to get to the workshop.

In our trainings, we embrace a holistic view that informs our entire approach to workshop design and facilitation. It's grounded in the belief that everything you really need, you already have. We see our participants through a lens of wholeness, and we lead experiences that allow them to discover that they already have everything they *really* need to live full and meaningful lives: namely, the inner resources of insight and empathy.

> " *The next Buddha may take the form of a community, a community practicing understanding and loving kindness, a community practicing mindful living. This may be the most important thing we can do for the survival of the earth.* "
>
> —Thich Nhat Hanh

*Insight* is seeing clearly the inner nature of things. Insight helps us to overcome a separate sense of self and discover our hidden wholeness. *Empathy* is our natural ability to understand one another by feeling what others feel—their pain and their joy. We choose to base our inquiry on these two innate human abilities because they are universal among us, and when cultivated, they mature into a wise and compassionate way of being together.

We foster each person's full participation in the workshop. *Full participation* means being there sensorially, emotionally, intellectually, and spiritually. The principle is "see for yourself." We encourage our participants to see for themselves through direct experience—not just ideas—that will enliven their inherent capacity for insight and empathy.

Humans are complex, self-organizing beings that, given the right conditions, tend toward harmony and the integration of the body, mind, heart, and spirit. In our trainings, we suggest that participants take on and practice an attitude of being "already whole" as a framework for being together. Early on in her workshop, Melanie was willing to adopt a provisional mindset of being fluid and a work in progress, instead of clinging to a view that she was broken, as a way of getting started toward this already-wholeness.

## Meet, Join, and Belong: Forming Intentional Community

Intentional communities form around a given purpose or vision. In transformational workshops, group members commit to a common higher focus; for example, growing into something that may be new, different, greater, or deeper than before. The leader helps the group get clear about the purpose and establish agreements.

Agreements are guidelines that aid in setting a culture of cooperation based on shared values.

Consciously meeting, joining, and belonging is essential to the life-changing workshop, because we get to know ourselves through our relationships. "The key to your heart lies in the heart of another."[iii] We are shaped in every way by interactions—with ourselves, others, and the environment. It was in our family of origin that our identity first began to form. Today, the caring presence of others in an intentional group can give you the support of being included, valued, and respected.

## Self-Awareness: The Key to Transformation

At the center of our model is self-awareness. By tapping into deeper levels of awareness, our participants come into contact with obstacles, hidden assumptions, and beliefs that stand in the way of full self-expression.

---

**Moments of Self-Awareness**

What have some of your aha moments looked like? Here are aha moments from some of our participants:

- I got myself! And then I got over myself!
- I'm not seeking answers outside of me. I know myself better.
- I recognize my emotional states and see the gift underneath.
- Releasing my shame, I can affirm myself and who I really am.
- I'm listening to others with less need to tell them what to do.
- I'm facing the inner voices that have kept me locked up most of my life.
- I love everyone in the circle!

---

Figure 2.4 Examples of Moments of Self-Awareness

Through body sensing and breath sensing, Melanie noticed how much tension she held in her neck and shoulders. She noticed the thoughts that came up whenever she had to speak into the group. She became more aware of her social anxiety and how running from the group would give her a quick fix. But she saw that if she could sit with her discomfort long enough to resist the urge to escape, she could get the greater reward of connecting with others. And over time, she felt a growing sense of hope.

---

[iii] This is a core teaching of Swami Kripalu.

How do you cultivate self-awareness throughout your workshops? You continually direct attention toward the *outer workshop* and the *inner workshop*. The outer workshop is what's happening in the room. The inner workshop is the individual thoughts and feelings bubbling up in the leader and each participant. As each person practices directing nonjudgmental attention to their own inner workshop, they're more able to manage emotions and be more flexible and open to what's happening in the outer workshop.

Self-awareness allows us to relate more positively with others and the environment, and to take in more of the big picture. Ultimately, self-awareness helps us stay connected to our deepest intention. Aha moments happen when a small window opens for beliefs to change, and new ways of being become possible.

### Embodied Leader: Present, Not Perfect

Think of someone who has touched your life and helped you believe in yourself. How did it happen? Were they a "sage on the stage" or more of a supportive "guide on the side"—someone who encouraged you in taking your next steps? In what ways were they authentic and heartfelt?

As the leader, you are the steward of the group and the guardian of the good. When you are *embodied*, you show up wholeheartedly, embracing your own imperfections with kindness. You monitor and manage yourself and the group—perceiving, sensing, and acting on many levels. When you're present, not perfect, you're not caught up in your thoughts. You model everything you've invited your participants to be: aware (mind), connected (heart), grounded (body), and intuitive (spirit).

As a workshop leader, how you teach is more valuable than what you teach. It's not about charisma. It's about being clear, consistent, appreciative, encouraging, caring, and optimistic. Real power comes from warmth, presence, and the ability to self-regulate and respond more naturally to whatever comes up in your group. Your participants will experience you as genuine and connected. In Melanie's workshop, the constant and reliable presence of the leaders helped Melanie feel safe enough to risk trying something different and new.

What does an embodied leader do in a transformational workshop? You are both teacher and facilitator—what we call the "twin roles."[10] As a teacher, you design and deliver the workshop content. You set goals, demonstrate skills, communicate information, and manage the group's learning. As a facilitator, you guide and support the group process by delegating responsibility and negotiating energy—that is, mediating the emotions, behaviors, and interactions of the group. A facilitator helps people to surface, explore, and transform hidden assumptions, beliefs, and values. We'll explore the twin roles more deeply in Part III of the book.

## Mind-Body Experiences: What You Practice Grows Stronger

The mind and body are not separate. Psychology and physiology are two ends of the same continuum. *Mind-body* is our shorthand way of referring to the whole self, including the heart and spirit. Mind-body experiences enhance our intuition and creativity through direct encounters with ourselves, others, and the natural world. In groups, this fosters connection, community, and group identity through collaborative inquiry and interactions.

Research tells us that the brain is shaped by experience. Neuroplasticity is the brain's extraordinary capacity to change itself so that what you practice grows stronger. For better or worse, experience drives the changes. Through experiences, participants can enhance their awareness of perceptions, thoughts, emotions, and behaviors, and they can gain life-changing insights. Negative patterns that are observed without judgment can be disrupted, and positive experiences can be reinforced.

Mind-body experiences are designed to engage different aspects of people: mind (through journaling and guided meditation), body (through movement and conscious breathing), heart (through partner sharing and well-wishing), and spirit (through rites, rituals, and invocation). In Melanie's story, the participants became active learners through a variety of experiences, such as partner yoga, group sharing, somatic awareness exercises, and conscious communication.

Mind-body experiences are the vehicle for delivering the workshop content. The best ones follow a three-step process—safety, experience, and integration. We refer to this as the *transformational learning cycle*, which is a facilitated process of self-discovery.[11] When people feel *safe* enough to explore their own direct experience, deeply and without judgment, curiosity overcomes fear. Immersion in *direct experience* is followed by a period of *integration*, which is an active process of meaning making through reflection. Cycles of safety, action, and reflection spiral through the workshop, cultivating inner resources and deepening the experience of wholeness in relationship with others.

Learning from experience is life changing. Melanie was able to loosen her grip and step out of her psychological story by learning to regulate her physiological state of being. When she no longer identified with her story, she could practice being herself without her story. We'll explore the transformational learning cycle more deeply in Part II of the book.

## Group Wisdom: Interbeing

*Group wisdom* is the mystery that emerges when we practice the conditions for transformation. It arises in shared, transpersonal, sacred space in which self-directed individuals exchange energy and information in relationship.[iv] Intentional groups can be wiser than the wisest people in them, so chasing the expert is not as wise as forming wise groups.[12] When each person becomes a knower, a truth teller, then everyone benefits, and the leader doesn't have to be the expert.

Being together on a conscious journey of cooperative inquiry bonds the group in a way that allows individuals to witness themselves from multiple perspectives. They cultivate a relational field by identifying similarities, accepting differences, building empathy, and gaining insight. A group identity begins to form where each individual is valued, seen, and connected. Participants report having a palpable feeling of immediacy that lifts up the whole group, and there's a kind of knowing that surpasses ordinary limits.

By attending to the conditions for transformation, you co-create a synergistic atmosphere that ultimately serves the needs of each individual, as well as the common good. In Melanie's words, "I could see how each person in the group was a catalyst for my own growth." In the same way, Melanie's honesty prompted John's growth.

When we see things as they are, we become aware of our inherent connectedness, what Thich Nhat Hanh calls interbeing. A sense of right action comes alive in us, and we are clearer, kinder, and more useful in the world.

### IN SUMMARY

Together, a holistic view, intentional community, self-awareness, embodied leadership, mind-body experiences, and group wisdom create the conditions for transformation, regardless of the workshop topic. Each person gets what they need and leaves the workshop with a renewed sense of purpose in life. The ultimate impact of the transformational workshop is to create a more conscious and compassionate world.

This understanding of how to create the conditions for transformation is supported by contemporary science, especially research in neuroscience, biology, psychology, sociology, and quantum theory. While we are not aware of specific scientific studies

---

[iv] Dan Siegel defines *mind* as the exchange of energy and information in relationship. We believe this is a helpful basis for understanding how group wisdom is formed when individuals come together. See Siegel, D. J. (2012). *The developing mind: How relationships and the brain interact to shape who we are.* Guilford Press.

on the impact of transformational workshops per se, there's an exciting and growing body of research in the areas of mind-body practices, mindfulness, meditation, and group formation that points to some of the mechanisms underlying the conditions for transformation that we describe. If you're interested in exploring these inferences and connections, we've summarized relevant research in Appendix A.

In Part II, you'll see how you can use the transformational learning cycle to design mind-body experiences that are especially relevant for your workshop participants, and in Part III, you'll learn more about the skills and tools of the embodied leader, including your twin roles as teacher and facilitator.

---

**Putting it into Practice:**
**Journal Prompts**

- What conditions are present when you feel safest in groups or workshops?
- Think of a time when you experienced an aha moment, felt a shift in understanding, or suddenly awoke to new possibilities. What led up to these breakthroughs?
- If you are currently teaching or designing a workshop, what do you want your participants to get out of it?

---

Figure 2.5 Putting it into Practice: Journal Prompts

# Part II

# Designing Your Workshop

*The bud*
*stands for all things,*
*even for those things that don't flower,*
*for everything flowers, from within, of self-blessing;*
*though sometimes it is necessary*
*to reteach a thing its loveliness,*
*to put a hand on its brow*
*of the flower*
*and retell it in words and in touch*
*it is lovely*
*until it flowers again from within, of self-blessing.*

—Galway Kinnell

## Hisla's Story

# I Have a Healing Heart Now

In Chapter 3, we explore how connecting to your own life story—your gifts, strengths, and challenges—can help you envision and design a workshop that comes from your own experience. In Hisla's story, a heart attack brings a psychiatrist face-to-face with her own vulnerability. Hisla discovers that her healing journey is a gift she can use to help others, through leading workshops.

It took a heart attack to open my heart. It was the Fourth of July weekend, and I was anxious about the drive from Philadelphia to Washington, DC, to visit Rich's sister. We stopped for breakfast at Hymie's Deli, and I remember leaving food on my plate as we got up to pay the bill. Suddenly, I was struck with a jolt of electricity. The pain hammered my chest and left arm—right through my elbow. It felt like a heavy, lead-weighted blanket of pain. A debilitating weakness came over me. I knew this was serious. I knew I was having a heart attack.

I began to pray silently to myself and thought of my daughter in New York City, now a world away. How would she get along without me? Helpless and unable to move, the threat of death was palpable. Rich helped me into our car, and I continued to beg for God to save me as we sped through the crowded streets.

From the age of 28, I began to harden my heart. That year, I lost both of my parents within a few months. When my father died, my heart shut down a little. When my mother died, it shut down a little more.

It shut down even more in medical school that same year. Entering my psychiatry specialty, I was told to not show my emotions: "Don't cry in front of patients. Don't hug them. Don't touch them, except during physician exams. Stick to your boundaries." When my child-patients ran up to hug me, I peeled them off. I couldn't accept their affection or offer them physical comfort, because that's not what a doctor—let alone a psychiatrist trained to be an objective observer—is supposed to do. I was shut down at work, and I was shut down at home.

Things have to break before they can heal. In fact, I've come to see how my heart attack was a gift. It forced me to stop and examine my life. Looking back, I realized my stress levels were through the roof. I endured long workdays where I rushed my lunch and ignored the tension at work and home. The added pressure I placed on myself to be more guarded with my patients had built up over the years, and I'd nurtured the belief that physicians were immune to illness. I learned that day in the deli just how wrong I was.

I have a healing heart now—a heart that is learning to reveal itself. I now realize the full extent of my closed and bulletproof composure. I was certainly not a "heartless" person; I was just guarded and protected. I didn't risk showing my feelings or my fear of rejection. My heart attack was the first time I really allowed myself to feel vulnerable—not only to life and death, but also to my sadness and longing. I've discovered many blessings in being more vulnerable and available to life—being more human. I've met wonderful people and experienced new and beautiful adventures I wouldn't have had if I hadn't reached out to others.

I believe that heart attacks are a way the body reminds us to be grateful and share what we have learned with others. One way I'm doing that is by creating programs to support medical professionals. I've learned to be a compassionate doctor, and I now encourage other physicians to share emotional connections and physical touch with their patients. I'm using my healing to help others heal.

From what I learned through my own recovery, I've created a workshop for women with heart conditions who feel alone or ashamed and want support. In the workshop Hug Your Heart: Using Mindfulness to Heal Heart Conditions, I share my own story and help my participants learn how to manage stress, practice meditation, deal with anxiety associated with heart conditions, practice positive psychology, visualize new versions of themselves, and write and share their story with others.

One activity I do in the workshop is to help participants create a mantra of positive intentions for tuning in to their own wisdom and self-support. In the workshop, I share some of my own mantras:

- My independence has served me, but it has also hardened me. I am seeking balance.

- I am learning to listen to my body as a way of removing some of the armor.

- I am learning when to say yes and how to say no to what doesn't serve me.

- I am learning to love myself.

- I am learning to let others give me things and accept help.

A poem by Dorothy Hunt talks about undressing your heart, and it has been very meaningful to me on my journey. In my workshop, we read it together as I share my story with others and expose my vulnerability. Instead of feeling victimized or sorry for myself, I find strength in caring for others and accepting their care for me. I feel happy. I feel loved. My loneliness has disappeared, and I realize that people want to help. They want to touch me with kindness, and when I let them, I find deep satisfaction and connection. I don't need the bulletproof vest. I can let my guard down and take a chance. I undress my heart and become vulnerable and open, and I help others do the same.

This story was written by Dr. Hisla Bates, MD, and edited by the authors. Hisla is a psychiatrist in private practice in New York City. You can see more of her work at www.DrHislaBatesMD.com or on social media.

# Chapter 3

## Workshops and Your
## Work in the World

*Now I become myself. It's taken*
*Time, many years and places;*
*I have been dissolved and shaken,*
*Worn other people's faces . . .*

—May Sarton

*I*n Part I, we explored transformation and how you can create the conditions for a life-changing workshop. In Part II, we turn to how to design your workshop using your own life experience as the starting point, why it's important to you to lead workshops, and what is uniquely yours to give.

In Hisla's story, her heart attack was the turning point that revealed a deeper condition—the hardening and hiding of her heart. Suddenly, she felt the urgency to focus on what really mattered—fulfilling a powerful vision for the rest of her life. This became the basis for her workshops.

If you look at the biographies of leaders and healers who have had a great impact, you often find that their work came directly out of challenges. Think of the healing work of Moshé Feldenkrais or Frederick Matthias Alexander, which emerged from their own severe health issues. Think of Harville Hendrix and Helen Hunt, who developed couple's therapy out of their own relationship difficulties. Or think of Byron Katie, whose depression led her to an epiphany about how to help others.

Connecting to our own life story—both our challenges and our strengths—is the pathway to being an embodied leader.

What were your challenges, and what did you learn from them? What are your innate gifts and strengths?

> ❝ *I discovered that when I believed my thoughts, I suffered, but that when I didn't believe them, I didn't suffer, and that this is true for every human being. Freedom is as simple as that. I found that suffering is optional. I found a joy within me that has never disappeared, not for a single moment.* ❞
>
> —Byron Katie

Rumi says, "Let yourself be drawn by the stronger pull of what you really love." Your passion draws you forward. One way to get started with the design process is first to have a vision for your workshop. Then, explore the connection between your topic (what your workshop is about) and your own experience of transformation. Next, design mind-body experiences that engage your participants' bodies, minds, hearts, and spirits. Part of the design phase is sequencing your workshop as a journey with a beginning, middle, and end. Then you're ready to deliver your workshop. Finally, after your participants leave, keep in touch by following up. See Figure 3.1 and the four phases checklist in the Appendix C.

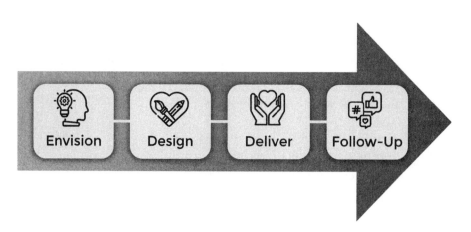

Figure 3.1 Phases of Creating Your Workshop

In the following chapters, we'll walk you through the steps of this process, starting with creating a vision for your workshop as an expression of your work in the world.

## WHAT HAS LIFE ENTRUSTED TO YOU?

What were your turning points? The more deeply you connect your own life to your workshop, the more alive you will be with your group. Therefore, get clear about what you're called to teach (your topic) and why it's important to you (your story). Where these two intersect is where your workshop lives in you. See Figure 3.2.

Figure 3.2 The Intersection of Your Topic and Your Story

## Your Topic: What is Your Workshop About?

What was Hisla's topic? What was she called to teach? Her topic grew directly from her life experience. By identifying her own challenges, she created a compelling workshop vision: to support medical professionals in sharing emotional connections and physical touch with their patients.

If you don't already have a workshop topic in mind, reflect on the following questions to help you generate ideas from your own life. If you already have one, use these questions to validate or refine your idea.

**Reflect on Your Workshop Topic**

- What's the fire in your belly? What lights you up? What breaks your heart?
- Where in your life are you already fulfilling your calling?
- Who are you called to serve? What do these people have in common? What are their challenges?
- Embody your promise to the world by saying the following: "I promise, no matter what, no matter when, that I will use my life to serve others by . . ."

Figure 3.3 Reflect on Your Workshop Topic

Wherever you are in the process, try to have a provisional workshop topic in mind. Write it down. It doesn't have to be fully formed; you can come back later to refine it.

## Your Story: Embracing the Lessons of Your Life

Bring yourself into your workshop design by exploring where your topic and your life experience meet. Try to figure out what your story is really about. The essence of Hisla's story was a serious health event that forced her to stop and examine her life. She learned that things have to break before they can heal, and she came to realize how her heart attack was a gift. Now she is using her healing to help others heal.

Looking at the narrative of your life gives you perspective. Here are some prompts to get you started.

### Reflect on Your Story

Imagine yourself as the hero of your own personal growth adventure.

- What were the pivotal events in your plotline? Who were the key people?
- What were the obstacles and triumphs along the way?
- What shifted? What changed? How are you different (and perhaps the same)?

Figure 3.4 Reflect on Your Story

Share your reflections with someone whose feedback you value. Tell your story from your heart, not just from your head. Step out of the literal recounting of it and tap into metaphor, images, or descriptive words. How did it feel to you? What insights came to you? Tell it and retell it in many different ways until you get to the essence, or as Galway Kinnell said, "until it flowers again from within, of self-blessing."

In our workshops, we find ways to share our personal stories. In post-workshop evaluations, participants often report that hearing the leader's story was a turning point for them. Revealing yourself through story can empower participants to reclaim their own personal narratives.

### GENERATING IDEAS

There are many ways to generate ideas for your workshop design. We use a brainstorming method called *mind mapping*. It is an intuitive way to get ideas about mind-body experiences, information you want to share, resources, assumptions, and values on paper without analysis.

Here's how to prepare for mind mapping:

- Use a large piece of chart paper or a standard piece of paper.
- Use colored pencils, pens, or crayons to encourage your creative side.
- Find a quiet place with enough space to lay out your materials.
- Set aside enough time—at least 30 minutes.

One way to begin mind mapping is meditation.

---

**Mind-Mapping Meditation**

- Sit comfortably and quietly with your materials in front of you.
- Breathe deeply and tune in to your body.
- Once you feel centered, begin to form a question about your deepest wish for the workshop. These questions might be helpful:
  - What has life entrusted to me?
  - How did I learn this?
  - What does this group need from me?

Figure 3.5 Mind-Mapping Meditation

---

**Mind-Mapping Instructions:** In the center of your blank paper, write down the main idea or topic of your workshop. Keep it simple—just a word or phrase. Next, let your imagination freely associate. Try not to edit, filter, or censor. Suspend all judgement (don't label anything "good" or "bad"). Have fun and play with possibilities.

Remember, the cost of early criticism is killing off possibilities before they arise. As words or images come to mind, jot them down. You can use colors, circles, or squares to highlight main ideas. Draw lines and arrows to make connections. Continue putting ideas on paper: thoughts, feelings, images, activities—whatever arises. There's no right way to do mind mapping. There's only your way.

Mind mapping is a creative process to get at the heart of your workshop: *why* you're doing it. Now it's time to synthesize and organize—to get clearer about *what* you're going to do. Depending on the direction your mind map took, you might use the following questions to bring your ideas into focus.

*" Creativity is . . . seeing something that doesn't exist already. You need to find out how you can bring it into being, and that way be a playmate with God. "*

—Michele Shea

- What's essential? What's at the heart of the workshop?

- What ideas from the mind map are jumping out and pulling you forward?

- What are your workshop outcomes and promises?

- What are the main activities and experiences you want to include?

- What surprised and delighted you?

Sifting and sorting your mind map will help you clarify ideas and see what's emerging. Keep this list handy as you move through the coming chapters.

---

### Mind-Mapping Tips

- Loosen up, get silly, and don't stop 'til it's over!
- Take a short break and do something active. Take a walk, play with your pet, or dance to the oldies.
- Draw images if words aren't coming to you.
- As themes or clusters emerge, link them together.
- Feel free to change the central idea if it no longer resonates with you.
- Come back to your mind map a day or two later and add to it. It can be an iterative process.
- Search the Internet for images of mind maps to help you get started.

Figure 3.6 Mind-Mapping Tips

## IN SUMMARY

The more deeply you explore what formed you and shaped the journey of your life, the more you will understand your motivation for offering workshops. When you have a felt sense of your purpose, it resonates in you, and your participants will feel it.

Once you're clear about your motivation and your *why*, the next chapter will help you to dive into the *how* of creating the conditions for transformation in your workshops by using mind-body experiences.

**Putting it into Practice:**
**Journal Prompts**

- How did exploring your story and your topic move you forward?
- What can you celebrate from your mind-mapping journey?
- What did you discover about yourself or your topic that's insightful, memorable, or even uncomfortable?

Figure 3.7 Putting it into Practice: Journal Prompts

# Beth's Story

## Embracing the Shadow

In Chapters 4, 5, and 6, we explore more deeply how experience drives change in both transformational workshops and life. We look at the theory and practice of creating mind-body experiences that produce lasting positive outcomes. In Beth's story, a psychotherapist uses her own "shadow work" to design a highly experiential workshop that encourages participants to notice and befriend their difficult inner voices.

All of us have hidden parts that we don't normally want to own or share with others—shadow parts. Typically, we try to ignore or push away what we don't like about ourselves, with blame and shame. In doing so, we not only alienate our whole selves, but we also miss out on the wisdom and gifts these other parts of us have to offer.

My Buddhist meditation practice has given me guidelines about how to bring compassion and friendliness to even my most challenging stuff. And my training as a psychotherapist has given me perspectives on human behavior and thought. But it wasn't until I experienced *shadow work* during a nine-month certification training in mind-body yoga therapy that I discovered my inner rules-obsessed, perfectionist-librarian character hanging out right next to my inner leather-clad, thrill-seeking, reckless biker. Shadow work helped me uncover insights about why and how I kept getting in my own way and working against my own best interests.

I wanted to help others experience this kind of life-changing insight.

As I set about to design my workshop, I first articulated my overarching goal: to bring shadow work to life, taking it beyond a mental exercise. I wanted to give my participants a chance to voice their shadow parts (rather than avoid them). This meant listening to how those shadow parts felt and to what they were trying to show us. I wanted to create a space for participants to immerse themselves in the experience and get as close as possible to their shadows.

My theater background in college and my use of psychodrama in therapy with my clients led me to explore shadow characters more broadly than practitioners following only the classical approach. A seed of an idea began to form: What if my participants could play out the role of the shadow character instead of only playing themselves, as is common in classical psychodrama? And what if, in addition to archetypal characters like heroes and gods, there were infinite ways of imagining ourselves, like a huge cast of characters in a play that spans every genre? Perhaps within each of us there would be a dragon or a weeping willow tree or a badass motorcyclist—or perhaps all of them were in there together.

I felt the energy behind this idea, and I dug deeper into the design. What kind of structure might work to do this? What questions might help these shadow parts reveal themselves? How could I give them a chance to speak up? Perhaps if they were invited to give an interview like a famous celebrity, they would find they had something to say. They could reveal those words rather than keeping them concealed.

The ideas coalesced into a shadow-work session that would take place on the Saturday evening of a weekend residential retreat that I was co-facilitating with a colleague. I designed the session so that everyone would get a chance to embody one of their shadows, and I scheduled enough time to group participants into threes so that each shadow could be interviewed by one participant while the other participant took notes.

To help participants get into character, I filled a giant trunk with costumes and props: hats and crowns, scarves, robes, swords, wands, wings, wine bottles—anything I could get my hands on. As I envisioned it, during each round, one person from each trio would come to the center and select a costume and props and return to their group to give an interview as their shadow part. At the end of each round, participants would rotate until everyone had a chance in each role.

I created a notes sheet for interviewers with questions that were designed to give the shadow a chance to speak freely about who they were, what they wanted their person to know, how they wanted to be treated, and anything else they felt moved to say.

I was so excited about this exercise. I had put time and thought into planning it as the peak experience of the workshop. All the previous activities would lead up to this moment, with enough safety built up so that each person's shadow characters could just go for it. Or so I thought.

When I first introduced the shadow-work exercise during the Saturday afternoon session, there was a round of nervous laughter that turned into resistance. One by one, each participant expressed their concerns: They were too emotionally tired. It felt too risky. It seemed too goofy. It wouldn't be useful. They didn't want to do it.

I hadn't expected this. Sure, I had expected discomfort, but I hadn't foreseen so much outright resistance. I certainly hadn't expected one of my own shadow characters to show up—the perfectionist-librarian who believes that if something doesn't go according to plan or is not a perfect success, then it's a failure (and, therefore, I'm a failure).

Taking a deep breath, I gave the group a chance to process their feelings and to review the group agreements, which stated that all activities were optional. My co-leader and I encouraged everyone to be involved to the degree that they were willing—even if they only took the roles of interviewer and recorder and not the role of shadow. I breathed deeply and wondered, *Will it take off or fall apart?*

The first round of brave volunteers came forward. They all picked lighter and easier unclaimed parts of themselves. The flower leis, ukulele, and Mardi Gras beads were popular props that round. But something happened as they gave their interviews. As they allowed themselves to welcome and really take on the voices and experiences of those unwanted parts, I heard both laughter and crying.

Because the groups were unevenly numbered, I got to participate in a small group and conduct an interview in the last round. The person I interviewed costumed her shadow character—also a perfectionist—very primly. The perfectionist was smug and arrogant throughout the interview, showing absolutely no concern about the impact of her attitude, and remained firmly convinced of her own rightness. It was hard to see how this participant was going to see any gift from her shadow.

Then came the last question of the interview—Is there anything else that you want to say?—leaving the door wide open for whatever wanted to be shared. The perfectionist took a long pause, a deep breath, and then began to cry. "I'm sorry. I'm so sorry." Through her tears, the shadow felt the hurt that she had unintentionally caused in her misguided attempt to try to protect against disappointment and failure. I could feel my own inner perfectionist nodding along in agreement. Person and shadow finally found some compassion for each other.

In the end, every person chose to take a turn in the shadow role. When the group talked about their experience, many people shared that it was the most difficult and transformative experience of the weekend. Several were surprised that, despite intentionally picking shadow characters they thought would be easy to deal with, very deep emotional issues came up. There was something powerful about embodying and giving voice to a part of them that had been hidden away, shamed, or silenced for so long. There was something powerful in being listened to kindly and with curiosity.

I think back on all the time I spent designing this session. I certainly had expectations about how it would play out. But what actually transpired was so much more than I could have imagined. I'm so glad I listened to that part of me that wanted to help others in this way.

This story was written by Beth Charbonneau and edited by the authors. Beth is a psychotherapist and makes her home in Maryland. Visit www.bethcharbonneau.com to see more of her work.

# Chapter 4

# What You Practice Grows Stronger

*Much mental and therefore neural activity flows through the brain like ripples on a river, with no lasting effects on its channel. But intense, prolonged, or repeated mental/neural activity—especially if it is conscious—will leave an enduring imprint in neural structure, like a surging current reshaping a riverbed.*

—Rick Hanson

*I*n the last chapter, we discussed weaving your personal narrative into the design of your workshop, revealing why you're called to do this work. Your unique voice, presence, and story will enliven the workshop in a way that only you can provide.

All human learning begins with and is shaped by our experiences. The next step is to create mind-body experiences for your participants that embody what you want to teach in a way that will have a lasting positive impact. Beth gave people a way to uncover self-sabotage experientially by deepening the impact of shadow work to reveal life-changing insights. The mind-body experience of role playing allowed her participants to investigate and hear the hidden wisdom in "negative" self-talk.

In this chapter and the next, we'll lay out the theory and practice of how to create mind-body experiences for your workshop—and how to make the learning stick.

## TRANSFORMATIONAL LEARNING: EXPONENTIAL LEARNING

The work of a transformational teacher is not about telling people what you know and expecting them to change and grow. Teaching through direct experience has far greater potential for healing, growing, and awakening. By actively engaging the whole person—the body, mind, heart, and spirit—participants will be more successful at focusing attention, solving problems, and remembering solutions.

> " Our bodies don't exist to carry our heads around. Any thinking has the whole body participating. "
>
> —Candace Pert

In general, there are four possible growth curves: negative growth, no growth, linear growth, and exponential growth. Transformational learning enables *exponential growth,* energizing individuals to become agents of their own learning.

Learning endures longer when a leader guides learners to take time to focus on what's rewarding and meaningful about an experience. When the leader directs awareness to how growth feels in the body, participants can consciously absorb and savor the experience. By letting it really sink in, the learning is internalized and becomes a part of the participant's emotional memory. It ignites motivation to continue growing and learning, and the impact will last long after the program is over. In other words, you help your participants learn how to learn.[13]

## TWO FORCES SHAPE THE BRAIN: CONDITIONING AND NEUROPLASTICITY

For better or worse, what you practice becomes a part of you. The brain is continually shaping, conditioning, and reconstructing itself based on the messages and experiences that are repeated in our thoughts, words, and actions.

We know that the brain is good at learning from negative experiences but comparatively poor at learning from good experiences. As Rick Hanson explains, the brain is Teflon to positive experiences and Velcro to negative experiences. Because of our *negativity bias*, pleasant experiences often slip away without notice, while unpleasant experiences stick. Painful or harmful experiences are then rapidly converted into lasting changes in neural structure or function, and they become the default mode of thinking and behaving. In yoga, these conditioned patterns are called *samskaras*, or energy blocks. Any energetic experience not lived out remains trapped inside the body until it is released. As long as you repeat these patterns unconsciously, you are not free.

Learning from experience is encoded into the brain's neural circuitry by the twin mechanisms of conditioning and neuroplasticity. *Conditioning* is how the brain learns and stabilizes our past patterns of response through repeated experience. *Neuroplasticity* is the brain's ability to transform itself physically and alter our learned responses by growing new neurons and connecting them in new ways.

Through focusing attention, conditioning and neuroplasticity can work together to change patterns of behavior. As Linda Graham writes in her book *Bouncing Back*, "When you focus attention on the conditioned pattern you want to rewire, you activate the neural networks of that pattern and cause the neurons to fire again. When you know how to harness the neuroplasticity of your brain in that moment, you can alter the pattern."[14]

The key to transformation is self-awareness. A transformational leader helps participants bring attention to hidden assumptions, which are often part of our default stories or identities, such as the lost child or hard-hearted person. We do this through the safe witnessing of habitual thinking and judgments. For example, if you bring to mind a habitual negative thought and shine the light of self-awareness on it, then the thought can be seen for what it is—a thought among many thoughts, like a tree in a forest of trees. When we see with this larger lens, the negative loses its hold over us, and the reality of who and what we are can emerge.

## MIND-BODY EXPERIENCE: "ORCHESTRATED IMMERSION"[15]

In his work on self-directed neuroplasticity, Rick Hanson points to various factors that lead to lasting change in the brain. Learning is enriched and deepened when experiences are personally relevant, emotionally stimulating, new and different, reinforced through repetition, and engaged through multiple modalities.[16] Mind-body experiences are the vehicle for exponential learning in a transformational workshop. They connect people to themselves, others, and the natural world.

Mind-body experiences are an invitation to go on a journey of exploration and self-inquiry. The value of experience is that it is engaging. It lets people find answers for themselves, have a stake in what they create, and then share their discoveries with others. The Chinese proverb says it this way: "I hear and I forget. I see and I remember. I do and I understand." The path of direct experience is to know for yourself what you can rely on. Direct experience develops your capacity for insight and empathy, and cultivates your ability to respond rather than react to life.

As a workshop leader, you can design and create an environment where participants become deeply interested in direct, firsthand experience. You can also give them ways to reframe the negative and, conversely, remember the good and the wholesome, such as insight, empathy, resilience, self-esteem, and positive mood. In Beth's story, a participant role-played a shadow aspect of herself and became painfully aware of the self-inflicted hurt she had suffered as a perfectionist. She found forgiveness and self-acceptance.

Mind-body *experiences* are often derived from, or are inspired by, the mind-body *practices* of yoga, tai chi, qigong, and other practices from wisdom traditions. In fact, transformational workshops and retreats are often designed with mind-body practices as an integral part of the agenda. Huston Smith describes these practices as spiritual technologies that link the heart and the mind. There's increasing evidence that the postures, breathing, relaxation, and meditation of mind-body practices have a synergistic effect on human functionality—enhancing fitness, self-regulation, awareness, and spirituality (see Figure 4.1).

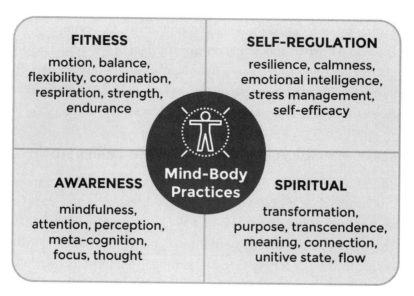

Figure 4.1 Synergistic Benefits of Mind-Body Practices[17]

Harvard researcher Howard Gardner recognized that all of us learn and experience reality differently, through multiple intelligences.[v] In transformational workshops,

---

[v] In his book *Frames of Mind* (1983), Gardner articulated seven sensory modalities. He has since expanded the list, which now includes musical-rhythmic and harmonic, visual-spatial, verbal-linguistic, logical-mathematical, bodily-kinesthetic, interpersonal, intrapersonal, naturalistic, and existential intelligences. At the

mind-body experiences can be diverse, creative, and multi-modal, as seen with Beth's role playing and shadow interviews. In your workshops, how can you create opportunities for everyone to grow and learn?

## INTEGRATING MIND AND BODY: TOP DOWN OR BOTTOM UP?

In transformational workshops, we use our current understanding of the mind-body connection intentionally in the following two ways: Mind-body experiences can either start in the body and impact the mind (*body-based experiences*) or start in the mind and impact the body (*mind-centered experiences*). Mind-body experiences, regardless of whether they are based in physiology or cognition, have an integrating or unifying effect on the whole person.

### Bottom-Up Integration

Bottom-up or body-based experiences start in the body and trickle up into the mind. Examples include controlled breathing, mindful movement, yoga or qigong postures, singing, dancing, drumming, shaking, tapping on the body, and progressive muscular relaxation. Movement and exercise enhance optimal learning states. If you ask participants to stand up and stretch their legs after mental exertion, you're using the body to freshen the brain and clear the mind. Breathwork and movement are two evidence-based embodied practices that can be integrated into mind-body experiences.

> *An anxious mind cannot exist in a relaxed body.*
>
> —Edmund Jacobson

### *Breath*

The quickest way to enhance attention, positively impact mood, cope with stress, and reduce anxiety and depression, is to slow the pace of your breathing. The breath is the gateway to the autonomic nervous system. When stressed, the breath tends to be short and shallow, whereas slow and full breathing reduces tension and promotes relaxation. Our bodies and brains interpret long, slow breathing as a sign that we are safe and available to learn. Research has shown that six to 10 breaths per minute is optimal for enhancing stress resilience.[18] Slow-paced breathing trickles up and

---

time of writing this book, Gardner was considering adding the "pedagogical" modality to his list. This affirms that teaching others is one of the fundamental ways that people sense, experience, and learn.

promotes creativity, mental and emotional flexibility, and more conscious and non-reactive behavior.[19]

### *Movement*

Movement can be as simple as standing and stretching, tensing and releasing, or dancing to music. Strong evidence supports the connection between movement and learning. Evidence from imaging sources, anatomical studies, and clinical data shows that moderate exercise enhances cognitive processing and increases the number of brain cells. Even light physical activity increases the connectivity between brain areas and improves memory.[20] When you use intentional movement in your mind-body experience, you influence the mind.

---

**Two Types of Breathing Exercises**

**Attentional Focus (Monitoring—or Following—the Breath)**

Follow your breath. Observe the sensations of the breath wherever you feel them in your body. Let the breath be just as it is, without changing it. When your mind wanders, return to noticing the sensations of breathing. Just notice. Continue for two to five minutes.

**Intentional Focus (Slow-Paced Breathing)**

Gradually lengthen the breath to a count of four for both the in-breath and out-breath. Pause. Now focus on extending the exhalation without forcing or straining. Inhale for four counts and extend the exhale to six counts. Continue for two to five minutes.

---

Figure 4.2 Two Types of Breathing Exercises

## Top-Down Integration

Top-down or mind-centered experiences start in the cognitive domain and trickle down into the body. Examples include meditation, visualization and guided imagery, intention setting, reflection, journaling, affirmations, and poetry. Depending on your intention, these practices can be included in a mind-body experience to focus the mind, stimulate creativity, generate insight, or soothe the nervous system. There are several ways you might integrate these top-down practices into a mind-body experience.

### Invoking Mindfulness

Invite participants into nonjudgmental awareness by saying the following: "Take a deep breath. Relax your body. Notice what you feel, without judging the thoughts or feelings. Simply watch and allow." Alternatively, you could facilitate a body scan, inviting participants to focus on parts of the body sequentially. Starting from the feet and moving to the head is generally more stimulating, while beginning in the head and progressing toward the feet is more calming.

### Intention Setting

Invite participants to imagine experiencing the successful results of their efforts: "Imagine yourself a year from now. You've just accomplished your goal. How do you feel? What does it look like? Working backward, what steps would you take to achieve this success?"

### Affirmation Using Past Success

Guide participants to think of a previous experience of accomplishment and apply it to a present life circumstance: "Do you remember a time when learning was fun, when creativity was natural? What were the conditions then that made the difference for you? How can you generate those conditions now?"

### Small Group Interviews to Activate Mindsets

Ask participants to suspend assumptions and to freely imagine as they interview each other: "If it were impossible for you to fail, what would you be doing right now? If you only had a year to live, how would you be living your life? What would you be doing differently?"

### Journal Prompts to Face the Dragon

Use this journal prompt to help participants confront the discomforts that we habitually avoid: "What's the worst that could happen if you arrange that job interview, apply to that college, ask for what you want, or address another challenge in your life?"

## IN SUMMARY

When your participants learn through direct experience and active, conscious participation, the impact will continue after the workshop is over. Mind-body experiences are the vehicle for exponential learning, and they can either be body based or mind based. Keep this distinction in mind as you design your own mind-body experiences in the next chapter.

**Putting it into Practice:**
**Journal Prompts**

- Recall a group experience that was profound or impactful. What experiences do you remember from that workshop? Were there any that you might use in your own workshop?

- If you already lead workshops, how might you use some top-down and bottom-up practices to enrich your workshop?

- If you find that you are working harder than your participants, how can you step back and allow them to step forward and have a greater stake in the workshop?

Figure 4.3 Putting it into Practice: Journal Prompt

Chapter 5

# From Idea to Mind-Body Experience

*What I find inspiring is to take a concept and guide someone to the possibility of experiencing it from the inside. The challenge is how to create an environment where people are eager and willing to grow.*

—Sudhir Jonathan Foust

*L*ife experiences have the power to change us, as do intentionally designed mind-body experiences. In the last chapter, you gained a theoretical framework for mind-body experiences—what they are and why they're important for a transformational workshop. In this chapter, you'll see how to design mind-body experiences suited for your workshop.

## YOUR WORKSHOP PROMISES

Mind-body experiences connect to your workshop promises—your intended outcomes. They serve to move your participants toward your promises. It's helpful to ask yourself how each aspect of your workshop serves your overall workshop outcomes.

Recall from Chapter 2 the three types of workshops: conventional, experiential, and transformational. These three categories provide a useful way of thinking through

61

your outcomes. Figure 5.1 shows examples of the kinds of outcomes associated with each type.

| TYPE | OUTCOME | PARTICIPANTS WILL BE ABLE TO: | |
|---|---|---|---|
| **Conventional** | Knowing | Understand ... | Classify ... |
| | | Define ... | Describe ... |
| | | Recognize ... | Explain ... |
| | | Discuss ... | Locate ... |
| | | Remember ... | Recite ... |
| **Experiential** | Doing | Execute ... | Differentiate ... |
| | | Implement ... | Organize ... |
| | | Solve ... | Use ... |
| | | Demonstrate ... | Perform ... |
| | | Synthesize ... | Create ... |
| **Transformational** | Being | Grow ... | Become aware of ... |
| | | Adapt ... | Be nonreactive to ... |
| | | Learn ... | Show compassion for ... |
| | | Be with ... | Listen and notice ... |
| | | Receive ... | Be at peace with ... |
| | | Observe ... | Let go of ... |
| | | Attune to ... | Accept ... |

Figure 5.1 Outcomes for Conventional, Experiential, and Transformational Workshops[21]

In Beth's workshop, she wanted her participants to understand that there's a shadow side in each of them (knowing outcome). She wanted them to become able to embody their shadows (doing outcome). But most of all, she wanted her participants to normalize and accept their shadows by listening to them, showing compassion, and remaining nonreactive (being outcomes).

Getting clear on your workshop promises will inform how you design mind-body experiences by infusing your workshop with your own energy. Write down three to five promises for your workshop. These might come from the mind map and brainstorming work you did in Chapter 3, or you might come at them from a fresh perspective now.

### INSIGHT AND EMPATHY

As a leader, you are designing opportunities for participants to enhance insight and empathy through mind-body experiences that offer direct encounters with themselves, others, and the natural world.

Let's first look at *insight*. It's tempting to simply tell (i.e., give information to) our participants what we want them to learn. Information is valuable, but it comes from external sources. Insight, on the other hand, comes from within. Insight is the meaning participants make of their experience. Information and insight work hand in hand to move your participants along the path of discovery.

Before participants engage in an experience, they may be asking themselves, *Why would I want to do this? What's in it for me?* Knowing that, how will you encourage participation, link the activity to their intentions, and create safety, especially if there is perceived risk involved or the hurdle of trying an activity that's new to them? It's important to give a context and purpose for the experience.

Providing information prior to the mind-body experience is called *front-loading*. Here, participants get the information first and then go through an experience that helps them apply that information (such as in the meditation example). Front-loading sets a more controlled and less ambiguous tone for the experience that allows your participants to understand in advance what they're doing and why they're doing it. This is part of *informed consent*, an ethical approach whereby participants can choose to participate or not. Front-loading is especially recommended for mind-body experiences that are higher risk, or if you know you have participants who have a history of trauma.

---

**Example: The Setup for Meditation**

If you're asking people to sit in silence and meditate for 10 minutes, give them reasons to participate:

- **Activate Curiosity and Appeal to Personal Relevance.** "Does your mind wander? Do you sometimes find it difficult to focus?"
- **Normalize Mind Wandering.** "Mind wandering is quite normal—it's the mind's basic survival mechanism for being on the lookout for danger."
- **Give Evidence.** "In fact, a Harvard study by Killingsworth in 2010 found that people experience mind wandering about 47% of the time."
- **Explain the Benefits.** "Meditating is a form of *attention training* to help you be calmer and clearer in daily life."

Figure 5.2 Example: The Setup for Meditation

---

It's also valid to provide information *after* the experience. This is called *back-loading*. This approach implies that you have previously given your participants permission to opt out at any time during the workshop. We recommend periodically reminding participants to decide for themselves when and how to opt out. Back-loading works best in more advanced groups or after the group has been well established. When you back-load an experience, there's more ambiguity and uncertainty. Without a framework, your participants have less of a scaffold to construct meaning. This can lead to more open-ended, creative outcomes.

Whether you decide to front-load or back-load the context for an experience, the important thing to remember is that you are inviting people to create their own meaning from the experience. It is the experience itself that opens up possibilities for new meaning.

---

**Example of Front-Loading Versus Back-Loading**

In our workshops, we explore the twin roles of an embodied leader: teaching and facilitating. We've designed an experience to generate insight related to balancing the twin roles. We give each person a peacock feather and have them walk around with the feather while performing increasingly complex tasks (balancing the feather on one hand, looking at others while balancing the feather, passing the feather to someone else, etc.). We've tried both front-loading and back-loading the twin roles concept:

- **Front-Loading:** When we front-load the experience by explaining the twin roles first, participants usually experience aha moments directly related to the teaching concept; that is, the challenges of balancing teaching and facilitating. The outcomes are more streamlined in terms of the conclusions participants draw from them. This can be helpful when we don't have much time for processing and integration.
- **Back-Loading:** When we back-load the experience and don't provide the model ahead of time, aha moments come from life itself. They're more varied, create broader connections, and can be surprising.

These approaches are equally valid, and we've found powerful insights emerge when leading the experience both ways.

---

Figure 5.3 Example of Front-Loading Versus Back-Loading

Now let's look at *empathy*, the innate ability to sense another person's emotions and to imagine what they might be thinking or feeling. Empathy is the quality of understanding that allows an individual to see outside of themselves, take on the perspective of another, and perceive the world in a new way. Sometimes just a simple expression of empathy toward another is enough to give that person a sense of feeling felt, of being understood or known. Empathy is deepened when we're given opportunities to relate to others through mindful interactions in a workshop.

To enhance empathy in a transformational workshop, you must co-create an environment that cultivates real intimacy and makes people feel safe enough to reveal (rather than conceal) their feelings and needs. Invite participants to share what's present for them, speak and listen from the heart, and witness others without judging, rescuing, fixing, or giving advice.

---

### Co-Listening Practice

Co-listening is a form of listening and speaking meditation done in pairs. It promotes self-awareness and empathy, lowers the barriers to true self-expression and bonding, and allows people to be seen and heard.

**Setup:**
The leader invites a welcoming space for the inner voice. She gives instructions and explains the benefits of doing the experience. Then the leader and assistant demonstrate and ask for questions.

Participants choose a partner and sit diagonally across from one another, close enough to be heard easily, perhaps touching, possibly holding hands. They decide who will speak first. The speaker has his eyes closed (with an option to gaze down instead). The listener keeps her eyes open, softly focusing on the speaker. The leader begins the experience with a signal (such as a bell or chime) and keeps the time, approximately five minutes. The leader ends with a signal to change roles.

**Steps:**
1. With eyes closed, the speaker starts by reporting what's going on in his physical body, beginning by saying, "I am aware of _____," and letting that stream of consciousness evolve. The speaker is invited to speak without judgment or expectation, to allow themselves to speak without editing or censoring, and to stay at the level of awareness rather than commentary or storytelling.

2. With eyes open, the listener silently listens, holding the space without judgment or expectation, and being aware moment by moment of her own reactions and responses, but not expressing or acting on them. There is compassion but no fixing or analyzing.

3. The roles are reversed.

When co-listening ends, participants simply thank each other. There is no analysis or review of what was said. Everything shared is confidential and may not be mentioned without permission from the speaker.

---

Figure 5.4 Co-Listening Practice

A cornerstone of our training is a practice called *co-listening*, which cultivates self-awareness in the speaker and empathy in the listener (see Figure 5.4). After a recent training, a leader changed only one aspect of her workshops: She added co-listening. "I trimmed my content down, added co-listening, and allowed more time for group sharing. The participant feedback was awesome, and I've made co-listening a permanent part of my workshops. I also noticed more people were buying my books at the bookstore, even though that was not my goal!"

Regardless of your topic or content, a transformational workshop primes participants to take greater emotional risks than in everyday life. You encourage participants to express themselves, to be seen and accepted by others, and to explore their interconnectedness. This can be as simple as doing an activity together, followed by time to share about the experience with the others in the group.

In Beth's workshop, she designed ways for participants to relate to themselves (by role playing) and to another (through the interview process). While the workshop attendees resisted at first, eventually they participated willingly because Beth had created a safe and caring community to explore their inner lives.

## DESIGNING FROM YOUR OWN EXPERIENCE

Reflect on your own journey—the ways in which you've gained a deeper understanding of life (insight) and also a deeper connection to yourself and others (empathy). By getting curious about how this happened, you'll be able to design mind-body experiences that give your participants similar opportunities to deepen their own wisdom and compassion.

The series of questions in Figure 5.5 can help guide you through a process of translating your own life lessons into an experience for others.

While reflecting on these questions, look for the essence of your experience rather than focusing on the details. It sometimes helps to express this essence in adjectives or as a metaphor. These adjectives or metaphors can help you bridge the gap between your knowledge of the topic and what you hope participants will gain from the experience. In our feather activity, balancing the feather is a metaphor for balancing the twin roles of teaching and facilitating while leading a workshop. By reflecting on and sharing their subjective experiences, participants discover their own intuitive understanding of teaching and facilitating, and benefit from the learning that happens through group feedback.

> ### Mind-Body Experience Design Questions
>
> - **Topic:** What's the topic of your workshop? What information do you want to share? What skill do you want to teach?
> - **Relevance:** Why is this important to you? What difference has it made in your life?
> - **Method:** How did you learn this? What insight and/or information lit you up or moved you forward? What experience or experiences caused you to see things differently?
> - **Impact:** How did connection to yourself and others play into your journey?
> - **Experience:** What experiences would help someone else travel along a similar road?

Figure 5.5 Mind-Body Experience Design Questions

How can you design mind-body experiences that are open ended enough to be inclusive, and specific enough to direct attention toward your topic? For Beth, her insight about the shadow sides of her personality (perfectionist-librarian and badass motorcyclist) inspired her to create an experience using characters with props, costumes, and role playing. The metaphor of "character" provided enough room for participants to find and explore roles that were personal to them while safely guiding them to engage with the vulnerability of their shadows.

Furthermore, from her own experience, Beth knew that there were important elements of relationship and connection inherent in shadow work. First, there was the connection between each participant and his or her shadow. Second, she designed an interview process with an interviewer and a note-taker, creating opportunities for connection. These intentionally designed invitations to relate and connect to oneself and others helped to deepen insight and empathy.

Let's look at another example. Let's say your topic is mindfulness, and you'd like to use eating mindfully as a concrete example of mindfulness in everyday life. It's all too common for people to rush through a meal without even tasting their food. Mindfulness practices, such as bringing present-moment attention to the physical act of eating, can rebuild connections with internal cues of hunger and fullness, allowing people to feel more in control and enjoy the experience of eating. You might begin by having participants connect to their breath and body, and have them notice their feet on the ground and their thoughts, sensations, and emotions right before eating. Then, you may invite them to tune in to their senses—to the color, texture, and smell of their food. Offer opportunities to slow down, such as suggesting they put the fork down between each bite and notice the changing tastes in their mouths.

Finally, offer a time for sharing with another and the group as a whole to bring greater appreciation for a common universal human experience.

Some workshop topics are more ambiguous or complex and will challenge you to think more creatively. For example, if you're designing a workshop on creativity, fear, or self-compassion, it's helpful to explore it in detail. How did you get to where you are? In a creativity workshop, for example, you might reflect on your own journey and see what shifted your perspective. How did you shuffle the deck, or how was the deck shuffled for you? Let's say you experienced a creativity breakthrough when you were painting on vacation and forgot your favorite brushes. You were surprised (and pleased!) to discover new techniques as you used unfamiliar brushes. Drawing on this experience, your creativity workshop could include an experience of doing something in a new way; for example:

- using your nondominant hand to eat a meal
- getting over fear of failure by deliberately doing something challenging (starting a conversation with a stranger)
- practicing slowing down by taking five minutes to observe your subject before painting the first stroke, settling yourself before writing the first word, or listening to silence before sounding the first chord

The value of immediate experience is that participants gain the opportunity to look at reality with new eyes, answer to their own voices, and build a world that originates from their own experiences.

In the next chapter, we'll explore a design tool to help you construct your mind-body experiences using a three-step process. You can also refer to the Transformational Learning Cycle worksheet in Appendix C.

## DOMAINS OF EXPERIENCE

Think about how athletes, musicians, soldiers, dancers, actors, and rescue workers bond through intense shared emotional experiences. In transformational workshops, mind-body experiences can offer the same possibility for empathy and emotional bonding between participants.

Experiences may be active, reflective, personal, or relational. A *reflective experience* engages the imagination, memory, or intuition. Examples of reflective experiences include guided meditation and body scanning (mind-centered experiences). A *personal experience*, such as journaling or silent meditation, is practiced alone. An *active experience* engages the mind-body connections through physical movement, as with stretching or dancing (body-based experiences). A *relational experience* creates interaction between or among individuals, such as when sharing and doing partner yoga. Figure 5.6 shows these four domains of an experience.

Beth designed an experience that was highly relational (the interview process) and active (dressing up and embodying the shadow). As we saw from her story, this drew resistance from some of the participants. The safe environment that she and her co-leader had fostered, coupled with their skillful facilitation, helped each participant step into the experience. Besides each participant's individual insight, this produced an additional reward in terms of group bonding.

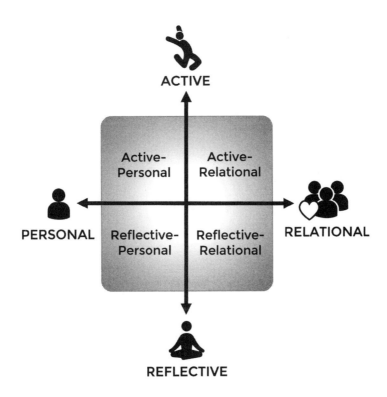

Figure 5.6 Domains of Experience

Below are examples of mind-body experiences in each domain.

### Personal-Reflective Domain

- visualization
- contemplation
- silent meditation
- deep relaxation (e.g., *savasana*)
- body scan (sensing)
- listening to music or poetry

## Personal-Active Domain

- conscious breathing
- drawing
- nature walk
- stretching
- sculpting
- tai chi/qigong/yoga
- conscious laughter
- self-massage
- meditative chanting
- rhythmic movement
- writing a letter to yourself

## Relational-Reflective Domain

- deep listening (listening without agenda, listening without speaking)
- praying for another person
- practicing loving-kindness or *metta* (sending well-wishes to oneself and others)
- sharing with a partner or group (e.g., pair sharing and group sharing)
- interviewing a partner

## Relational-Active Domain

- singing or chanting
- massage
- partner stretches
- role playing
- skits
- group visioning
- music making
- dance
- charades
- group sculpture
- blindfold dance
- mirror dance
- demonstration
- reading aloud
- mask making
- drumming
- support circles
- public declarations

Any one of these experiences can be used in multiple contexts and with different topics. For example, visualization is a powerful mind-body experience. It falls into the personal-reflective domain and is appropriate for most groups. If you were leading a workshop for people making a career transition, one of your workshop promises might be for the participants to develop an action plan that reflects their values and aspirations. Part of that process is knowing what to let go of. Consider how guided visualization can be used for this purpose.

> **Guided Visualization for Making Decisions**
>
> Ask participants to imagine a quality or behavior taken to the extreme. This can help them become clear about making alternative choices.
>
> Invite them: "Call to mind one area of your life right now that feels heavy. Imagine that it's a rock on your back. Allow that rock to get very heavy. Feel how heavy it is. What things in your life add to the heaviness? What choices could you make to get that weight off your back? What can you let go of?"

Figure 5.7 Guided Visualization for Making Decisions

Whether a participant leans into an experience or pulls back often depends on the perception of the threat versus safety of the experience. Each mind-body experience exists on a threat-safety continuum, which is entirely unique for each individual. There are many factors that could influence a person's perception of an experience, including temperament (e.g., introverted versus extroverted), life story (including trauma history), and cultural norms (e.g., personal space, eye contact). Offering your participants the choice to opt out of an experience without judgment honors each person and empowers them to make choices that are right for where they are at that moment.

Before you launch a mind-body experience, do a test run. Whether you are creating a theatrical mind-body experience (as Beth did using props and role playing) or simply using the body and the breath, you as a leader must be comfortable with the experience. Visualize it happening, including the sequence, props, music, and timing. Better still, practice it with willing test participants to make sure it's clear and can be accomplished as planned in the time allotted. You can also consult a colleague to get an opinion about how the experience will work and contribute to your workshop promises.

## IN SUMMARY

Mind-body experiences are not formulas. They are tools to invite your participants toward your workshop promises. Experiences that have moved you personally will likely resonate more intensely with your groups. You can keep a file of experiences that have touched, moved, and inspired you. Customize them for your workshop with questions and prompts that are aligned with your context and intended outcomes.

Although you can design an experience with certain outcomes in mind, you can't guarantee those outcomes. Experience is subjective. As Kripalu workshop leader Bhavani Lorraine Nelson says to her participants, "We guarantee that your experience will be exactly what it is." Trust the process and allow people to have their experiences. Invite them to pay attention to what's happening in the moment and to share their experiences with others. This is part of the holistic view.

Mind-body experiences are woven into the tapestry of your workshop in a specific way. They're nested in a three-part cycle with a setup (safety), buildup (experience), and payoff (integration). We call these steps the *transformational learning cycle*. More on the transformational learning cycle will follow in the next chapter.

**Putting it into Practice:**
**Journal Prompts**

- What are your workshop promises, and why are they important to you?
- As you reflect on the four domains (active, reflective, personal, and relational), do you lean toward one or two more than the others?

Figure 5.8 Putting it into Practice: Journal Prompts

# Chapter 6

# The Transformational Learning Cycle

*The basic formula for drama is setup, buildup, payoff—just like a joke. The setup tells us what the game is. The buildup is where you put in all the moves, the forward motion. . . . The payoff answers the question, Why are we here anyway? What is it that you've been trying to give? Drama must move forward and upward, or the seats on which the audience is sitting will become very hard and uncomfortable.*

—Anne Lamott

The conventional workshop model is primarily about information. The experiential model is more about skills. Transformational workshops include information and skills, but they are more about a way of being and rely on experience to drive the changes. Mind-body experiences are the centerpiece of a *transformational learning cycle* made up of three phases: safety, experience, and integration. As the workshop designer, you'll weave the threads of safety, experience, and integration into the fabric of your workshops in an unfolding series of learning cycles toward your overall intended outcomes (your workshop promises).

In the last chapter, we focused on the central feature of the transformational learning cycle—the mind-body experience. In this chapter, we'll describe the other two features—safety and integration.

## INTRODUCING THE TRANSFORMATIONAL LEARNING CYCLE

The structure of a transformational learning cycle is *setup* (safety), *buildup* (the mind-body experience), and *payoff* (integration). It's just like telling a good story with a beginning, middle, and end. To begin each cycle, you want your participants to feel safe enough to take risks and be vulnerable. Within that safe environment, mind-body experiences are opportunities for discovery—in the middle of the cycle. Integration comes at the end of each cycle and offers multiple ways to remember, make new meaning, and generate lasting outcomes. The learning has to really sink in; otherwise, it will dissipate without leaving a trace.[vi] Experience arises, registers, and passes away. The primary pathway to promote growth, healing, and development is to have positive experiences and internalize them.

Figure 6.1 shows the transformational learning cycle, which cannot occur without the engagement of the mind, body, heart, and spirit. When you complete one cycle, you can begin the next one.

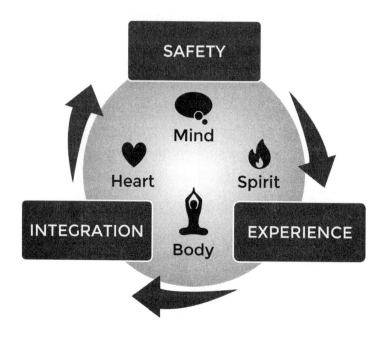

Figure 6.1 The Transformational Learning Cycle

---

[vi] In other words, "passing states" are less likely to become "lasting traits." See, for example, Hanson, R. (2016). *Hardwiring happiness: The new brain science of contentment, calm, and confidence.* Harmony.

The transformational learning cycle helps to create what brain-based researchers call *optimal learning conditions*:[22]

- a low-threat, high-challenge state of mind (relaxed alertness)
- multiple complex and authentic experiences (orchestrated immersion)
- the opportunity to make meaning of experience (active processing)

When leaders weave these threads of safety, experience, and integration throughout their group work, participants feel held in a fabric tough and tender enough to handle the emotional intensity and complexity of change, making it safe yet challenging, predictable but not inevitable.

A transformational workshop repeats this spiraling pattern, each experience preparing the group for the next cycle and offering opportunities for participants to move along a path of self-discovery.

## A COMPARISON: CONVENTIONAL AND TRANSFORMATIONAL

Let's consider an hour-long hospital lunchtime wellness workshop on mindful eating. Figure 6.2 shows two approaches: a conventional workshop and a transformational workshop using the transformational learning cycle.

| AGENDA ITEM | CONVENTIONAL APPROACH | TRANSFORMATIONAL APPROACH |
|---|---|---|
| **1. Welcome & Introductions** | People sit in rows as a leader stands at a podium. The leader welcomes everybody and introduces herself and the topic, shares the objectives, and describes the methods. | People sit in a circle. The leader welcomes everyone with a brief story about her experience with an eating disorder and how mindful eating helped her to recover. Participants are then asked to reflect and journal on their relationship with food, including while growing up (e.g., recalling how mealtimes were at home or at school), and what prompted them to attend this workshop. |
| **2. Learning About Mindful Eating** | The leader shows a slide presentation with the research behind mindful eating and quotes from experts. | Using all of their senses and honoring the food and themselves, the group is invited to go on a mindful journey while eating a single raisin for a full minute. Participants are then invited to turn to a neighbor and share their experiences, including any insights about their usual eating habits. |

| AGENDA ITEM | CONVENTIONAL APPROACH | TRANSFORMATIONAL APPROACH |
|---|---|---|
| **3. Developing a Mindful Eating Plan** | The leader presents a list of ways eating mindfully can be used to achieve healthy eating goals and invites participants to put them into practice. | Participants are asked to take a few moments to consider one change they are willing to make this week in their approach to eating, and one person in their life who could support them to make this change. |
| **4. Closing** | The leader offers a handout on all the information that was provided in the slide presentation. | Participants are invited (but not required) to share with the group the small change they are committing to in the next week. They receive a handout of the principles of the practice and research behind mindful eating to take home. |

Figure 6.2 Two Workshop Approaches

The conventional approach alone is what many of us are used to. It's easier to plan and deliver but may not have the impact that you desire. The transformational approach—which incorporates conventional and experiential elements—demands more creativity and imagination on the part of the leader. It includes an intention to be interactive and inclusive, and to provide opportunities for participants to make their own meaning through direct experience. The transformational approach is more likely to result in real shifts in thinking and behavior, because sharing with others and making commitments enriches and reinforces the direct experience.

Notice how the transformational learning cycle is used in this approach. The leader creates familiarity and trust by telling her story, and participants are asked to reflect internally on their relationships with food. Rather than simply conveying information, participants are invited into the direct experience of eating a raisin mindfully. They integrate the experience by sharing their reflections with each other and making a commitment for the next week. In the final integration, everyone is invited to let the group witness their commitment.

This could be considered a low-risk experience for some. But for those who have a complicated relationship with food, it could trigger discomfort. Even if you think an experience is low risk, don't underestimate the need to establish safety and trust. When designing an experience using the transformational learning cycle, imagine what the level of trust might be within the group, as well as where the group is in its overall journey. We'll get into more detail about how to do that later in this chapter.

**SAFETY**
*Relaxed Alertness*
*20%*

- Create a safe physical and emotional space for experience with a low-threat, high-challenge state of mind.
- Offer a living context and purpose for the experience.
- Give clear instructions, examples, and exceptions. Demonstrate the experience if necessary and ask for questions.

**INTEGRATION**
*Active Processing*
*30%*

- Debrief: help participants make meaning of the experience by guiding them through facts, feelings/thoughts, insights, patterns, and action.
- Layer integration: from individual reflection to sharing in pairs (or small groups) to the large group.
- Help participants feel complete with a closing ritual.

**EXPERIENCE**
*Orchestrated Immersion*
*50%*

- Allow for self-discovery by guiding participants into multiple complex and authentic experiences.
- Foster a balance between action, reflection, sensing, interaction, and application.
- Monitor the experience. Note and list issues for integration.

Figure 6.3 Details of the Transformational Learning Cycle

A common design flaw is to shortchange safety or integration. In the flow of the workshop, integration often gets rushed at the end due to lack of time. In transformational workshops, experience drives the changes, so a good portion of the time (about 50%) is devoted to experience, with integration taking up about 30% of the time, and safety about 20%. Figure 6.3 summarizes the transformational learning cycle and the approximate percentage of time you might allot to each phase, depending on the experience and your intention.

We described the experience phase of the cycle in Chapter 5. In the sections that follow, we'll describe the safety and integration phases.

### SAFETY: RELAXED ALERTNESS

When you invite participants to show up authentically in a group setting, you are asking them to get past the inner critic, to be open, and to become somewhat vulnerable. When people feel safe enough to explore their direct experiences without judgment, then curiosity can overcome resistance. This makes safety—physical, emotional, and psychological—essential.

But safety doesn't mean there is no risk. For most of us, being vulnerable can feel risky. It threatens our well-defended self-image. The key is to lower the threat by reducing the fear of being judged or criticized.

---

### Quick Checklist for Creating Safety

☐ Show up early and get acquainted with the room (to create safety for yourself).

☐ Provide an overview or agenda.

☐ Start with centering (e.g., pause and breathe for a minute).

☐ Let participants introduce themselves.

☐ Reveal something about yourself.

☐ Set up agreements or norms.

☐ Give clear instructions and ask for questions.

---

Figure 6.4 Quick Checklist for Creating Safety

Here are some questions you can ask yourself to see if you have created a supportive, empowering, and appropriately challenging environment:

- **Have you created enough physical and emotional safety?** Is the room at a comfortable temperature and appropriately lit? If you are offering a guided deep relaxation, for example, are valuables in a safe place? Are the doors closed? Will you be undisturbed? Have you revealed enough about yourself so people get a sense of you as a real person? Are you monitoring the pacing and tone of your voice to help participants feel more comfortable and trusting?

- **Have you offered a context?** Have you reviewed what's been done so far and previewed what's ahead? Have you given a reason for doing this experience? How does it tie into the larger intention for the workshop?

- **Are your instructions clear?** Have you used examples? Have you said that every activity is voluntary? Have you given exceptions and choices for people to opt out? If a demonstration is needed, have you planned for one? Have you invited questions?

- **Is the experience appropriate for the energy level of the group right now?** If not, what else might you do to prepare them? Wake up the body? Calm the mind? What will help them enter this experience wholeheartedly?

- **Have you planned enough time?** Is there time for participants to have an experience *and* actively process it?

Create safety by using *living language*. State the purpose of the experience and provide a context. Is it clear, brief, digestible, and evocative? Review, preview, and build bridges between experiences. Without this continuity, the journey can feel bumpy and disjointed. For deeper experiences, do a demonstration. As senior Kripalu workshop leader Sudhir Jonathan Foust says:

> I never ask anyone to do something I am not willing to do. My stance is that I'm going to jump in first and then say, "Come on in! The water's fine!" So, whenever I or my staff do a demo, we focus on being authentic. Feeling safe creates the possibility of transformation. I put all my energy into creating safety, and I don't move on until everyone is ready.[23]

Introduce a mind-body experience either with directive language (e.g., "Feel the weight of your arms.") or with softer, invitational language (e.g., "If you wish," or "If it feels right for you."). Use open-ended invitations—such as "Feel what's happening in your body," rather than "Feel the delicious stretch that's happening in the back of your leg"—to give participants permission to enter into their own experience fully. It may not feel "delicious" for everyone. Give permission for a variety of responses. For example:

- "Release any judgments about doing it right."

- "*Everyone else is doing it right* is a common thought. As best you can, accept whatever comes up as being just right for you."

- "This experience may bring up different, even contradictory, responses in you. Allow yourself to notice and feel whatever arises."

- "Stay present for your own experience. Don't worry about what others may be experiencing."

- "Notice what it's like to be present, not perfect."

Create safety with the choice to opt out, at any time. Offer a clear and simple way to make that choice. For example:

- "This is an experience that you can choose to do or not. If you start the experience and feel it's not right for you, you can stop at any time."

- "This activity can bring up emotions. If you need to care for yourself right now, it's okay. Feel free to step aside and observe. There's no judgement for choosing not to participate."

- "If you feel overwhelmed and sense that you need help, raise your hand and one of the staff will support you."

## INTEGRATION: ACTIVE PROCESSING

Integration is the final step in the transformational learning cycle. After the mind-body experience—a *divergent process* of uncertainty, exploration, and wonder, in which something new may be activated—there's a sort of homecoming. Integration is a *convergent process* of bringing ideas, feelings, and experiences together. It's a time to reflect, link patterns, consolidate, install new understanding, and make conscious the meaning from the experience.

Without the closure of integration, participants may feel incomplete. If integration gets cut short, it may leave them unresolved or unable to consciously apply what they learned.

> **❝** *The installation phase of learning is the fundamental weakness—and opportunity— in much coaching, psychotherapy, human resources training, and mindfulness programs.* **❞**
>
> —Rick Hanson

Transformational groups depend on participant interaction. The foundation of group work is pairing up (also known as pair share, turn-and-talk, and dyad). Sharing reinforces experience, aids in vicarious learning (learning from others), and can lead to real shifts in thinking and behavior. Groups of three (also known as triads) or four take more time but can be effective for certain goals; for example, if support, witnessing, or note-taking is needed. Interacting in small groups or as a whole group likewise provides opportunities to generate ideas and to create possibilities for group wisdom.

You can support participants by *layering* integration—that is, starting with the individual and then moving to the group. Here is one way you could layer your integration:

1. Give participants five minutes to write about their experience (journaling).

2. Ask participants to pair up with a neighbor and have each share for two minutes from their journals (pair sharing).

3. Ask participants to share a highlight with the whole group. In a *structured round*, each participant in the group shares. In an *unstructured round*, the leader asks for a few volunteers to share ("popcorning").

Layering allows participants to sift through their own experience first. Pair sharing with a neighbor reinforces personal learning and allows everyone to be seen, heard, and feel connected. Sharing in the whole group is higher risk and should be voluntary. Hearing the experiences of others enhances vicarious learning and appreciation for our common human condition.

Another way to layer integration is to direct attention to levels of perception and thought through questions and prompts. The five levels are facts, feelings/thoughts, insights, patterns, and action.[24] You might notice that these levels loosely correspond to the Foundation for Experience pyramid in Chapter 1. This kind of layering unpacks experience in a holistic way.

If participants role-play during the experience, they will need to "de-role." They can thank each other for participating in the role playing, and they may ask, "How are you feeling now? Are you okay to continue?" The leader may invite the whole group to take a breath in and a breath out before moving on to integration.

---

### Questions for Integration

During integration, use questions such as:
- What happened for you? What were the facts of your experience?
- How did you feel? What were you aware of?
- What does that mean to you? How was it significant?
- Did it remind you of anything? Are there any patterns here?
- How would you characterize this experience? What metaphor captures this experience?
- How can you apply that, repeat it, or do it differently next time? What plan of action might help you?

At the end of integration, consider the transition. With the intention of getting closure and moving to the next experience, use questions such as:
- How are you feeling now?
- What was useful about this experience?
- Are you complete? Are you okay to continue?
- Is there anything else you want to say or do before we continue?

---

Figure 6.5 Questions for Integration

## HOW LONG IS A CYCLE?

Transformational learning cycles can be of any length, depending on the nature of the experience, the time allotted, and your goals. Figure 6.6 shows examples of safety, experience, and integration for the first 10 minutes of a workshop.

| | LEADER'S INTENTION | EXPERIENCE/ACTIVITY |
|---|---|---|
| 1 | To set up the experience with an introduction. (one minute) | **Introduction (Safety):** "Is your life busy? Do you have a lot on your plate? Have you really arrived here now? Or is your mind still at home? I'd like to invite you to visualize something that may help you be more fully present for our workshop." |
| 2 | To help participants become fully present. To arrive and "land" in the moment. (four minutes) | **Guided Visualization (Experience):** "Close your eyes, or gaze softly down, and take a deep breath. Review what it took for you to get here—planning, scheduling with family and work, travel, et cetera." (Pause) |
| 3 | To help participants commit to their intentions and reconfirm interest in the workshop content. (three minutes) | **Journaling (Integration Layer One):** "Remember when you first thought about coming to this workshop. What did you want when you registered for this program? Consider your personal intention for attending this workshop. Take a few minutes to jot down your thoughts in your journal." |
| 4 | To affirm and anchor intentions, to initiate a sense of belonging, to encourage self-revelation, and to enhance communication between participants. (one minute each, for a total of two minutes) | **Pair Sharing (Integration Layer Two):** "Now, turn to a neighbor, perhaps someone you don't know, and in groups of two, share your intention for being here. Decide who's sharing first. You have one minute each. Begin." |

Figure 6.6 Example of the First 10 Minutes of a Workshop

The primary mind-body experience in this 10-minute transformational learning cycle is the guided visualization. It's set up with a short set of instructions (safety). Following the visualization, participants reflect on the experience, considering what it means for them (first layer of integration). Then, participants connect with another and share out loud (second layer of integration).

A longer cycle might include a presentation of information at the beginning, a longer mind-body experience or a series of related mind-body experiences, and a group popcorn discussion as a third layer of integration.

## IN SUMMARY

Trust the transformational learning cycle to help you create optimal learning conditions for your participants. *Setup, buildup, payoff* is a tried-and-true method of designing experiences that have surprisingly creative outcomes and lasting value.

The ultimate payoff is group wisdom, the most overlooked and underappreciated opportunity in workshops. Groups can be smarter than the smartest person in them. Group wisdom transcends the individual and is unique to each group.

In the next chapter, you'll see how to design a workshop sequence by stringing together transformational learning cycles throughout the stages of the workshop.

*" For me, the promise of this work is that we all learn more and more how to meet one another in our wisdom. Then our challenges will appear not as threats to our way of life but as opportunities to grow into life itself. "*

—Peter M. Senge

**Putting it into Practice:**
**Journal Prompts**

- How can you create more safety in your workshops?
- Do you allow enough time for integration? How can you provide more time and space for active processing?

Figure 6.7 Putting it into Practice: Journal Prompts

*Meira's Story*

# Growing in Trust Over Time

In Chapter 7, we explore transformational workshops as a journey unfolding in a sequence or with an intended trajectory. As a leader, you design mind-body experiences to fit the goals of the group process for each phase of the journey. Meira's story follows an emergency room nurse and wellness coach in a two-year therapeutic mindfulness training for people suffering with chronic and traumatic stress. We see how the teaching team fosters a consistent and reliable culture of self-care and nonjudgment, using trauma-informed practices throughout the training.

I used to work as an emergency room nurse in an inner-city hospital, where I learned about healing the physical body from acute illness and trauma. I later became an integrated health and wellness coach and expanded my model of healing to include a more holistic approach. A few years ago, I felt called to deepen my understanding of people's innate resilience and ability to heal from the effects of chronic and traumatic stress. I was excited to find a three-year training that taught a method of therapeutic mindfulness, based in neuroscience, that could be healing and transformative for those suffering from the effects of chronic stress and trauma. It would be a significant commitment of three four-day sessions with a cohort of participants for the first two years, followed by two six-day sessions without a cohort in the third year. I felt ready to deepen my skills and understanding in treating traumatic stress and its effects on physical and emotional health.

I showed up the first day full of eager anticipation. I recognized similar looks of nervous excitement on the faces of the other participants in our 25-person cohort. We were embarking on a journey that would take us to yet unknown places over the course of the next two years of working together as a cohort. The physical space was minimalist and beautiful—the pieces of art hanging on the wall were simple yet elegant, and the program room felt spacious and peaceful.

Our instructor and the assistants began the session by introducing themselves and then inviting introductions from the participants. As we went around the room, I was filled with awe and respect for the diversity of background and experience in the room. I was grateful to be part of a group of like-minded individuals who shared similar interests and intentions for helping bring deep healing and transformation to those suffering from trauma. I had a sense that I was about to enter a powerful personal experience that was part of something bigger than each of us as individuals.

For the first few classes, I was intrigued and excited about the content we were learning, and I felt I would pick up the technique easily and naturally. But as the training progressed, I started to realize that this modality was an intuitive art as well as a science, and it would take years to master.

I hit a wall with the humbling realization that I was just a beginner. I had learned enough to know how much I didn't know, and I got discouraged. I was frustrated at being a novice and at times noticed others in the group feeling similar emotions. My negative thoughts were gaining momentum: *I should be getting this. Maybe I don't belong in this training.* Fortunately, our instructor calmly addressed these collective concerns. He knew it was a normal part of the process, and he also knew the aha moments would happen in time.

During the second year, I discovered that this wasn't a typical training. The content was intense—we delved into the treatment of specific types of trauma such as assault, terrorist attacks, and torture—and at times it was overwhelming. The training moved back and forth between instructional and experiential teaching, and it was not uncommon for me or others to get emotionally triggered. The instructor made self-care a priority by encouraging mindful awareness of how the training content felt in our bodies and thoughts. He normalized our uncomfortable feelings by conveying, "It's okay. This is completely normal. Remember to be kind to yourself."

Personal inhibitions quickly broke down as the leader and assistants encouraged us to actively care for ourselves in whatever way we needed. It wasn't unusual for people to be listening to the lecture while laying down on a blanket, doing yoga postures, or even going to a corner of the room to take a nap. Permission for self-care whenever needed was central to our group culture, and I never felt judged for doing whatever I needed to support myself.

Those first two years were very intense, but the knowledge and skill of the instructor and the support of the group helped to keep me motivated through the challenging times. Very powerful were our groups of three (triads) for practicing techniques and doing deep work. We rotated through triads so we had the opportunity to work with everyone in the group, and we always had an assistant nearby to help when needed. These small groups created a sense of safety as we witnessed and supported each other. In our triads, we were able to develop our skills, work through our individual triggers, and develop compassion and respect for our fellow participants. Because of the large group size, these small breakout groups became a backbone of support. Our cohort became a self-supporting system through the group process. But this didn't just happen automatically. The leader had established a safe environment, and the norms and structures allowed everyone to be supported.

The shakiness of the first year—when all of us were struggling with feelings of failure and doubt—gave way to strength and confidence in the second year. In my own journey through those two years, I experienced my breakthrough somewhere around the two-thirds point. I went from feeling like a novice to a confident practitioner without even realizing what had happened. I noticed a similar process in my fellow participants—although the breakthroughs happened at different points for everyone. We grew to trust the leader, the process, and the group as we navigated our way through our individual and collective journeys.

We gathered together for our final session of the second year with a sense of satisfaction and awe, but also some sadness, as most of us would be going our separate ways. We had gone through so much together as a group, and now each one of us was going to continue on as an individual in the third year of training. And this was okay. Somehow, the strength of the group implanted itself in each of us as individuals somewhere along the way, and while I was saying goodbye to this particular formation of the group, I knew that all of the collective wisdom and skill of the group now resided in me.

We threw a party during that final session to celebrate our journey and to say goodbye to each other. The celebration started with everyone having the chance to share with the group what the experience meant to them. It was very emotional—lots of tears. After that, we broke out the wine and Indian food. We ate, drank, and danced into the night. I was amazed at the transformation that had taken place in each of my fellow sojourners, as well as myself. I knew I would never be the same and that these changes in me would bring healing and empowerment to others.

This story was written by Meira Alper, RN, BSN and edited by the authors. Meira is a trauma-informed health educator and somatic-experiencing practitioner. Visit www.integrativehealingpath.com to see more of her work.

# Chapter 7

# A Journey of Discovery: Navigating and Sequencing Your Workshop

*A hero ventures forth from the world of common day into a region of supernatural wonder: fabulous forces are there encountered, and a decisive victory is won: the hero comes back from this mysterious adventure with the power to bestow boons on his fellow man.*

—Joseph Campbell

A workshop is like setting out on a journey of discovery. As the group travels together, you guide your participants through conscious encounters with themselves and one another. Whether it's a series of workshops in a three-year training program, as in Meira's story, or a three-hour workshop, there's an arc that develops over time.

After you've designed your primary mind-body experiences, it's time to step back and look at the overall plan, or trajectory, of your workshop. This includes your promises, the flow of the mind-body experiences, and the transitions between experiences and stages. The design needs to cover the "distance" of your workshop, no matter how long or short the program. In this chapter, we'll describe a framework that gives you a sense of direction and the confidence to trust the process and your progress to stay on course.

## WORKSHOP TRAJECTORY:
## A JOURNEY ACROSS THE UNKNOWN SEA

A participant in our training said, "I knew what I wanted to teach, but I didn't have a way to structure it. But once I put my workshop into a trajectory, I had a map. I could see the big picture, and everything came together." David Whyte coined the term "crossing the unknown sea" as a metaphor for work and identity.[25] We use this same metaphor as a way of looking at the sequencing of a workshop: First, get everyone on board by creating a safe space. Help people get acquainted and fully engaged. Then, set sail on a sea of discovery by introducing the workshop content and exploring group boundaries. The midpoint of the voyage requires navigating unknown waters and claiming new territory. When you arrive at your destination, you put the journey into perspective by reviewing discoveries, celebrating outcomes, and creating closure. Finally, you offer ways to keep the journey alive, after the workshop has ended. Great voyages live on in our hearts and minds. Figure 7.1 shows these stages of the journey with the basic intention of each stage. While the stages are more obvious in a longer workshop, we've found that the model also applies to shorter workshops.

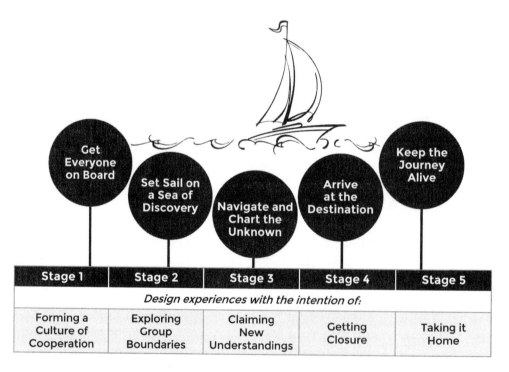

| Get Everyone on Board | Set Sail on a Sea of Discovery | Navigate and Chart the Unknown | Arrive at the Destination | Keep the Journey Alive |
|---|---|---|---|---|
| **Stage 1** | **Stage 2** | **Stage 3** | **Stage 4** | **Stage 5** |
| *Design experiences with the intention of:* | | | | |
| Forming a Culture of Cooperation | Exploring Group Boundaries | Claiming New Understandings | Getting Closure | Taking it Home |

Figure 7.1 Intentions for Each Stage of the Journey

In the pages that follow, we'll explore how to accomplish the intentions of each stage through the design and sequencing of mind-body experiences for your workshop.

## STAGE 1. GET EVERYONE ON BOARD: FORMING A CULTURE OF COOPERATION

The first stage of the journey is about getting everyone on board. In this stage, design your mind-body experiences around forming a culture of cooperation. Set a purpose and give an overview of the workshop. Create buy-in with individual intentions so participants have a stake in the outcome. Establish safety with group agreements, housekeeping, and logistics.

In Meira's story, the teaching team created physical and emotional safety with a serene and peaceful space, and by helping people to get curious about each other, their backgrounds, and their motivations for coming together to bring deep healing to the world. As the leader, you're really allowing participants to get to know each other in a way that invokes the mystery of meeting and joining. As Meira said, "I was about to enter a powerful personal experience that was part of something bigger than each of us as individuals."

Consider mind-body experiences that are lower in risk and more reflective. In certain instances, it might be appropriate to bring in higher risk activities early on. For example, a workshop focused on exploring personal limits might begin with higher risk experiences, whereas a workshop designed to support healing would need safer, lower risk experiences at the beginning and greater sensitivity throughout.

Depending on the nature of your workshop, it may be useful to use a pre-workshop survey to get to know your participants in advance, why they've come, and what they expect. A pre-workshop survey can also head off potential misunderstandings or disappointments and help your participants get clear whether the workshop is a good fit for them.

---

### Pre-Workshop Survey: Sample Questions

- How did you hear about this workshop?
- What aspects of this workshop most interest you?
- What do you hope to gain from this workshop?
- What is your background in the topic of this workshop?
- Is there anything you'd like us to be aware of regarding your participation in this workshop?

Figure 7.2 Pre-Workshop Survey: Sample Questions

## STAGE 2. SET SAIL ON A SEA OF DISCOVERY: EXPLORING GROUP BOUNDARIES

Setting sail is about boundaries and belonging—getting sea legs. In this stage, participants may seek clarification, and they may try to push limits. As interaction deepens, conflict can arise. They need to have a sense that they can be themselves in the group—that they can be real and authentic. Remind them, as Oscar Wilde said, "Be yourself. Everyone else is already taken!"

Participants need the leader to show up. Be willing to model self-acceptance, and to normalize the awkwardness of moving out of one's comfort zone. Reinforce the value of honest self-inquiry and vulnerability.

Mind-body experiences during this stage are crafted to create opportunities for deeper interactions and inviting the group's creativity forward. You need to be clear about what really matters. Aim the group toward the big picture. Ask them, "What's possible here?" Encourage them to enjoy the journey: "Have fun! You have a license to fumble here, and you can always have a do-over. Be an explorer. Surprise yourself!"

In Meira's story, the activities were more interactive and higher risk, more deeply personal and sensitive. The leader fostered a culture of self-care and nonjudgment. They designed breakout groups to support higher risk interactions, including an observer to witness the dyad protocols. This triad structure gave participants a backbone of support for each other. Assistants provided another layer of support for the minigroups, freeing the leader to focus on the big picture.

## STAGE 3. NAVIGATE AND CHART THE UNKNOWN: CLAIMING NEW UNDERSTANDINGS

At this stage, participants have been tested together. They're more confident and creative. As group wisdom emerges, the leader can step back and let the group take more ownership. Craft your mind-body experiences to allow for increasing readiness to share discoveries, surface and clear baggage, and go beyond perceived limitations. Experiences can be higher risk in this stage, but only when there is enough trust in the group to (1) handle upsets and confusion and (2) reveal hidden assumptions and beliefs.

In Meira's story, there were shared moments when people "got it" and grew to trust that the group could hold them. It happened at different times for each participant and coincided with the organic development of the group as a self-organizing and self-monitoring body.

## STAGE 4. ARRIVE AT THE DESTINATION: GETTING CLOSURE

As the workshop comes to a close, be aware that there may be a paradox of feelings. Participants may feel uplifted and fulfilled, but they may also feel apprehensive about leaving the group. Some may feel overwhelmed—on the one hand, filled to overflowing with so many good ideas, and on the other, challenged about how to implement them. Offer personal and reflective experiences to help them internalize what they've learned. Highly relational experiences can bring attention to trust and acceptance in the group and will support participants to get closure.

Closing rituals honor the journey and acknowledge endings and feelings of loss. For example, a structured round gives each person a chance to sum up their feelings, thank the group, and say what they gained from the experience of the workshop. You may offer a time to journal first, followed by group sharing, using a prompt such as:

- What I'm leaving behind is _____.
- What I'm taking with me is _____.

As a way of helping participants sustain and build on their workshop experience, invite them to write down and share intentions, next steps, or short-term goals. This helps to make the transition from the workshop to the everyday challenges of work, family, and community. Goals can be written down and shared with partners and/or the whole group. One model uses SMART as an acronym.[26] SMART goals are:

- specific
- measurable
- attainable
- relevant
- time bound

A commitment to book an upcoming workshop by calling three possible venues within one week is a goal that meets these criteria.

To improve the impact and effectiveness of your workshop—to see whether they "caught what you taught"—have an evaluation questionnaire ready. Have them fill it out before they leave, while the experience is fresh in their minds and hearts.

> ### Post-Workshop Evaluation: Sample Questions
>
> - Please rate your overall experience in this workshop (*excellent, above average, average,* or *poor*).
> - What part of this workshop was most valuable to you?
> - What areas of improvement would you identify for the workshop leader or for the workshop content?

Figure 7.3 Post-Workshop Evaluation: Sample Questions

Make time for goodbyes. In Meira's group, the closing circle and party let them express gratitude, share emotions, and celebrate accomplishments. Meira's group had been together for two years, but for groups that meet for shorter periods—even a half day—closure is essential. You may have been in a workshop that ended abruptly and experienced the unsettling feeling of it not getting complete.

You can also get feedback during the course of your workshop by using an *exit ticket* in between sessions. An exit ticket measures what participants learned and helps you plan for the next level of learning. A basic prompt is, What questions do you still have after this session? Appendix C provides more examples of exit tickets and evaluation forms.

## STAGE 5. KEEP THE JOURNEY ALIVE: TAKING IT HOME

Returning home, participants often feel motivated and elevated by the experience of the group. But that feeling fades. How can you keep the momentum going to encourage and support their interactions after the workshop is over?

Before your participants leave, you can form small accountability groups that will stay in touch going forward. Have the minigroup members exchange contact information and decide on their first meeting time.

As a leader, find ways to stay in relationship with your participants. You can send out periodic emails, newsletters, or bulletins keeping them connected to each other, the workshop content, and to you. (Make sure you have their contact information!) Offer connections on social media. Follow up and ask them how they're doing with a post-workshop survey that invites them to reflect and/or take another action step. You can also consider online programs, coaching, or mentoring to support your participants after the workshop.

Finally, honor your own process and make time to reflect on your own journey. We recommend that you do this before reading participant feedback in order to honor your own experience. Make a list of pros and cons. Savor the good first by remembering what went well in the workshop. Really let it sink in so it sticks like Velcro! Celebrate your wins, then think about how you might make it even better. Claim your experience and document everything for the next time you roll out this workshop.

Figure 7.4 summarizes the intentions for each stage and how to accomplish them.

| | INTENTION | DO THIS BY . . . |
|---|---|---|
| 1 | Get Everyone on Board: Forming a Culture of Cooperation | ■ Creating a safe space.<br>■ Building connections and trust.<br>■ Setting purpose and intentions.<br>■ Getting buy-in. |
| 2 | Set Sail on a Sea of Discovery: Exploring Group Boundaries | ■ Providing new information.<br>■ Increasing interaction.<br>■ Offering ways to explore comfort zones.<br>■ Building collaboration. |
| 3 | Navigate and Chart the Unknown: Claiming New Understandings | ■ Celebrating new insights.<br>■ Stretching beyond group limits.<br>■ Challenging unhelpful beliefs and behaviors.<br>■ Supporting the group in resolving conflict. |
| 4 | Arrive at the Destination: Getting Closure | ■ Offering a closure ritual.<br>■ Encouraging meaning making.<br>■ Offering an opportunity to say goodbye.<br>■ Facilitating transition out of the workshop. |
| 5 | Keep the Journey Alive: Taking it Home | ■ Helping to transfer new insights and understanding to daily life.<br>■ Offering opportunities to stay connected.<br>■ Providing additional resources.<br>■ Reviewing and improving your workshop. |

Figure 7.4 Moving Through Each Stage of the Journey

## CREATING A PLAN FOR YOUR JOURNEY

Put your mind-body experiences into a plan—an agenda—that outlines your entire workshop from beginning to end. You can deviate from the plan and make course corrections as needed, but you must keep your destination in sight.

You might create a script for each segment to think through what you will say and what your participants will do. Capture only the highlights in your overall agenda. Too much detail can be distracting and take you out of the present while leading your workshop.

Every piece of the workshop has its own place, but you need to ensure they're connected. Once you have the major experiences in place, turn your attention to the transitions and entry and exit points—the "connective tissue" of the workshop. Between major experiences, help people get closure before moving on. For example, previewing and reviewing helps people relate each part to the whole picture. You can also ask participants to take a big breath in and a long breath out before moving to the next experience. (You can also use this brief pause to glance at your agenda.) Silence frames experience. Pause and allow people to settle and savor, maybe by allowing five minutes for reflection and journaling before ending a session.

As you create your agenda, consider the following:

- **Timing.** Estimate the duration. You might also write in target start and end times to help you stay on track and know what needs to shift if you deviate.

- **Who Will be Doing it.** If you're co-leading with one or more other leaders, clearly name the prime mover of every experience. Knowing who will be doing what keeps everyone on track and ready for their role—to lead or support.

- **Experience.** Name the experience in shorthand for quick reference.

- **Description.** Describe the details of what you and the participants will be doing for each part of the transformational learning cycle (safety, experience, integration).

- **Purpose.** Briefly describe how the experience relates to your intention for the session.

- **Materials/Setup.** To stay organized, note the materials or preparation needed for each learning cycle, such as handouts, music, pens, paper, writing boards, or journals.

Figure 7.5 is an example of a detailed agenda for an opening session (Stage 1: Get Everyone on Board).

## Opening Session Agenda
### (90 minutes)

| TIME | WHO | EXPERIENCE | DESCRIPTION | PURPOSE | MATERIALS/ SETUP |
|------|-----|------------|-------------|---------|------------------|
| 5m 9:00-9:05 | Ken | Introductions | Meet the teaching team | Building connections and trust; creating a safe space | Music upon entering |
| 5m 9:05-9:10 | Ken | Reflect with Pair Share | Prompt: *What did it take to get you here?* | Getting acquainted and connecting | None |
| 10m 9:10-9:20 | Lesli | Circle Name Game | Whole group claps in rhythm, each person says their name in turn, and everyone else repeats it. | Building connections and trust | None |
| 5m 9:20-9:25 | Ken | Intention Meditation | Prompt: What's your intention for this week? | Setting purpose and intentions | None |
| 20m 9:25-9:45 | Ken & Lesli | Movement: Partner Yoga | Embodiment exercise of group yoga:<br>▪ Demonstrate.<br>▪ Invite everyone to find a partner (with opt-out).<br>▪ Lead partner yoga (switch halfway).<br>▪ Prompt: What do you notice? Body … Mind … | Building connections and trust | Music |
| 20m 9:45-10:05 | Ken | Sharing Circle | Prompt: *State your name, where you're from, your work in the world, and headline your intention for the week.* | Getting buy-in; building connections and trust | Newsprint with the questions; blank newsprint to scribe; microphone |
| 10m 10:05-10:15 | Ken | Group Agreements | Collaboratively set group agreements:<br>▪ Explain agreements.<br>▪ Brainstorm agreements; scribe on newsprint.<br>▪ Invite everyone to verbally "Agree." | Creating a safe space; getting buy-in | Blank newsprint to scribe Agreements |
| 10m 10:15-10:25 | David | Overview and Logistics | ▪ Hand out workshop manual.<br>▪ Review agenda for the week.<br>▪ Go over housekeeping with Q&A. | Creating a safe space; setting purpose and intentions | Workshop manual; agenda for the week |
| 5m 10:25-10:30 | David | Closing Journaling | Prompts:<br>▪ *What key learning did you take away from this session?*<br>▪ *Do you feel supported? If not, how will you get support?* | Reinforcing the learning; activating self-empowerment | Workshop manual; music for closing the session |

Figure 7.5 Example of Opening Session Detailed Agenda

Remember, a transformational workshop is not a presentation. You're not reading from a script unless, for example, you're leading a guided visualization, reading poetry, or quoting someone. An agenda is a map to keep you on course. If you're a leader who thrives on spontaneity and would rather go with the flow, create an agenda anyway, and keep it available in case you need it. Glance at your agenda when needed. Most importantly, stay present and connected to the group.

You'll find a template for creating a basic agenda in Appendix C.

## IN SUMMARY

Ultimately, you want a plan that helps you navigate your workshop and that's also flexible enough to allow for creativity and spontaneity. Designing your workshop can be exciting, challenging, and at times tedious. But it's worth it! Be open to possibilities, trust the process, and stay true to who you are and what you want to do.

In the next chapter, we'll explore how to design and describe your workshop through the lens of personality and temperaments in order to be more holistic and inclusive.

---

**Putting it into Practice:**
**Journal Prompts**

- Which stage of the journey resonates with you most?
- When in your own life did you experience a workshop where you felt supported? What did it look like? What did it feel like?
- Are you more comfortable with structure or with spontaneity? How might you expand your comfort zone?

Figure 7.6 Putting it into Practice: Journal Prompts

# Chapter 8

# Champion Your Workshop: Meet People Where They Are

*Groups that are too much alike find it harder to keep learning, because each member is bringing less and less new information to the table. Homogeneous groups are great at doing what they do well, but they become progressively less able to investigate alternatives.*

—James Surowiecki

*H*ow can you design a workshop that is balanced, well rounded, and meets people where they're at, including their expectations, aspirations, and preferences? How can you honor both what is universal to all of us and unique to each individual?

This chapter gives you a framework to understand human nature through the lens of personality traits and how that nature might impact the design of mind-body experiences. By using this model, you can describe your workshop with language that is holistic and inclusive, and that will attract the people you want to serve.

## THE BASIC ELEMENTS: A PERSONALITY MODEL

Personality theories assert that we all have predispositions in the way we perceive life—tendencies and preferences that underlie our interests, needs, values, and motivation. Naturally occurring human differences have been noted throughout history and still hold value today.[vii]

Biological anthropologist Helen Fisher found that personality is shaped by two essential forces, temperament and culture. Temperament is our biology. Culture is our conditioning. Her research found personality traits to be linked with four neural systems: serotonin, testosterone, dopamine, and estrogen and oxytocin.[27]

The Basic Elements Model, developed by Jim Harden and Brad Dude, is a simple and contemporary personality framework based on the four elements: earth, air, fire, and water.[28] Figure 8.1 shows the relationship between the Basic Elements Model and two other well-known models—Jung's archetypes and Fisher's neural systems.

|  | ARCHETYPES (JUNG) | NEURAL SYSTEMS (FISHER) |
|---|---|---|
| **EARTH** | Sensing-Judging (SJ) | Serotonin |
| **AIR** | Intuitive-Thinking (NT) | Testosterone |
| **FIRE** | Sensing-Perceiving (SP) | Dopamine |
| **WATER** | Intuitive-Feeling (NF) | Estrogen/Oxytocin |

Figure 8.1 Comparison of Personality Models

Becoming familiar with personality traits can help you understand your own nature and unique personal expression. Your unexamined preferences and predispositions may lead you into the trap of designing workshops through the lens of your own sensibilities while overlooking those of others. The better you understand yourself, the more skilled you will be at designing workshops.

Figure 8.2 presents characteristics that are generally associated with each of Harden's and Dude's elements. Read through the lists and reflect on your own preferences. Notice if there are elements that you identify most strongly with (your dominant and secondary temperaments), feel neutral about (your tertiary temperament), or feel very negative about (shadow temperament).

---

[vii] Examples appear in Indian Ayurveda and traditional Chinese medicine. In addition, in 450 BCE, Hippocrates identified four key personality traits: phlegmatic, choleric, melancholic, and sanguine.

| EARTH |
| --- |
| ☐ Reliable |
| ☐ Traditional |
| ☐ Organized |
| ☐ Sensible and Practical |
| ☐ Down-to-Earth |
| ☐ Lives in the Present |
| ☐ Strong Work Ethic |
| ☐ Often Projects a Parental Attitude |
| ☐ Needs Structure and Order |
| ☐ Expects Preparedness in Self/Others |
| ☐ Protector of Home and Family |
| ☐ Hates Wasting Time |
| ☐ Driven by "Shoulds" and "Oughts" |
| ☐ Dislikes Change |
| ☐ Often Feels Underappreciated |
| ☐ Loyal to Family and Co-Workers |
| ☐ Detail Oriented |

| AIR |
| --- |
| ☐ Analytical |
| ☐ Unemotional |
| ☐ Loves Intelligence |
| ☐ Curious |
| ☐ Critical of Own Capabilities |
| ☐ Sees and Articulates the Big Picture |
| ☐ Loves the Theoretical |
| ☐ Expects Perfection in Self and Others |
| ☐ May Appear Arrogant |
| ☐ Thinks Logically and Globally |
| ☐ Tends Toward Skepticism |
| ☐ Often Oblivious to Others' Emotions |
| ☐ Analyzes Personal Relationships |
| ☐ Enjoys Being Alone |
| ☐ Fixated on Self-Improvement |
| ☐ Visionary and Future Focused |
| ☐ Expects Others to See the Obvious |

| FIRE |
| --- |
| ☐ Action, Action, Action |
| ☐ Uninhibited and Innovative |
| ☐ Thrives in Crisis Situations |
| ☐ Improviser |
| ☐ Loves Life |
| ☐ Flourishes in the Unknown |
| ☐ Good at Troubleshooting |
| ☐ Must Have Change |
| ☐ Resists Being Told What to Do |
| ☐ Takes Things Lightly |
| ☐ Humorous |
| ☐ Loves Travel and the Unexplored |
| ☐ To Wait is to Die |
| ☐ Will Rebel if Trapped in a Routine |
| ☐ Lots of Short-Term Relationships |
| ☐ Goals Are Nice, but They Often Shift |
| ☐ Thrives on Adventure |

| WATER |
| --- |
| ☐ Personal |
| ☐ Caring, Empathic, and Compassionate |
| ☐ Is a Romantic |
| ☐ People and Relationships Come First |
| ☐ Strives for Harmony and Cooperation |
| ☐ Sees Value in Contributions of Others |
| ☐ Seeks Significance and Meaning |
| ☐ Sensitive to Feelings of Others |
| ☐ Flair for Writing and Speaking |
| ☐ Spiritual |
| ☐ Has Difficulty Saying No |
| ☐ Looks on the Bright Side of Life |
| ☐ Hates Being Lied to |
| ☐ Committed to Love |
| ☐ Sacrifices for Team and Organization |
| ☐ Good Motivator |
| ☐ Benevolent |

Figure 8.2 Self-Assessment: The Basic Elements Personality Traits[29]

**What's Your Slogan?**

Participants in one of our trainings came up with these fun slogans:

**Earth:** "Make a list!"

**Air:** "Can't live without us!"

**Fire:** "Just do it!"

**Water:** "No person left behind."

What's your slogan?

Figure 8.3 What's Your Slogan?

## IMPLICATIONS FOR DESIGN

Why does this matter in designing mind-body experiences? Many leaders design workshops for people with the personality they're most comfortable with. Consequently, leaders may lead the way that they themselves like to be led. Earths like structure and clarity, Airs love concepts and theory, Fires crave action, and Waters value connection and relatedness. When you design a workshop, take a step out of your comfort zone and imagine experiences that might engage all four elements.

Take a look at Figure 8.4, which shows types of experiences and structures that most appeal to each of the four elements. Which experiences appeal to you? Do they match the element you identified in Figure 8.2?

| EARTH • STRUCTURE | AIR • CONCEPTS |
|---|---|
| ■ Clear agendas and time frames | ■ Talks |
| ■ Explicit instructions | ■ Constructs, models, and theories |
| ■ Concrete outcomes | ■ Logical ideas |
| ■ Consistent methods | ■ Clear relationships between ideas |

| FIRE • ACTION | WATER • CONNECTION |
|---|---|
| ■ Movement | ■ Discussions |
| ■ Activities | ■ Small group sharing |
| ■ Spontaneity | ■ Intimacy |
| ■ Demonstrations | ■ Team building |

Figure 8.4 Elements and Preferred Experiences

Depending on the goals of your group, you may lean toward one or two elements. However, you'll be more effective by weaving in other elements as well. For example, in a workshop that's movement oriented (fire), such as a qigong workshop, you can bring more balance by providing the theory of qigong (air), creating opportunities to share thoughts and feelings (water), and starting sessions with a clear schedule and set of expectations or outcomes (earth).

When you step back and look at your overall design, is it well rounded? Does it meet the needs of the four elements?

## COMMUNICATING YOUR WORKSHOP TO THE WORLD

How can you champion your workshops? If you want to bring your workshop to the world, you need to describe it in a way that lives and breathes what you love about it. Capture the essence of your workshop with an appealing title and tagline. You also want a paragraph that describes it. When you advertise your workshop, potential participants first see the title and tag. If they're interested, they'll read more about it.

### Your Title and Tagline

There's no formula for workshop titles and taglines, but when people see them in a catalog, email campaign, flyer, or website, you want it to:

- catch the eye of potential participants
- make it clear who it's for and what it's about
- appeal to their emotions and aspirations

Below are titles and taglines for three of our workshops:

- Facilitating Transformational Workshops: Group Dynamics and the Power of Presence
- Designing & Leading Transformational Workshops: The Craft of Mind-Body Teaching
- Creating Transformational Workshops: An Introduction to Mind-Body Learning

What do you notice about these? Are they descriptive? Is it clear what the workshops are about? If you were looking to improve your ability to create, design, lead, or facilitate a workshop, would these titles and taglines catch your eye? Why or why not?

Now it's your turn. Here's a process you can use to come up with your title and tag. First review the work you've done so far—especially the lists that came out of the synthesizing process after mind mapping. On a piece of paper or in your reflection journal, start writing down phrases that you think capture the essence of your workshop. Come up with as many phrases as you can without stopping. Don't judge them or evaluate them. Write as many as you can. Can you come up with 10? 20?

Once you've done that, go through the list and circle or underline the phrases that you like best. Say them aloud or review the list with a friend. Which phrases sit well with you? Which ones give you a hit of inspiration? Try putting together combinations for title and tagline.

See if you can narrow your list down to one title-tagline combination that can serve as a proxy until you're ready to go live. No need to make a final decision now. Pick one and test drive it for a while. Then return to the list to refine, edit, or pick a new one to try out.

## Your Workshop Description: The Blurb

*The blurb* is a paragraph that describes three things about your workshop: the nugget, your methods, and the outcomes.

Your title and tagline give the big-picture topic. What's at the center of your topic— the gold, *the nugget*? How can you describe it with another layer of detail? Is there any essential background information? Briefly describe the problem you're trying to solve and the solution you are offering. For example, if burnout is the problem, self-care might be the solution.

Your *methods* are how you plan to offer your solution to the participants. Briefly describe what your participants can expect to experience in the workshop. Here are a few sentence starters:

- "Through examples and storytelling, you will . . ."
- "By practicing visualization and affirmation techniques, you will . . ."
- "In small groups and voluntary paired activities, you will . . ."
- "Through mindful movement exercises, you will . . ."
- "With the presentation of concepts, models, and cutting-edge research, you will . . ."

Use the lists from your mind-map process to see if some of your methods are articulated there.

The *outcomes* are what participants can expect to get out of the workshop. Again, review your mind-map and synthesis lists to see what outcomes you've already come up with. For example, for Creating Transformational Workshops: An Introduction to Mind-Body Learning, a weekend workshop, we tell potential participants that they will take home:

- self-discovery tools that link the heart and mind
- keys to collective wisdom and ways to spark group creativity
- interactive techniques to energize, connect, and empower people
- marketing tips to champion workshops
- accountability partners and a peer-support network

Brainstorm five to ten outcomes that your participants can expect to take away from your workshop (you may have already done this in Chapter 5).

As you consider your methods and outcomes, keep in mind the four elements and what would appeal to each type of person. Using the Basic Elements Model as a framework can help ensure that your workshop appeals to a wide range of people, and it might also help you come up with ideas you may not have thought of.

Finally, put your topic, tagline, and blurb together. The Messaging Your Workshop worksheet in Appendix C can help you do this.

## IN SUMMARY

In Part II, you explored how to design your workshop by first putting yourself at the heart of it and connecting your topic directly to your own experience. You learned how to create mind-body experiences that fulfill your workshop promises. You saw how repeated transformational learning cycles of safety, experience, and integration spiral through the trajectory of your workshop, each stage having its own intentions and impact. To fine-tune your workshop design and description, we described the Basic Elements Model as a way to understand personality differences and to include the interests and needs of a wider range of people.

Part III explores what it means to be an embodied leader. It's about showing up and delivering your workshop with presence.

**Putting it into Practice:**
**Journal Prompts**

- How comfortable are you with your element?
- Have you used any experiences that include your least comfortable element?
- How can you support yourself to use mind-body experiences that include all four elements?

Figure 8.5 Putting it into Practice: Journal Prompts

# Part III

# Leading Your Workshop

*All streams flow to the sea because it is lower than they are.*
*Humility gives it its power. If you want to govern the people,*
*you must place yourself below them. If you want to lead the people,*
*you must learn how to follow them.*

—Tao Te Ching (translation by Stephen Mitchell)

*Vivian's Story*

# Letting Go and Holding Space

In Chapters 9 and 10, we turn to the inner life of the leader and explore how cultivating presence can help you show up and deliver your workshop effectively and wholeheartedly. In Vivian's story, a workshop leader struggles with doubt, fear, and self-judgment, as well as an urge to stick rigidly to her agenda. In the end, she gives way to the wisdom of the group by relinquishing control and allowing what wants to emerge in the group.

What started as fun was quickly turning into a pit in my stomach. On one hand, I was in awe at what was going on in front of me. On the other hand, I wanted to be practical and in charge, and to keep my class on plan. I was worried about going off the rails and not getting through the agenda that I had so carefully prepared.

I was facilitating a workshop I created called Evolutionary Improv, which combined movement, storytelling, and improvisation for personal transformation. The intent of the workshop was to shift people's relationships with their personal stories, and I had structured it so participants would both be encouraged and supported to discover and explore hidden parts of themselves.

This was my first time leading the workshop as a series, and I had six people enrolled. I had offered the group the groundwork and theory of improv during the first two sessions, so they were up to speed cognitively. Now we were focusing on the dynamics of the practice. The workshop was very interactive, and the exercises each week were different, except for the warm-up period, which had the same structure each week.

On that night—the third in the series—the group began to riff a bit during the warm-up. I had designed the opening exercise as a somewhat freeform activity to help participants drop into their bodies, connect with their primal nature, and make the transition between the workday and the workshop. But on this night, they started to interact nonverbally with each other within the space. Chirps, chortles, growls, and other noises erupted around the room. I had planned about 10 minutes for this phase of the warm-up, and I'd anticipated some amount of crawling around and interacting with animal-like sounds and behavior. But what was unfolding before me was pushing the limits of what I was comfortable with. I was losing control.

The energy began to build, and soon there was a hive of activity. There was buzzing and running and grunting and jumping. Then it morphed into childlike chasing and teasing. It grew into a free-for-all, with sounds of yips and yelps and laughter filling the room.

The group was alive and inclusive. Everybody was interacting, participating, and engaging in ways that I had not seen before. Nobody was off to the side, left out, or doing their own thing. I was delighted at first, laughing and enjoying the wave of energy. At the 10-minute point, I thought, *It's cool—I can let this piece go a little longer.* But as 15 minutes turned into 20 with no decrease in energy, my inner calm crumbled.

I noticed myself getting tense, holding my breath, and starting to fidget. I was painfully aware of the minute hand marching steadily forward, each tick and tock representing a point and counterpoint in the great internal dialogue that was unfolding in my mind:

*You gotta stop this.*

*Why would I stop this? It's amazing!*

*But what about your other exercises? If you lose control of the class, they won't respect you.*

*But this is amazing.*

*Perhaps, but what are you going to do to stop this?*

*Why would I do that? This class is for them. They come here after work and want to have fun. Let them! Besides, this isn't medical school. There's no set curriculum to get through.*

Then, something in me clicked. I took a deep breath, then another, connecting with my own body, feeling my tension and my nervous stomach. After my third deep breath, the voices died down, and a knowing began to emerge.

I knew that no one was going to be harmed if this went on too long and kept me from the rest of my plan. I knew that if I interrupted it, I would be doing so out of fear and ego. Fear! That's what was wanting to stay in control, and I recognized this as a pattern throughout my life. A new voice spoke up: *I choose not to allow fear to run the show. I choose to surrender and allow the class to do what it will.*

A wave of relief immediately washed through my body as I voiced that intention to myself. I relaxed and began breathing deeply again. I returned my attention to the show in front of me and felt freed to attend to that moment—to hold the space and witness. With an open heart and mind, I sat back, smiled, watched, and waited.

A full 45 minutes later, they lost steam. Eventually they were all lying face up in a circle, with their heads toward the center. Little chirps and twitches and funny phrases continued to pass between them as the experience came to its natural conclusion.

I smiled to myself and gently brought their attention back to the room. And then my role shifted from witness to guide, and I helped the group integrate what had just happened. I asked them to reflect on what they just experienced. To my surprise, they were aware that the exercise had gone on much longer than planned, and they thanked me for not stopping it. It was unlike anything they'd ever experienced, and they were grateful for being able to experiment so openly and safely. They said it was "the most fun improvisation ever" and that it created "a feeling of being unconditionally accepted" and " totally and completely included." With a sense of gratitude and awe, I moved forward with my now-modified agenda.

As I reflect on that night, I see that it was just as much a learning experience for me as it was for them. It was an exercise in surrender and trust for all of us. I had to let go of my own agenda, put my participants first, and believe that what was happening in the moment was more important than my preconceived ideas of what I thought I had to provide. I had to first recognize my own fear and then reconnect with my internal source of discernment and trust.

In hindsight, I can see how that night was a turning point for the group. That all-inclusive camaraderie and trust created appreciation, depth, and a feeling of support that grew throughout the series. One woman reported that she always felt like she was on the outside but was suddenly now as integral to the group as everyone else. It was life changing for her, for the others, and for me. For the rest of their lives, every member of the group has that moment of togetherness and acceptance to remember. And I have the lasting memory of letting go of fear and trusting my intuition. What a gift!

This story was written by Vivian Geffen and edited by the authors. Vivian is an authenticity coach and applied improvisation facilitator. She makes her home in Los Angeles. You can see more of her work at www.creativitymuse.com.

# Chapter 9

# The Embodied Leader

*Quiet friend who has come so far, feel how your breathing makes*
*more space around you. . . . be the mystery at the crossroads of*
*your senses, the meaning discovered there.*

—Rainer Maria Rilke

Can you sense when someone is not present for you—when they're distracted, or unavailable? James Joyce wrote that the character Mr. Duffy "lived at a short distance from his body." All of us are caught up at times at a short distance from our bodies. But how much more alive to the present moment are you when you drop into the body? How is your presence your most important skill for leading transformational workshops?

Take a moment right now to pause. Feel where your body makes contact with the chair. Take a big breath in and a long, slow breath out. Pause. Feel how your breath and your body move together. Notice your shoulders, your jaw, and your belly. Pause. Take another big breath in and a long, slow breath out. Notice how present you feel now.

Part III is about showing up for and delivering your workshop—creating the space and holding it with your skillful presence. This chapter will build a foundation for exploring what an embodied leader is, ways to cultivate presence, and why nothing much matters if you don't show up wholeheartedly as best you can. "Present, not perfect" is our mantra.

## PRESENCE

Garry Trudeau said in jest, "I'm trying to create a lifestyle that doesn't require my presence!" It's quite common to be absent. Minds wander—have you noticed? A Harvard study found that people are distracted 47% of the time.[30] That is, our attention is on something other than what we are doing. How and where you place your attention determines how present you are and how present other people perceive you to be.

> " *When we feel present, our speech, facial expressions, postures, and movements align. They synchronize and focus. And that internal convergence, that harmony, is palpable and resonant—because it's real. It's what makes us compelling.* "
>
> —Amy Cuddy

Presence is not charisma, and it's not perfection. When you're present, you're connected to your experience and intuition, and you respond naturally in the moment. *Present, not perfect* means you don't try to become someone else or some idealized version of yourself.

When you focus your attention on what you are experiencing now, you feel present. You can strengthen presence by training the mind to be focused, open, and flexible. Every mind (and especially the untrained mind) wanders, ruminates, and anticipates—we time travel. When you consistently bring your attention to the present moment, it allows you to let go of distractions, especially the future and past, and develops the ability of the mind to focus. Once you are able to stabilize your attention, your mind opens to take in all of your internal and external experiences—thoughts, sensations, emotions, other people, and the environment. With a mind that is able to focus and be open, you can cultivate flexibility—letting go and being available to the next moment in a fresh way. Experience changes and flows, and the trained mind is able to respond naturally to this flow. These qualities of mind—focus, openness, and flexibility—are trained through the practice of mindful awareness.

## MINDFUL AWARENESS

What does *mindful awareness* mean? *Mindfulness* is focusing attention on the present moment without judging. *Awareness* is knowing where your attention is and when you are distracted. So, mindful awareness is the ability to know where your attention is and to direct it to what you are experiencing in the present moment. As we discussed in Chapter 4, you can practice mindful awareness from the top down or from the bottom up.

Top-down practices include meditation, such as using a point of focus (the breath, sounds in the room, or a mantra). Bottom-up practices include physical activities like yoga, qigong, tai chi, and simply taking three deep breaths. The intention in all of these practices is to synchronize the mind, body, heart, and spirit, and to cultivate the feeling of being centered, relaxed, and available.

### A Mind-Body Experience: Centering Meditation

**Scan your body.** Let your attention come to rest on sensations wherever you feel them (in your face, neck, shoulders, belly, etc.).

*Pause.*

**Bring your attention to your breathing.** Notice that the breath comes in through the nose and down, filling the lungs. The breath comes up and out, emptying the lungs. *Pause.* Feel the lifting and falling of the chest, the rising and falling of the belly.

**Notice the still moments.** Become aware of the stillness between the in-breath and the out-breath.

*Pause.*

**Allow thoughts and feelings.** Let them be, without trying to change them in any way.

*Pause.*

**Open your eyes.** Notice your surroundings.

Figure 9.1 A Mind-Body Experience: Centering Meditation

What gets in the way? When attention moves toward expectations, judgments, and self-referential thoughts (like *me, my, or mine*), we get disconnected from direct experience and connection to others. Sometimes, self-doubt comes up when you are leading a workshop, as it did in Vivian's story: *If you lose control of the class, they won't respect you.* Sound familiar? There are lots of ways to get distracted, get off your game, or just give up.

Mindful awareness brings you back to what is actually happening in the room, for yourself and your participants. Mindful awareness helps you be centered, relaxed, and available by dropping down to what's happening on the intuitive, emotional, and sensory levels—below your interpretations. For example, Vivian recognized that the group was actually fully engaged and having fun together, regardless of the voices in her head. She was able to discern what the group needed. Seeing and accepting things as they are opens up a wider field of possibilities. More choices emerge. Vivian allowed the group to go on beyond the usual limits, and they were grateful. She modeled presence by practicing mindful awareness.

Figure 9.1 describes a practice of mindful awareness. You can use this exercise as a meditation for yourself and for centering a group.

## RIDING THE WAVE: SKILLFUL SELF-REGULATION

There are many workshops taking place at one time. There's an *outer workshop* and there's an *inner workshop*. Everyone is having an internal experience, including you. Because you are the leader, your actions, attitudes, and thoughts are the most contagious in the room. Your inner workshop influences everything else.

Are you able to stay with your feelings when you're under emotional pressure? When the mind and heart are racing, and tension builds up like a wave, most people want it to stop. They react by avoiding, denying, or distracting—jumping off the wave. Then may come troubling thoughts: *I should get things under control. I'm not enough. My workshop's no good!* You might want it to be different, better than it is—to "fix" it. But when you struggle and try to resist what's happening, energy gets trapped in the body as tension, pain, and dis-ease. Resisting shuts you off from the flow of life.

What would happen if you just let yourself feel—witnessing your experience without judging or interpreting? Is it possible to just let your feelings move through you like a wave moves through water? If you stay present with the breath and focus on sensations, you can anchor the mind in the body and allow the wave to rise, crest, and recede.

Riding the wave of experience[31] is a skillful way to self-regulate and calm the nervous system, helping to restore rhythm and presence. When you let yourself ride the wave, awareness expands, and reality seems larger. Self-limiting thoughts are revealed, and new choices and thoughts arise: *This moment is perfect as it is. I am enough as I am. I can do this.* Vivian was closed down, trapped in fear, until she took a deep breath. And then things began to shift.

## DISRUPTING THE PATTERN: PAUSE, BREATHE, AND DEEPEN

How do you ride the wave? When you get triggered and find yourself in a reactive pattern, how do you come back to the present? In the moment when everything in you wants to revert to the path of least resistance, remember to pause and take a breath. In the space that opens, move your attention to your body. Maybe even create an "inner smile," relaxing your face.

*Pause, breathe, and deepen* is a formula you can use to get present. It helps you to accept the moment as it is. It naturally readjusts your mindset, returning you to feeling centered, relaxed, and available. Notice your triggers and how you use your knee-jerk reactions, such as talking too much or freezing up and white-knuckling the microphone, to discharge nervous energy. Pause, breathe, and deepen. When you're present, you'll know what to do next. When you're present, you'll see solutions that were invisible to you before. This is the discernment that arises from presence.

For example, what if a participant challenges your authority? This is one of the most uncomfortable experiences for a facilitator. When your authority is challenged, it's natural to want to defend yourself. Instead, take a breath, direct your attention inward, and notice what's happening in your body. Pause, breathe, and deepen. As you become more present, other responses become possible:

- Get curious rather than deflecting or defending. ("I get that you aren't satisfied with my answer. Can you help me understand what I might be missing?")

- Focus on the group welfare. ("I hear that you have a request, and I would be glad to meet with you at the break to discuss it. Right now, for the sake of the group, would you be willing for us to continue with our agenda?")

- Apologize for mistakes. ("I realize that we went longer than planned. I apologize for not sticking to the schedule. If I think this will happen again, I will let you know ahead of time and ask you if you're willing to go over time.")

- Express a willingness to adjust the program based on group needs. ("I've received feedback that some of you don't feel your needs are being met. I'm willing to adjust the program accordingly, and I'd like to have a conversation to better understand the extent to which this may be true for everyone and what we might do about it.")

We'll discuss how to respond to upsets, obstacles, and confusion more in Chapter 15.

Being real can feel risky because it makes us vulnerable to being hurt. As a leader, you give permission to others to be vulnerable by first being vulnerable yourself. Being real creates trust, and without trust, nothing worthwhile happens.

## COMMUNICATING WITH PRESENCE

Whether speaking or not, you are communicating through your body language, posture, and eye contact. One study breaks down communication into three categories: nonverbal (facial, posture, eye contact), vocalization (tone), and content (words).[32] See Figure 9.2.

| | |
|---|---|
| Nonverbal | 55% |
| Vocalization | 38% |
| Words | 7% |
| **Total** | **100%** |

Figure 9.2 Methods of Communication

What's the conclusion? Your words have the least impact on your participants. When you're feeling strong or energetic, you naturally stand up straighter and face forward. When you're feeling weak or depleted, you naturally slump and face away. When you lack confidence, your eyes may shift. And when listening to people, your face speaks volumes about what you're thinking and feeling.

All powerful communication is rooted in presence, and the quality of your presence as a leader is felt, and it ripples through the group like a pebble in a pond. Be mindful of nonverbal communication, especially when you're uncomfortable and riding the wave.

How do you communicate authentic presence? First, notice your body. Are you facing toward or away from the other person? As much as you can, see if you can face squarely—your legs, torso, and head. A square, upright posture communicates interest, attention, and presence.

Next, notice your eyes. Are you looking gently into the eyes of the other person, or are your eyes shifting or darting around? As you speak to a group, mindfully look from face to face, making eye contact as you go. See if you can do this while maintaining the flow of your words.

What about your facial expression? Mirroring someone else's expression is a form of reflecting and encouraging—it affirms the other for who they are at that moment and invites them to share more. Most of us have a resting expression that we default to when we're not mindfully aware. Sometimes your resting expression can communicate the complete opposite of what you're thinking or feeling. Ask a close friend for feedback on your resting expression.

**A Mind-Body Experience:
Communicating With Presence**

From a standing position or while seated upright, face squarely forward with the spine elongated and a calm and relaxed face. Place your hands on your belly. Breathe deeply, feeling your breath move your hands. On an out-breath, sigh out loud, feeling the sound coming from the deepest part of your breath. On the next out-breath, say "hello" using the whole breath to support your sound. No need to push. Relax the sound out.

On another out-breath, say, "Hello, my name is _____." You can also practice with any introductory sentence (e.g., "Thank you for coming to the workshop today."). Try it with your hands on your belly and then take away your hands and see if you can maintain the feeling of connectedness to the belly breath.

Figure 9.3 A Mind-Body Experience: Communicating With Presence

How about your voice—not your words, but the quality of your voice? An authentic voice is natural and free of anxiety. It's compelling and can draw listeners in. A voice that is present begins low in the body and is shaped and empowered from what the Japanese call the *hara*, the abdomen. It resonates from the belly and moves into the heart and upward into the throat and mouth, where voice meets language and purpose. Practice embodying your voice from the ground up. Let feelings flow into images, ideas, and words. Singing and reciting poetry are great ways to develop your powerful and authentic voice.

## IN SUMMARY

Embodied leaders monitor themselves and the group, perceiving, sensing, and acting on many levels. When you're in the thick of things, remind yourself to pause and ask these key questions: *How might I drop into this experience? How can I be more open? How can I help my participants to be more open?*

When you're open, you're able to see where your attention needs to be. You're able to respond more naturally to whatever comes up in your group. You'll be surprised and delighted by what the group comes up with.

In the next chapter, we'll explore the work of an embodied leader through the twin roles of teacher and facilitator. By balancing these roles, you can move gracefully between content and process, awareness and energy.

**Putting it into Practice:**
**Journal Prompts**

- What takes you out of the present when leading a group?

- How do you self-regulate and bring yourself back to the present?

- How can you improve your communication (verbal and nonverbal)?

Figure 9.4 Putting it into Practice: Journal Prompts

# Chapter 10

## The Twin Roles of Teacher and Facilitator

*If we want to grow as teachers—we must do something alien to academic culture: we must talk to each other about our inner lives—risky stuff in a profession that fears the personal and seeks safety in the technical, the distant, the abstract.*

—Parker J. Palmer

Workshops are like music. They have rhythm and mood. The kind of leader you are depends on the kind of music you want to make. A march is structured and rhythmic. A waltz has more flow. Swing is much looser. Jazz, however, is altogether different. In jazz, the music emerges as the musicians flow, listen, and improvise within a structure.

Transformational groups are more like jazz. Jazz requires a deeper level of trust, intimacy, and creativity. The jazz leader needs to feel the music, know the musicians, and trust when to step in and when to let go, when to provide structure and when to provide space. This is a balancing act. In this chapter, you'll discover the four guiding intentions of an embodied leader and how to accomplish them through the twin roles of teacher and facilitator.

## THE WORK OF AN EMBODIED LEADER

Transformational leaders engage their whole being. They're connected in the heart, grounded in the body, and in touch with spirit. The leader does four things: informs, supports, inspires, and guides.

You *inform* by giving information, essential ideas, and concepts. Participants want to know how what you're teaching fits into the big scheme of things. Start with a living context. Get everybody on the same page. Use information that's alive and has meaning for you.

You *support* by sensing the ongoing needs of the group for safety, satisfaction, and connection. This might lead you in the moment to take a break, acknowledge someone's contribution, or offer encouragement. Support helps create a safe container for vulnerability and risk taking. It starts the first time you communicate with your participants before the workshop, and it continues when you follow up afterward with additional resources.

You *inspire* with your heartfelt presence. As Sudhir Jonathan Foust says,

> Teach from the radiance of your own self-discovery. I see younger teachers who are not yet experienced teachers, but their sincerity wins the day, every time. People will forgive them for their inexperience, because they get a hit of the *shakti*, the energy, of their own aspirations and love for what they're doing.

Don't leave your own inspiration at home. Bring your poetry, your music, and your stories.

You *guide* by using intuition—your source of insight and empathy. Learn to recognize and act on your instincts in the moment, offering clarification, a question, or an intervention. Guide your participants using whatever language (invitational, suggestive, or directive) is appropriate at the moment.

Stay connected to these four intentions in mind, heart, body, and spirit as you balance the twin roles of teacher and facilitator.

## THE TWIN ROLES

As a transformational leader, you can think of yourself as writer, designer, producer, director, and leading role in your workshop. Within all that, you're doing two things—managing content and facilitating process in your twin roles as teacher and facilitator.

Teaching is aimed toward awareness (*chitta* in Sanskrit) that's conscious, cognitive, rational, logical, linear, sequential, and time bound. Facilitation is all about the energy (*prana* in Sanskrit) of intuition, imagination, creativity, vitality, possibility, and the timeless and unbounded. See Figures 10.1 and 10.2.

|  | **TEACHER** | **FACILITATOR** |
|---|---|---|
| **Location in the Body** | Mind (*chakras* 5, 6, 7) | Body (*chakras* 1, 2, 3) |
| **Focus** | Intention: Focusing on content (concepts, information, goals, objectives, materials, skills) | Attention: Entering into the process (sensations, breath, feelings, interactions, behaviors) |
| **Brain Function** | Analytic (cognitive, rational, linear, sequential) | Intuitive (imagination, creativity, vitality, timelessness) |
| **Gender** | Masculine energy of directedness (yang) | Feminine energy of flow (yin) |
| **Source of Energy** | From the sky down (top down) | From the earth up (bottom up) |
| **Primary Tools** | Insight and awareness | Empathy and compassion |
| **Tasks** | Synthesizing, organizing, evaluating, clarifying, timekeeping | Mediating, encouraging, appreciating, feeling the tone, managing the environment |

Figure 10.1 The Twin Roles of Teacher and Facilitator

A teacher creates the structure and curriculum. She sets goals, establishes an agenda, chooses learning methods, communicates information, demonstrates skills, and manages the way the group gains expertise. She invites people toward greater wholeness in learning, thinking, communicating, planning, and decision making. A teacher is a manager, synthesizer, timekeeper, clarifier, and evaluator. She helps participants to be connected knowers.

A facilitator's role is different. *Facilitate* means "to make easy." A facilitator "makes easy" the group process by working with energy and delegating and sharing responsibility. She mediates the interactions, behaviors, and feelings between participants and helps people to surface, explore, and transform hidden assumptions, beliefs, and values. As a delegator of responsibility, a facilitator shifts the focus back to the self-discovery process in order to investigate and transform patterns that are no longer useful, and to help participants take ownership of the results. During the course of the workshop, a facilitator gradually relinquishes control, allowing the group and individuals to be empowered and access their own agency. She is a mood setter, an emotional-pulse taker, and an encourager. Facilitators help participants be relaxed, alert, and available so they can be fully present for themselves and others.

Your heartfelt connection (the fourth *chakra*[viii]) brings the twin roles together. The heart connects us to ourselves and to others. The yin and yang of facilitator and teacher meet in the heart.

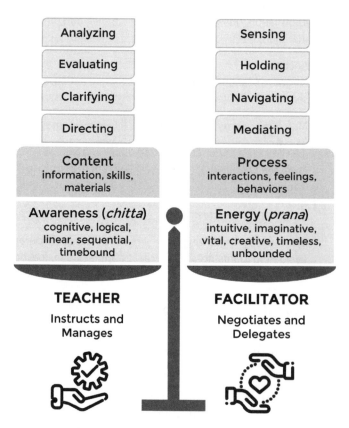

Figure 10.2 Balancing the Twin Roles[33]

## SHAPE-SHIFTING

As teacher and facilitator, you have power and influence. How do you use it? The group expects you to use your authentic power to guide them toward goals. If you

---

[viii] *Chakra* is Sanskrit, meaning "wheel," and is used in yoga to refer to an energy center in the mind-body.

don't recognize your inherent power and influence, you can unwittingly undermine your hard work and affect the healthy functioning of the group.

Your role is to gradually delegate power and control to the group, empowering individuals to be self-determined within a group of other self-determining individuals. Your aim is to be a *self-disappearing act*—to put yourself out of a job—as participants stop being receivers and become knowers that are self-empowered and self-directed. Shape-shifting means being able to shift between directing, negotiating, and delegating.[34]

- **Directing ("Power Over").** Sometimes you have to take control of the group and assert your genuine power as the director. You'll probably use this hierarchical role to *decide for others* at the beginning of group formation, when there might be confusion, or when you need to intervene. For example, "We're going to begin with a round of introductions," or "Let's take a quick break," are statements that reflect this directing power.

- **Negotiating ("Power With").** Use your cooperative role to collaborate. This means sharing control with the group and *deciding with its members*. Questions such as "Would you like to continue on, or take a break now?" or "Would you like more time to complete this exercise?" exemplify this collaborative spirit.

- **Delegating ("Power From Within").** You are a delegator when you empower individuals to be self-determined and help them *decide for themselves*. You're guiding them toward their own sense of agency. Statements such as "Take the next 10 minutes to work on anything that would help you feel complete," or "There are two ways to do this next exercise; select the one that works best for you," invite independent decision making.

Choosing to be a director, negotiator, or delegator depends on the situation. Knowing when to shape-shift gives you flexibility to meet the group needs in the moment. Are you willing to give up control and let the wisdom of the group emerge, as Vivian did in her improv workshop?

Here are some ways that leaders might struggle with their own authority:

- **Disappearing Too Soon.** Moving from director to delegator before healthy boundaries are in place.

- **Denying Genuine Power.** Not claiming your true power and failing to step forward during confusion or upsets.

- **Resorting to Authoritarian Power.** Holding too tightly to authority in order to hide or suppress your own insecurity.

- **Cleaning Up Too Soon.** Tidying up messes before they run their natural course in order to overcome your own anxiety.

---

**Pause for Reflection**

Take a minute to think about the four ways that leaders struggle with authority. Do you see yourself reflected in one or more? What did it look like the last time you felt challenged in your authority? What could you have done differently?

Figure 10.3 Pause for Reflection

## BRINGING IT TOGETHER: THE THREE KEYS TO LEADING TRANSFORMATIONAL WORKSHOPS

As you balance teaching and facilitating, keep three goals in mind:

- **Create Safe Space.** Create a place where participants feel seen and heard.

- **Invite Full Participation.** Create an environment where participants can immerse themselves fully.

- **Attend to Challenges.** When obstacles, upsets, or confusion occur, mediate the energy between individuals and the group using top-down or bottom-up practices.

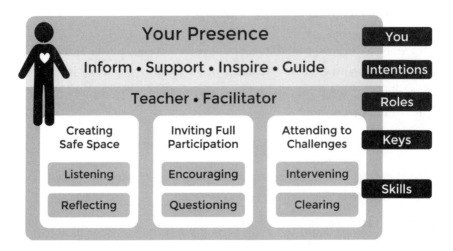

Figure 10.4 The Nested Aspects of an Embodied Leader

You'll see in the upcoming chapters how you can meet each of these goals with six facilitation skills: listening, reflecting, encouraging, questioning, intervening, and clearing. Your presence is central to all of these.

Figure 10.4 summarizes the nested relationship between skills, keys, roles, intentions, and your presence as the leader.

## IN SUMMARY

Next time you are witnessing an effective leader in action, notice how well she moves between the twin roles of teacher and facilitator. Notice how she informs, supports, inspires, and guides the group.

In the coming chapters, we'll explore the three keys to leading transformational workshops and the six skills of facilitation. As you continue, reflect on your own strengths and challenges in leading workshops.

### Putting it into Practice:
### Journal Prompts

- Where are your strengths? Facilitating or teaching? Both?
- Which of the three keys do you find the most challenging and why?
- Are you willing to create space within your group and then step back and let things unfold?
- What's the ratio of your speaking versus participants being actively engaged?

Figure 10.5 Putting it into Practice: Journal Prompts

# Katie's Story

# Runaway Workshop

In Chapters 11 and 12, we explore how workshop leaders create safe space while dealing with the natural ebb and flow of emotions and reactions in participants and in themselves. Katie's story is one of transformation. First, we see how a workshop gets away from her when her fear of confrontation and being judged overshadows her passion to serve. Then, we see how Katie turns things around in her next workshop and is able to stay present, set agreements, create time for integration, and deal with upsets consciously and kindly.

A big part of me wanted to just quit. *Never again!* I thought to myself as I drove home, tears streaming down my face. My adrenaline-filled body was pulsing and vibrating, toggling between utter shock and abject despair. I had spent months preparing for the retreat because I wanted to help people, not hurt and anger them. But hurt and anger were what ended up happening. I felt I had let my participants down, and I was devastated.

How had I gotten so in over my head? This question plagued me for months following the retreat, and I wracked my brain, trying to figure out what had gone wrong. I had held retreats before with many of these same women, and there had always been a normal ebb and flow. Sometimes things were easy, and other times difficult, but nothing like this had ever happened to me. In past retreats, people were mostly receptive, friendly, kind, and when necessary, forgiving. Until this one.

Don't get me wrong. I *love* my work. I'm passionate about helping people who are struggling to find peace with food, their bodies, and the scale. I'm dedicated to helping people with the psychological journey that ultimately determines success or failure after weight-loss surgery. I started leading retreats because I wanted to deepen the work I do with my individual clients. But this workshop started going south right away. One woman argued from the start about the room arrangements. Another completely withdrew from the group. I knew from my individual work with her that she liked being the funniest person in the room, but someone funnier showed up, and she would have none of it. Another woman seemed to be having some personal struggles, and her irrational behavior was impacting others. A small clique began to form. They decided they really didn't want to be there, and they complained loudly about small things. A couple of them even took phone calls during our session.

As the retreat progressed, I learned that some of them had been spreading gossip and lies about me and some of the other participants. I was so stunned that I began to shut down. My fear of anger, confrontation, and being judged overshadowed my passion to serve. Things continued to go downhill, and I did all I could to just make it to the close of the retreat.

I realize now that I didn't know what I didn't know. I had been blessed for the most part with relatively functional groups for my retreats. I didn't realize how group dynamics can radically change with the mix of people who show up. This group of participants seemed to have created the perfect storm, and I was not prepared for it.

With my ego bruised but my passion still intact, I realized I needed to sort out where things had gone wrong and how I had contributed to the meltdown. I wanted to learn how to better manage a retreat that has a variety of personalities and challenges. I knew I needed to stretch myself so that I could be better at my work. So, I decided to attend a weeklong training on facilitating transformational workshops, and it was there that I began to piece together what had happened at my retreat and what I could have done differently to better serve my participants.

I learned how to create a much safer space, how to lead a group with loving kindness while remaining the leader, how to get a group to take ownership of their experiences, how to make my retreats more experiential, how to be more emotionally present and less fearful of confrontation, and how to deal with the normal ebb and flow of emotions and reactions in participants (and in myself).

As I worked through my retreat-gone-south experience, I identified at least four things that I could have done differently: (1) being and staying present, (2) setting up group agreements, (3) creating time for integration, and (4) seeing and dealing with upsets.

### Being and Staying Present

As the group started to fall apart, so did I. Had I been more present, I would have noticed what was happening inside me—in my own "internal workshop." I'd have noticed my own reactions and could have practiced remaining open rather than shutting down. I could have connected more deeply with what energizes me about my work: I love people, and I love to help them. Had I been more present, I could have made an intention to stay present and listen— really listen—to my participants, like I do in my private practice. Instead, I got focused more on planning and less on just being with the group in a way that they could feel seen and heard.

If I had been more present, I could have supported the participants who were upset. I see now that I had responded only superficially to them. I didn't make time to meet them inside or outside the group. I just moved on without taking the time to listen and to help them express themselves more openly in the group. As a result, they became more raw and vulnerable as time went on.

### Setting Up Group Agreements

I could have started my workshop by establishing group agreements. Ensuring the participants agreed to use respectful communication (using the conscious listening and affirmation practice I learned at the training) would have helped me and my group settle in the space, acknowledge one another, and show up with an intention for positive interactions. Group agreements would also have given me something to fall back on when behaviors started to be harmful to the group.

### Creating Time for Integration

I now know the emotional impact mind-body experiences have on people. Participants need time and space to process and fall apart a little before they get back together. I failed to follow up each experiential exercise with enough time for people to process what happened and to integrate the meaning of it. This left emotions raw and exposed, which contributed to the escalation of reactivity and insensitivity.

### Seeing and Dealing with Upsets

I realize that I had ignored the process side of leadership. I was too attached to my prearranged plan, and I failed to respond to warning signs. My focus on goals came at the expense of not feeling the group's energy. The minute I saw a problem with a participant, I could have intervened before the bad feelings and gossip got going. Rather than sensing the mood and monitoring how people related to each other, I drew a blank. I failed to hear and respond to the underlying voice of need. I missed the big picture, the global view.

Perhaps most importantly for me, I learned that it's hard to lead groups when I'm trying not to get hurt. When my own unresolved feelings get in the way, it's hard to take risks. I realized that I had withdrawn rather than engaged. Being open to the group and to their challenges was too uncomfortable for me. When fear comes up in groups, my avoidance reaction kicks in. Left unmanaged, these waves ripple through the group, making the members feel wobbly and unsafe.

My own fear of rejection led me to distance myself from the group and to teach from my head. I needed practice being vulnerable in groups, as I had learned to be with clients one-on-one. And I needed to release control of outcomes and be more comfortable with uncertainty as a facilitator. But my own fears escalated a bad situation and made it worse.

I see now how the group is a mirror for my own journey, and I have learned so much from this experience. I've learned to be less reactive when faced with challenge and confusion. I am practicing, not immediately reacting, knowing that participants are just doing the best they can with the knowledge they have in that moment. I still have some rough edges when challenges and problems come my way, but I handle them much better because I know that I'm response-able: I'm able to respond rather than react.

Armed with my new skills and ideas, I got back in the saddle. I stepped into my leader role with new confidence. Since then, my retreats have been completely different. I've devoted more time to process and integration, starting off with group agreements. I give my participants a mini lesson on how to do reflective listening so they could be more sensitive to each other. Most importantly, I come to the space differently than before. I shed my shame and am fully present as we move together, find our voices, hug firmly, and laugh deeply.

One woman from my last retreat wrote to me: "I felt so safe experimenting at your retreat. I am completely changed. I know what I need to do now and the risks I will need to take. I know I'll be okay." When I read that note, I thought, *That's why I'm here—to stretch so that others will stretch*. I am humbled and honored to be able to do this important work.

This story was written by Katie Jay, MSW, and edited by the authors. Katie is a life and wellness coach, trainer, and workshop and retreat leader. She makes her home in Reston, Virginia. Visit www.nawls.com to see more of her work.

# Chapter 11

# The First Key—
# Creating Safe Space

*I've learned that people will forget what you said,*
*people will forget what you did, but people will*
*never forget how you made them feel.*

—Maya Angelou

$\mathcal{H}$ ave you ever been in a group that became dysfunctional? What were the symptoms? People talking over each other? Sidebar conversations? People coming late and leaving early? In many groups, an intentional culture is never set. How to be together as a group is not addressed. It's taken for granted that gathering around a common purpose is enough for participants to stay focused and productive. But this is a gamble. As we saw in Katie's story, her retreat devolved into chaos because she and her participants hadn't declared conscious group boundaries. In her group, when the rim of the circle wasn't firm enough to hold disagreements, strong feelings, and emotional discharge, people felt unsafe, unsupported, and began to act out in dysfunctional ways.

In this chapter, we'll explore five ways to gather a functional group by creating a container that can support emotionally safe and effective interactions:

- Get clear about your intention.
- Attend to the space.
- Set group agreements.
- Use conscious dialogue.
- Abide by ethical guidelines.

## GET CLEAR ABOUT YOUR INTENTION

*" To have a firm persuasion in our work—to feel that what we are doing is right for ourselves and good for the world at the exact same time— is one of the greatest triumphs of human existence. "*

— David Whyte

As a leader, if you don't know where you want to go, any road will take you there. A better plan is to get a sense of direction. Where do you want to go? What's in it for you, and what do you want for your participants?

An intention is a setting for the heart. It's a movement toward what you want. In yoga, intention, or *sankalpa*, is a way of being born from the heart. Right intention leads you toward harmony and protects you if worry or doubt arise.

Here's a three-part intention. It's a way of aligning your work with what you want and who you really are before the group arrives. See Figure 11.1.

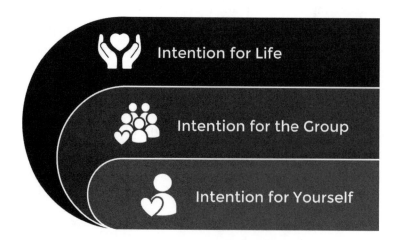

Figure 11.1 Three-Part Intention

## Part 1: Set Your Intention for Life

What kind of world do you want to see? What's your promise to life? What inspires you? What breaks your heart? As Stephen Cope says, "Every human has a dharma, a sacred duty, a true calling."[35] Here are some examples, expressed as already true in the present moment:

- I am a compelling force for good in the world.
- I am a catalyst for positive change.
- I express myself creatively and share it with the world.
- I am an enthusiastic champion of life's possibilities.
- I am an instrument of peace.

## Part 2: Set Your Intention for the Group

What do you hope to accomplish? How do you want to serve your participants? Getting to the essence of your promises—your core outcomes—will help you focus your intention. Here are some examples:

- We are being authentic and honest in relationships.
- We are exploring mindfulness in everyday life.
- We are developing and strengthening emotional intelligence.
- We are creating a vision for the next phase of life.

## Part 3: Set Your Intention for Yourself

How do you want to show up today? What is your mantra? How do you want to interact with the group? Getting clear about how you want to be as you lead the group can help you stay present. Here are some examples:

- I am present, not perfect.
- I am clear and focused.
- I am steady and determined.
- I am enthusiastic about what we will create.

Where your attention goes, energy flows. Taking time to get clear about your intentions for life, the group, and yourself will give you a sense of dedication and clarity in your work. See Figure 11.2 for ways that you can deepen your intention.

---

**Ways to Deepen Your Intentions**

**Visualize**

Find a quiet place. Close your eyes and imagine yourself after a session where you fulfilled your intention(s). What images come to mind? What do you see in your participants? In yourself? Allow the picture to expand in your mind. Let it become very clear.

**Journal**

Take a look at the questions posed in the three-part intentions (for life, for the group, and for yourself). Choose a question that calls to you from each section. Journal your answers.

**Connect to the Feeling**

How do you feel when you imagine that your intention is fulfilled? Try to sense the need that is satisfied when you connect deeply with the feeling. Where do you feel it in your body? Let the energy build so that you can recall it easily later on.

**Pause, Breathe, and Deepen**

Take a few moments to pause and feel. Take a breath or two and allow your three-part intention to land in your body and integrate.

---

Figure 11.2 Ways to Deepen Your Intentions

## ATTEND TO THE SPACE

One new leader failed to let the organizers know in advance that the workshop would be experiential. When she arrived at the venue, she discovered that the chairs were bolted to the floor in rows! It threw her plan into disarray. She confessed later, "The group eventually coalesced. Some even liked it. But it wasn't exactly the seamless experience I had hoped for!"

The physical space where your group will gather has the power to hold energy, evoke emotions, and elicit thoughts. It can help or hinder connection and openness. Think about the great European cathedrals with vaulted ceilings and stained-glass windows, the simple elegance of a New England Shaker meetinghouse, or a natural setting like the redwood forests in California. Inevitably, you'd feel different in each of these spaces.

When preparing your workshop space, attend to the décor, cleanliness, and lighting. You don't have to be an expert in feng shui to create harmony in the room. Imagine it from your participants' point of view. Having traveled hours to get there after a long week at work, they'll likely be tired but excited to have time for themselves. They're a little bit nervous about not knowing what to expect.

Imagine your first impressions in these two scenarios as you arrive at the venue.

**Scenario 1.** You're not sure you're in the right place because there's no sign outside the room. You open the door to find the teaching team in a meeting. They notice you and motion for you to come in. The overhead lights are a little jarring, the chairs are not well aligned, and there are a few piles of paper around the room. You're not sure if they're meant to be handouts, so you take one from each pile just in case. As you take a seat, you notice the room feels stuffy, the walls are bare, and the other participants seem equally unsure and nervous. You sit quietly and look through the handouts while you wait for the workshop to begin.

**Scenario 2.** You arrive at the meeting room, marked clearly with a sign. The door is open, and soft music is playing. You're greeted by one of the teaching staff, who welcomes you, asks your name, and chats with you briefly before inviting you to find a seat. The chairs are neatly arranged with an agenda, a pen, and a folder of handouts on each one. There are floor lamps around the room, casting a warm glow. Inspirational quotes are up on the walls, and the temperature in the room feels just right. You think to yourself, *Someone cares.* You smile at the participant next to you. She smiles back, and you engage in a conversation. You're both eager and excited for the workshop to begin.

Although it's easy to see which scenario features a preferable environment, there are times when you may not have a choice over your workshop setting. For example, your venue might be a basement, a school, a prison, a community center, or another place with constraints and limitations. Whether you have control of your workshop environment or not, acknowledge it, especially if the environment isn't what you would prefer. Once you have acknowledged the space, you can then think about how you will work within it.

Here are some thoughts. You can create a welcoming circle of chairs. A circle allows everyone to make eye contact. It promotes equality. It represents oneness and helps people to connect on the same level. Also consider placing an object in the center—maybe a candle or something from nature, like flowers—to focus participants' attention and anchor the energy.

Organize and arrange your materials to support your purpose. Be ready to welcome each person into the room, and invite them to sit in the circle.

First impressions are important. It's human nature to look for things that reinforce our first impression. If you start off on the right foot, your participants are more likely to overlook small missteps later on.

## SET GROUP AGREEMENTS: THE SPINE OF THE WORKSHOP

Transformational workshops are as much about how we *are* together as they are about what we *do* together. Written agreements are guidelines for group behavior and interactions, and they form the spine of your workshop. You can rely on them when you need to. Whereas rules are imposed from above, agreements are made between self-directing individuals. Agreements help to set a culture of cooperation based on shared values. For example, underneath the agreement for confidentiality is the respect for privacy.

In shorter workshops, there are three basic agreements (easily remembered by the acronym "INC") you can quickly propose to the group:

- **"I" Statements.** Speak from your own experience. Take responsibility for your own thoughts and feelings. For example, "It's warm in here" might be better stated as "I feel warm. "Likewise, "That doesn't make sense" might be better stated as "I don't understand."

- **No Cross Talk.** Honor each voice. Wait until a person finishes speaking before you start to speak. Refrain from judging, giving advice, offering solutions, or commenting on what other people share.

- **Confidentiality.** Everything shared is confidential and may not be mentioned outside the group without permission from the speaker.

In longer workshops, agreements can be more nuanced, generated by the group, documented, and mutually agreed upon. They can be added to or revised in real time. This builds ownership and delegates responsibility to the group.

Sometimes it's necessary to send agreements before the workshop begins. This might be appropriate for an intensive or longer program. This gives participants an awareness of the norms and expectations for the group and gives them a chance to evaluate ahead of time whether the program is suitable for them. Appendix C contains a sample "contract" that can be sent to individuals before the program starts.

Here are some other agreements to consider in addition to INC:

- Speak from your heart.
- Listen from your heart.
- Monitor your contribution rate.
- Practice letting go of judgment of yourself and others.
- Arrive on time and end on time.
- Refrain from gossiping, blaming, and complaining. Instead, speak to someone who can do something about it.
- Be an explorer.

Set agreements at the outset and monitor them during the workshop. Periodically inquire if any agreements need to be added or modified. You can ask everyone to rate how well the group is abiding by the agreements. One way to do this is to ask for a simple thumbs-up or thumbs-down. A thumbs-down could precipitate a short discussion to get more information and perhaps lead to modifications.

## CONSCIOUS DIALOGUE: A TOOL FOR COMMUNICATING CLEARLY AND KINDLY

Words that are used consciously have a healing and connecting effect. The Buddha offered five questions for "wise speech": Are my words well intended? Useful? Timely? True? Kind?

Notice that our three basic agreements—"I" statements, no cross talk, and confidentiality—are all about speaking or not speaking. Words can help or hurt, create safety or threat. Speaking with care is a way to initiate, maintain, and repair relationships. We want to invite people to approach and attach to the group and reduce defensiveness.

"I" statements are the foundation for communicating consciously. They help the speaker to identify, acknowledge, and take responsibility for feelings, needs, and requests. "You" statements can be misunderstood and lead to defensiveness. *Conscious dialogue*, based on Marshall Rosenberg's nonviolent communication model, is a protocol that guides people through a conversation based on self-awareness, including "I" statements, expressing honestly, and listening empathically. Leaders can help participants communicate consciously by teaching conscious dialogue and encouraging the use of it during the program. Figure 11.3 shows the steps of conscious dialogue.[36]

| STEP | DESCRIPTION | STATEMENT | EXAMPLE |
|------|-------------|-----------|---------|
| **Observation** | Describe observable behavior in a statement of fact. Avoid a judgment. | "When I see/hear . . ." | When someone consistently interrupts: "When you speak without raising your hand, I lose my train of thought." |
| **Feeling** | Identify the emotions that you are feeling in relation to what you observe. | "I feel . . ." | "I feel frustrated and distracted . . ." |
| **Need** | State your need or an outcome you would prefer or a state of affairs that you value (not what you need them to do for you). | "Because I need . . ." | ". . . because I have a need to be clear in my thinking and speaking." |
| **Request** | Ask the other person to do something specific and doable that would help or please you. | "Would you be willing to . . . ?" | "Would you be willing to wait until I finish before you speak?" |
| **Thank You** | Always end with a thank you. | "Thank you." | "Thank you for listening." |

Figure 11.3 Conscious Dialogue Steps

## THE ETHICS OF CARING IN WORKSHOPS: MONEY, SEX, AND POWER

Ethics play a central role in ensuring safety and inclusivity. Groups, like all healthy organisms, need to have good boundaries. Most of all, you as the leader need to be aware of your own motivation and behavior.

Where do leaders most frequently run into trouble in workshops? Money, sex, and power. You won't be blindsided by these powerful forces if you acknowledge that money is motivational, attraction is natural, and competition is normal. It is up to the leader to be mindful of these forces and to monitor healthy boundaries.

## Money

Money is a powerful motivator and can also be uncomfortable to deal with. For example, how do you get fair compensation without overcharging or deceiving? How do you avoid entering into unethical money arrangements? Be up front about what you charge. Be mindful of unhealthy dynamics that can arise from offers, gifts, or favors from participants. Avoid charging participants different rates within the same group, unless you have clearly stated your policy.

Many people use bartering as an exchange for services rendered. While this is a common practice, be aware of pitfalls that can result from an uneven exchange or an exchange that's perceived to be uneven. Beware, also, of a bartering relationship that creates potential entanglement between you and a participant ("dual roles"). Ensure that bartering agreements are clearly articulated and mutually agreed upon before the actual exchange of services. While it may feel unnecessary at the time, consider putting the details of a barter arrangement on paper for both parties to agree to.

## Sex

Acting appropriately with romantic or sexual attraction means acknowledging and accepting it, while maintaining ethical behavior. Pretending attraction doesn't exist and fanning the flames of attraction can be equally dangerous. Be mindful of how attraction to someone may be coloring your perspective, influencing your behavior, and affecting the energy of the group.

## Power

Leaders have power in relationship to participants. Workshop encounters may seem like a hall of mirrors. Unspoken needs, feelings, and wishes get projected between the leader and participants around the circle. Participants may idealize the leader or project their own needs onto the leader. Leaders may also let their unconscious needs negatively affect others. These needs are often based in our own insecurities and manifest in the longing to be a healer or leader, the need for respect or status, or the desire to have control. When these needs control our interactions, participants may temporarily surrender their usual worldview, succumb to the leader's will, and give their power away. Signs that a negative power imbalance is present include:

- participants idolizing the leader
- constant deference to the leader's opinion
- the leader's inflated personality overshadowing the group
- the leader giving more attention to some participants to the exclusion of others (such as being overly negative or adoring)

The tricky thing about abuse of power is that it's often invisible to the one in power—the leader. The more present you are, the more you will notice when the power dynamic has shifted in an unhealthy direction. If you become aware of an imbalance in power, be honest with yourself. What's behind it? What's your part in it? What might you be doing to inadvertently contribute to the dynamic? It's easy to be seduced by power.

Money, sex, and power are inherent in human relationships and group work. By maintaining healthy boundaries, we avoid the confusion and subtle manipulation that can creep into any relationship. Asking yourself the two questions in Figure 11.4 can help you identify potential ethical problems.

| QUESTION | RED-FLAG ANSWERS |
|---|---|
| What do I want from this relationship? | Any answer that lies outside the bounds of your role as group leader can be an ethical red flag. |
| Am I afraid of this relationship? | Fear is a messenger that can reveal something about your inner motivations. Fear that stems from unclear boundaries in the areas of money, sex, or power can be an ethical red flag. |

Figure 11.4 Questions for Ethical Practice

As leaders, we are stewards of trust. Being mindful of your own unmet needs for safety, satisfaction, and connection before and during your workshop is the best safeguard against unethical behavior. If you're part of a leadership team, have a conversation about these dynamics with your teammates before you begin group work, and invite the team to be mutually accountable. Often, it's easier to see early warning signs in someone else's behavior than in your own. If you find yourself in an ethical bind, you can bring your concern to your team or to a trusted colleague. Ask him or her to help you explore ways to restore balance.

The checklist in Figure 11.5 will help you create a safe and inclusive atmosphere.

**Checklist of Ethical Guidelines**

☐ Do no harm.

☐ Keep agreements with individuals and the group.

☐ Refrain from sexual or romantic behavior with participants.

☐ Inform participants before inviting them to do a mind-body experience. Tell them what they're going to do, advise them of possible outcomes, or do a demo.

☐ Act within your *scope of practice*, which is defined as the procedures, actions, and processes that are appropriate for (or allowed by) your professional license, education, experience, and competence.

☐ Keep all your workshop promises, including objectives, pricing, and schedule.

Figure 11.5 Checklist of Ethical Guidelines

## IN SUMMARY

Creating a safe space doesn't guarantee that your workshop will be challenge-free, but if you set a culture of cooperation, small problems will be less likely to escalate into larger ones. Think back to Katie's story. In her reflection about what she might have done differently, she lists some of the practices that we've just described.

Clear intentions, group agreements, conscious dialogue, strong ethics, and an inviting space help your participants to trust the group. When you show up with an open mind, a warm heart, and pure intent, your groups will reflect that.

In the next chapter, we'll explore the leadership skills of listening and reflecting.

**Putting it into Practice:**
**Journal Prompts**

- What unmet needs might lead you to cross ethical boundaries?
- Are you clear about your intentions for leading transformational workshops? How could you get clearer?
- Have you been in a runaway workshop, and what agreements might have prevented it from going off the rails?

Figure 11.6 Putting it into Practice: Journal Prompts

# Chapter 12

# The Skills of Listening and Reflecting

*A baby that is not reflected doesn't know itself. We must be seen.*
*We must be heard. We look inside for the inner beloved and can't*
*find it. So, we project it out onto others in trying to find love*
*outside ourselves. When we finally recognize "It's me," the inner*
*beloved—the inner marriage—releases me to love outside myself.*

—Marion Woodman

Creating safe and caring space isn't a one-and-done task. It's an ongoing practice of being reliable and consistent in your ability to be present for the group and their needs. People want to be seen and heard. They need opportunities to affirm themselves and each other to enable the group to evolve.

Here's an all-too-common experience from one of our trainees about a prior workshop:

> The leader told us we would get spiritual resources to embrace our emotional breakdowns and to quicken the pace of positive change in our lives. He told us we would engage in experiential exercises, and that we would leave with a clearer sense of our life's purpose and be able to apply insights. But what he said and what he did were two different things. There was a slideshow, a lecture, and he told a lot of stories about himself. Rather than leaving with a

clearer sense of life's purpose, I left frustrated and disappointed. There was no interaction with others, and I didn't feel seen. I didn't feel heard.

The group gauges trust by how the leader hears and responds to each of them. In this chapter, you'll see how you can intentionally create safe space where people are heard and reflected.

## LISTENING: HONOR EACH VOICE

"By listening, you minister to me," said Fred Rogers, world-renowned children's public television host. Listening is fundamental and so overlooked. All other facilitation skills rely on the ability to listen fully, without judgment or distraction.

Ordinarily, we listen from our own point of view; that is, we listen for what we already know (or think we know), reinforcing our own biases. When we go a step further and begin to listen beneath the words, from a feeling level, with body awareness, we begin to hear and see the world differently from a wider perspective and a deeper place. This *empathic listening* is listening to the heart of another. By not analyzing and judging what we hear, we can make room to listen for the truth of another's life. Putting aside our own agenda and shifting to the other person's worldview connects us more deeply to heart wisdom.

What gets in the way of listening? Tension, worry, fear, criticism, second-guessing, and thinking of what to say next are all patterns of not listening that affect us deeply. Ultimately, the unconscious tension of not listening erodes trust and destroys relationships. Listening doesn't always come naturally at first. It takes practice.

### Nine Ways to Listen Deeply

1. Slow down and put aside other tasks in order to fully listen.
2. Sit or stand at the same level as the other person.
3. Relax your body and sit or stand comfortably in an open, receptive position.
4. Create mental and emotional equality by recognizing the value in the other.
5. Take conscious breaths.
6. Establish and maintain eye contact.
7. Drop expectations of self and other.
8. Relax your face—your forehead, eyes, mouth.
9. Be natural and patient, trusting in the process.

Figure 12.1 Nine Ways to Listen Deeply

## REFLECTING: OBJECTS IN THE MIRROR ARE CLOSER THAN THEY APPEAR

There is a drive in all of us to belong and be part of the group. In our primal past, banishment from the tribe was a death sentence. Belonging has always been key to survival, and the need for it is hardwired in us through the autonomic nervous system, which scans for patterns of protection and connection in the faces, emotions, intentions, and actions of others.

We are social beings. Empathy, imitation learning, the evolution of language, and social-cue interpretation are believed to result from mirror neurons. These neurons are common to all humans and help us notice joy, sorrow, acceptance, and rejection in the faces and body language of others.[37] Neuroscientist Giacomo Rizzolatti said, "Our survival depends on understanding the actions, intentions and emotions of others. . . . Mirror neurons allow us to grasp the minds of others not through conceptual reasoning, but through direct simulation. By feeling, not thinking."[38]

We may not be able to see ourselves clearly at times, but others can. Feelings are both received and transmitted through us, even when we try to hide them. We need the mirror of another person to reflect us, including the unconscious parts. A leader who practices the skill of reflecting helps people see themselves as they are—like the moon, which reflects the sun without interpretation.

Reflecting can be done with or without words. Without words, we can reflect another when we match our gaze, face, and posture to theirs. This validates their feelings and emotions. It creates a sense of safety and awakens presence in ourselves and others.

Reflecting with words is called *reflective listening*, and it's a practice that helps a person to be fully heard and understood. All it takes is repeating, as closely as possible, what a speaker said back to them. We are often quick to offer an opinion or answer, but reflective listening opens up space for the other to be their own answer.

Reflective listening can be used to:

- Help you understand a participant better if, for example, you sense something is unsaid, unfinished, or incomplete in a participant's communication.

- Strengthen the relationships between group members by helping them value each other's communication. You can model and teach reflective listening to group members so they can use it in and outside the group.

- Clear the air between group members who are having a misunderstanding or dispute.

> **Practice Reflective Listening**
>
> You can help others be seen and heard in your groups by inviting the listener to repeat back to the speaker what they said as closely as possible:
>
> 1. "What I heard you say was [reflect back to the other person what they said to you, as closely as possible]."
>
> 2. "Did I get that right?"
>
> 3. "Is there more?"
>
> 4. "Thank you."

Figure 12.2 Practice Reflective Listening

At first, reflective listening may feel awkward or inauthentic, like a technique you're using on someone. After some practice, however, it will become a powerful way to promote understanding and become part of your skill set.

## IN SUMMARY

By practicing the skills of listening and reflecting in your workshop, you give your participants an experience of being seen, heard, connected, and valued. This is fundamental to creating a caring and safe space. It fosters opportunities for all to feel their own presence and the presence of others.

What happens when people feel valued? They begin to lean in and open up. In the next chapter, we'll explore ways to invite their full participation.

> **Putting it into Practice:**
> **Journal Prompts**
>
> - What gets in your way when you try to listen to another person?
> - When did you really feel listened to, and what did the other person do or say? What was your physical sensation of being heard? What happened in your heart and in your mind?

Figure 12.3 Putting it into Practice: Journal Prompts

*Lauren's Story*

# The Truth I Needed to Face

In Chapters 13 and 14, we explore how the leader can get participants engaged so they connect to others in the group, express themselves, and choose the course of their personal growth. Lauren's story is about a writing workshop that offers her a chance to look compassionately at some long-standing personal issues. A warm and welcoming environment helps her feel safe enough to open up. Inspiring poetry shared by the leader, as well as somatic and sensory experiences, become the catalysts for Lauren to make a life-changing decision.

The workshop is still so vivid in my mind. When I entered, music was playing. The workshop leader greeted us at the door and invited us to find a place in the neat circle of chairs and back jacks on the floor. *This is a big group for a writing workshop*, I thought. But the wet spring day, still wearing the cool air of a long New England winter, made the indoor activity more enticing.

I first fell in love with the Berkshire Mountains in western Massachusetts in the 1970s when I was attending college in New England. Twenty years later, unexpectedly, a neighbor I barely knew invited me to a day of "rest and relaxation" at Kripalu. I took the risk. I thought I was coming for some yoga and relaxation, and I had no expectations beyond that.

At that time, I was about to turn 50. I had three young children, and I was deep in an unhappy marriage, though few people knew it.

Because I was a child of divorced parents, I had vowed never to get divorced myself. But even after years of trying to revive my marriage with individual and marital therapy, it was basically dead. I was in despair, and I didn't see a way out. I wanted to break through my paralysis, but I suffered in the silence of intense isolation.

The first thing my neighbor and I did on that wet spring Saturday morning was to attend a writing workshop, The Poetry of Self-Inquiry: Write From Your Heart. I had no expectations and certainly no idea what a pivotal moment it was going to be in my life.

The aims of the workshop were to explore the use of writing exercises as a tool for self-discovery and to reframe our life story by writing it down. It sounded straightforward. The leader got us interacting right away: The first exercise was done in pairs and involved talking about where you would be and what you would be doing if you weren't here at this moment. Because of the warm and welcoming environment, I felt safe enough to open up to the person next to me and share that I was wrestling with some personal issues. But I didn't share the specifics of feeling hopelessly locked up in a life sentence.

After that first exercise, the leader gave us a little inspiration and encouragement. "There's a writer in each of you. By tuning in to your inner wisdom and letting your writing flow without judgment, you'll take home valuable insights about yourself."

Then he posed this question: "How do you make writing easier?"

Someone replied, "When I get peaceful, it's easier to write."

The leader replied with another question: "Does anyone here have a harsh internal critic?"

Hands went up, including his. He reminded us of Anne Lamott's advice about how to overcome perfection: to just write and let it go, to let it pour out of you, and to think of it as writing lots of "shitty first drafts." It's about practicing what it feels like to be present, not perfect.

The leader told us what to expect from our time together. We'd be writing poetry, but to get past our usual distracted mind and beyond the internal critic, we'd first listen as he read from poets describing what it takes to find your true voice in the world. Then we'd do a short walking meditation. I felt at ease knowing what to expect, and listening to the raw and beautiful words of others was just what I needed right now.

I was surprised when the leader led us in some mild stretching and breathing exercises before reading poetry to us. He told us it would help get us out of our heads and grounded in our bodies. Then he talked about what it means to be authentic. He introduced us to Rumi and Mary Oliver and Oriah Mountain Dreamer and other wonderful poets.

I was blown away as he recited the words of those great poets, and I've held them close to this day. Each poem spoke to me in a different voice, but the messages were the same: Being your authentic self is the most essential element in living your one lifetime well. This message resonated deeply within me. Authenticity is exactly what I was seeking to live and longing to express.

After reading poetry, the leader led us through a walking meditation. He invited us to just walk, feel our feet, and focus on sensations—our breathing, emotions, and thoughts. He encouraged us to notice the changing movements of our bodies, senses, and minds. As I walked, I felt my attention move from my mind to my body, and I felt at home as I settled into the sensations.

At some point, the leader invited us to shift attention from foreground to background—to widen the lens of attention, to step back in our minds, to breathe, and to allow things to be. He invited us to become the witness of our experiences, to realize ourselves as an unchanging presence outside of time and space, never in need, but present and wise. His words, which might have easily withered in the numbness I had been feeling, found fertile soil in my heart, which had been coaxed into opening.

Now it was time to turn to writing, and I wondered how we would shift from acceptance and allowing to putting words on paper.

We each took pen and paper, and the leader invited us to find a comfortable, private spot anywhere in the room. He encouraged us to clear away distractions and allow our attention to rest in the mystery of just being, feeling alive, and feeling the force of all life, creativity, well-being, and joy, independent of changing events.

I was open and vulnerable, and the leader's voice was soothing and comforting. As I held the pen loosely in my hand, the words began to flow.

I'd always loved to write, but the experience I had that day was like none I'd ever had before. The combination of those evocative poems followed by the walking meditation put me in a state of consciousness that allowed my poem to be born naturally and with ease. It was almost as if my pen was directly connected to my heart, and it began to move by itself. The poem that came out of me was so crystal clear, and in that moment, I heard my own voice. I knew what I had to do. As I wrote my poem, I sobbed silently and uncontrollably.

When the leader asked us to pair with someone else and read what we had written, I was vibrating and alive. I was on fire. Then we rejoined, the whole circle and the leader offered the group as a witness for anyone who wanted to share their work. Everyone who chose to share was a powerful example of vulnerability and courage. We closed the circle with an om, giving us a sense of calm grounding so we could reenter the world.

I was so surprised and blown away by what had emerged in the workshop. I left somewhat shaken, but I also felt deeply reconciled. I went to a dance session at lunchtime, which helped me integrate even more through my body all that was going on in my mind and heart. I finally had access to the essence of my problem and the truth I needed to face.

It was not a happy choice, and I deeply mourned the "intact family" that I wasn't going to have. The divorce process was long and painful, mirroring much of the marriage. But despite my sadness and fear of the future, I was no longer depressed. I was living authentically. I showed up in profound, new ways, supporting my children and fighting for their well-being. And I learned to do things I never knew how to do, from managing money to putting up curtain rods.

Some years after that day in the Berkshires, I fell in love with my soul mate, a friend I had known through my work. We married, and today we are blessed with our blended family and our wonderful partnership.

This story was written by Dr. Lauren Behrman and edited by the authors. Lauren is a clinical psychologist, mediator, and author in independent practice in New York City. Visit www.laurenbehrmanphd.com and www.mydivorcerecovery.com to see more of her work.

# Chapter 13

# The Second Key—
# Inviting Full Participation

*The soul lives contented*
*by listening.*
*If it wants to change*
*into the beauty of*
*terrifying shapes*
*it tries to speak.*
*That's why*
*you will not sing,*
*afraid as you are*
*of who might join with you.*

—David Whyte

*A* transformational workshop is not a spectator sport. As leaders, we are not celebrities performing in front of an audience. Our groups are collaborative and dynamic. Our group members are participants. We want them to speak up, raise difficult issues, try out new ideas, see the value of diversity, and have a stake in the outcome. We honor out-loud thinking, unformed conclusions, and "shitty first drafts." As Don Stapleton, a Kripalu teacher, says, "Slick is deadly." Self-censorship is a drag on creativity and group wisdom.

How do you help people dive in and participate, to connect rather than protect? First, create safe space (Chapter 11) by welcoming different views, needs, interests; by normalizing silence, disagreements, and strong feelings; and by encouraging thinking about possibilities. Wisdom traditions encourage adopting a beginner's mind—not having expectations and not already knowing how things will turn out.

The second key to creating dynamic, impactful workshops is inviting full participation. Doing this builds momentum by immersing participants in diverse, interactive experiences, from self-reflection to pair sharing. The more engaged and invested each participant is, the greater the transformational potential of the group.

In Lauren's story, the workshop leader used a variety of experiences to help participants settle in, connect with themselves and others, and be authentic and open to creativity. In this chapter, we'll describe eight practices for inviting full participation.

## WAYS TO INVITE FULL PARTICIPATION

Transformational groups depend on interaction. We live in an entertainment culture, so sometimes people have to be coaxed to participate. Consider Joan's experience:

> Joan came to the workshop with a familiar feeling: *I'm going to sit back, watch, and let the workshop and the leader do it for me.* Underneath that feeling was the notion *I need something. I don't know what it is. But just fix me. Something's broken, and I don't know what.* After the workshop, she realized how much had shifted. *I'm going away with a feeling of hunger.* The workshop inspired Joan to ask herself big questions: *Where am I headed in my life? Do I have a bright enough beacon to follow? How do I train myself to become more of who I already am?*

How did Joan go from wanting to be fixed to being self-directing, from being a spectator on the sidelines to fully participating in her journey? The transformational workshop gave Joan a place to move from observer to player.

But joining the game requires trust. Taking risks can be uncomfortable, yet it helps people to stretch and grow. Your role is to lead your participants progressively, starting with lower risk experiences and slowly introducing higher risk experiences.

## LOWER RISK EXPERIENCES: STARTING EASIER

Storytelling, journaling, and brainstorming are generally low-risk experiences. First, let's look at storytelling, which is a powerful way to teach. In many spiritual traditions, stories are used to illustrate profound truths and life lessons. Metaphors, imagery, self-disclosure, and humor create a living context to teach concepts. In Lauren's story, the leader used a very simple way to reveal something about himself to the group. He asked if anyone had a harsh internal critic, and then he raised his own hand, putting himself on the same level with the group.

Telling your own story shows your humanity and can have an impact on the willingness of group members to do the same. Use common sense when you self-reveal as a leader. Ask yourself what your motivation is and how it serves the greater good. If, for instance, you're still actively processing your life's story and experience an emotional charge when thinking about it, practice telling your story in a way that doesn't overly activate you. Telling your story to the group in a way that models your lessons learned (without being activated) can be a great gift to the group and to you.

Journaling is another way for individuals to collect their thoughts and reflect on their experiences. It preserves anonymity and can be used to set up a mind-body experience and process it afterward. Journaling can even be the primary experience itself, especially when followed up with pair sharing to deepen relationships, increase interaction, and foster trust. Invite your participants to keep an ongoing journal throughout the workshop or retreat, and give them short journaling prompts, such as:

- What surprised you? Any insights or aha moments?
- What do you want to remember?
- What new questions do you have now?
- What's coming up for you?
- Where do you need support? How might you get it?

Journal prompts invite participants to reflect on what's happening in the moment. Asking participants to reflect on their needs through journaling empowers them to get those needs met before the workshop ends. You can also target journaling toward workshop goals:

- Review your intentions. Are you on track? Has anything shifted?
- What is the key lesson you took from this session?

Finally, brainstorming is a way to generate, sort, and prioritize ideas. It can jump-start a discussion to explore issues, resources, and obstacles. To begin a brainstorm session, you can ask for a simple list of ideas, or you can first brainstorm categories for the list. Brainstorming pros and cons can help a group evaluate the merits of two different approaches without having to impose a right or wrong answer.

You can write the highlights on chart paper or a white board, using the participants' words. In brainstorming, there are no bad ideas. Get as many as possible. Try not to evaluate, restrict, or shut down the process. Maintain an open and encouraging attitude. You know you're having a great session when ideas are flowing too quickly to write them down!

## MEDIUM-RISK EXPERIENCES: STEPPING IT UP

Medium-risk experiences invite participants to choose how much they want to self-reveal. Continuums, scatter plots, breakout groups, and structured and unstructured rounds generally fall into this category.

Continuums and scatter plots invite participants to engage nonverbally in what's being discussed. In a *continuum* exercise, participants are invited to take a position along an imaginary line. Opposing viewpoints are represented by the two ends of the line, or continuum. For example, in our workshops we help leaders explore major feelings that might come up in a workshop, such as anger. We start the continuum with this question: How comfortable are you with anger in yourself? On one end of the continuum is "not at all comfortable," and on the other end is "very comfortable." As participants line up along the continuum, they are revealing something about themselves without having to use words.

You can build on a continuum by posing another question. In our workshops, we ask this follow-up question: How comfortable are you with anger in others? Then we invite participants to move to another position on the continuum if their answer is different. We then go a step further and invite those who changed positions to share their reflections on their reason for moving.

A *scatter plot* is similar to the continuum in that it provides an opportunity for participants to speak without using their voice. In a scatter plot, you pose a question that has multiple possible answers, and you connect different sections of the room to different answers. In our workshops, we build on the continuum by identifying each corner of the room with a big feeling (anger, sadness, fear, and joy). We pose this question: Which big feeling in you disturbs you most? Then we invite participants to walk to any point in the room that expresses their answer.

A scatter plot allows you to quickly see where participants stand (literally) in regard to a particular issue or question. You can build on the scatter plot by inviting participants to explain why they chose the position they did. You can also shift the question and invite people to move accordingly and then report on why they moved.

The scatter plot is a good setup for asking subgroups to explore an issue and generate ideas around the categories they chose.

A *breakout group* is a way of getting participants into smaller, more intimate groups to share reflections, complete a task, or do active processing. Small breakout groups are the primary "unit" of experiential learning, and they can be dyads (groups of two), triads (groups of three), or larger. Breakout groups can be used to energize and engage the group, break the ice, get people's attention, build relationships, boost confidence, help participants take more ownership, and generate information or reports. Breakout groups are also an expedient way to explore various aspects of a single issue simultaneously.

Dyad breakout groups (or pair shares) are quick and can be used informally and in the moment. The leader in Lauren's story used dyads at the beginning of the workshop and asked participants to share with each other "where you would be and what you would be doing if you weren't here at this moment." She used dyads again near the end when she had participants read aloud what they had written. This use of sharing in small groups opens multiple channels of communication and interaction. What starts as a leader-to-participant channel opens up to a participant-to-participant channel. Once participants start to interact with each other, you've enhanced engagement and ownership in the group.

> *How did the rose ever open its heart, and give to this world all of its beauty? It felt the encouragement of light against its being, otherwise we all remain too frightened.*
>
> —Hafiz

Triads are helpful when note-taking is needed; for example, when one participant shares, one participant listens and asks questions, and the third participant takes notes on what's being said. Triads are also helpful when an observer or witness is needed. The downside of triads is that they take longer, as there are three people who need to cycle through the experience rather than just two.

Another medium-risk experience is the *round*, which can be structured or unstructured. A round is a whole-group activity where all participants are invited to share. In an *unstructured round*, everyone is invited to share, but only if they want to. The final sharing activity in Lauren's story was an unstructured round. To initiate an unstructured round, you can pose a question and then invite participants to "popcorn," or call out, responses. You can also pass a talking stick or toss a beanbag from one person to the next to signal who will speak next. This helps participants to not talk over each other.

A *roving reporter* is another form of unstructured round. The leader brings the microphone to participants as they raise their hands. This ensures that participants speak one at a time and into a microphone. It also allows the leader to tactfully use body language or gently take back the microphone to manage session time.

In a *structured round*, each person shares by turn. A structured round is good for warming up a newly formed group, ensuring that everyone participates (including quiet members), taking the temperature (or mood), or sizing up an issue. Structured rounds are often used at the beginning to get acquainted and at the end to close the workshop or retreat so that everyone has an opportunity to express themselves.

In larger groups, structured rounds take more time. Depending on your purpose, you may want to impose a time limit for each person. If it feels right to do so, you can use a timer and/or timekeeper to help keep things moving. If you choose to use a timekeeper, let everyone know what the time limit is. For a five-minute share, you might signal the speaker at four minutes to let the person know it's time to wrap up. You can use a bell or chime to keep time, which is less intrusive than a verbal awareness.

Early on in the workshop, when the group is still forming and participants may be still hesitant to share, you can open the floor and show them the protocol by sharing first. Keep your sharing concise, and others will follow your example. If someone goes over the time limit, gently interrupt, thank them for sharing, and let them know there will be time later for more sharing.

## HIGHER RISK EXPERIENCES: DIVING DEEP

Two higher risk experiences are fishbowl and role playing. In a *fishbowl*, an individual or subgroup volunteers to enter the center of the circle while taking part in an experiential exercise. The group is asked to witness, holding the rim of the circle with compassionate presence. It takes courage to be the focus of a fishbowl, so be sure to build up enough trust in the group before introducing this activity. When handled with sensitivity, a fishbowl can be profoundly moving for those in the middle and on the rim.

*Role playing* is when one or more individuals take on roles and act out a scenario. This is helpful for trying out ideas (seeing their implications in role playing before putting them into practice in real life), giving voice to unspoken issues, illustrating a concept, conducting a case study, simulating a scenario, imagining a hypothetical situation, or practicing a technique.

Role playing and fishbowl are high-risk activities because they ask participants to imagine and try out different ways of being in front of others. Being seen and heard in the moment is emotionally revealing and demands a high level of trust. High-risk experiences are better done later in a workshop after group bonding is well underway. Choosing to opt out is always possible, so reinforce that option for role plays and fishbowls.

Role playing can be highly activating and requires more attention to safety and integration. First, demonstrate role playing and give clear instructions so that participants see exactly what they are being asked to do. Ending a role-playing session also requires skill and attention. Demonstrate how the role playing will end—how each person will "de-role." When debriefing role playing and fishbowls, let the ones being witnessed de-role first, and caution the others to be sensitive to the feelings of those who volunteered by first offering your own praise for their courage in stepping forward.

## INVITING FULL PARTICIPATION: WHY AND HOW?

Interactive practices can be used at any point in the transformational learning cycle (safety, experience, integration). For example, storytelling or journaling can be used to create safety and prepare participants for an upcoming mind-body experience. Any one of the eight ways can be used as a mind-body experience in itself, and most of them can be used for integration by actively processing each experience. If you use higher risk experiences, such as fishbowls or role playing, remember to set aside enough time for integration (e.g., through journaling, dyad/triad sharing, and whole-group sharing).

Inviting full participation involves risk taking, which is personal and subjective. For example, someone who wants to fit in might feel pressured to conform to the majority in a continuum. Someone who is reserved may experience anxiety in a structured round, where everyone is encouraged to share. And someone who struggles with intimacy or vulnerability may find pair sharing threatening at first. Moments of discomfort are normal and can lead to personal growth when supported with a kind and curious attitude. Every experience in the workshop is an opportunity for self-awareness and learning.

Figure 13.1 summarizes the eight ways of inviting full participation.

| EXPERIENCE | RISK LEVEL | DESCRIPTION | PURPOSE |
|---|---|---|---|
| Storytelling | Low | Facilitator uses metaphor, imagery, and humor to tell a story. Individuals make their own meaning. | Illustrate teaching concepts and create safety through self-revelation. |
| Journaling | Low | Individuals are given a chance to reflect and write their thoughts in a journal. | Diving in, searching, uncovering, contemplating, and opportunity for anonymity. |
| Brainstorming | Low | Individuals offer up ideas, and a scribe records them (list of items, pros/cons, categories). There are no bad ideas! | Generating creativity by exploring ideas or envisioning goals, methods, resources, issues, obstacles, and inspiration. |
| Continuum and Scatter Plot | Medium | Individuals take a position in the room in order to measure intensity, priority, or relationship to an issue. | Generating a visual range of view, energetic polling, ranking priorities, and speaking without having to talk. |
| Breakout Groups | Medium | Groups are formed (dyads, triads, larger groups) to complete a task or process something that just happened. | Relationship builder, icebreaker, attention getter, energizer, engager, confidence builder, ownership maker, and idea generator. |
| Structured and Unstructured Rounds | Medium | Structured: Each person in the group takes a turn. Unstructured: Voluntary sharing from individuals in the group (popcorn, talking sticks, beanbag toss, roving reporter). | Warm-up, equalizer, barometer, way to test the water, and opening/closing. |
| Fishbowl | High | A subgroup performs a task while the rest of the group gathers around to observe and witness. | Supporting, focusing, witnessing: being seen, heard, and supported by the group. |
| Role Play | High | One or more individuals take on roles and act out a scenario or practice a technique. | Act out ideas, unspoken issues, illustrations, case studies, simulations, and hypothetical situations. Practice techniques. |

Figure 13.1 Eight Ways of Inviting Full Participation

## IN SUMMARY

Transformational groups depend on individual and collaborative inquiry through participation in interactive experiences. As leaders, our aim is to cultivate ongoing awareness and meaning making through cycles of interaction and reflection. Small-group and whole-group sharing deepens understanding and supports vicarious learning.

In the next chapter, we'll explore two more facilitation skills that can be used to invite full participation: encouraging and questioning.

**Putting it into Practice:**
**Journal Prompts**

- In your workshops, how much "work" are you doing compared to your participants?
- How comfortable are you with using interactive experiences in your workshops? How might you support yourself?
- How could you use more pair sharing in your workshops?

Figure 13.2 Putting it into Practice: Journal Prompts

# Chapter 14

# The Skills of Encouraging and Questioning

*I have come to think that one of the most satisfying experiences I know—and also one of the most growth-promoting experiences for the other person—is just fully to appreciate this individual in the same way that I appreciate a sunset. . . . People are just as wonderful as sunsets if you let them be.*

—Carl R. Rogers

$A$s an embodied leader, you help individuals and groups grow and transform through what Carl Rogers called *unconditional positive regard*—accepting people without judgment and valuing them as doing their best. Holding this nurturing perspective is key as you monitor and negotiate the group interactions, moods, and behaviors.

A leader can invite full participation and mutual understanding through compassionate dialogue and by surfacing, examining, and reframing hidden assumptions. In this chapter, we'll explore the skills of encouraging and questioning, which stimulates new ways of looking at the world and allows participants to self-determine.

## THE SKILL OF ENCOURAGING

Research in neuroscience suggests that we have a negativity bias that predisposes the mind to focus on what's not working—*something's missing; something's wrong.* Leaders can counteract this negativity bias by reminding participants of what is working, what is right, and what has always been right. The skill of encouraging promotes what's positive and life affirming. It's what reminds participants that everyone already has everything they need. Encouraging (derived from the French word *coeur*, which means "heart") affirms that everyone has an internal compass for life, insight, and empathy.

As a leader, you reinforce the good by encouraging participants to trust their own abilities, to take responsibility for their experiences, and to own their places in the group. You give people permission to notice and express feelings by validating and normalizing fear, grief, anger, disappointment, etc. You support people to reveal rather than conceal. You encourage quiet participants to speak more, and you invite those who share a lot to consider stepping back in order to let others step forward.

Appreciation is one form of encouragement. It affirms the other for who they are, what they've said, or what they've done. Sometimes a simple thank-you or a smile is enough to express gratitude. However, specific expressions of gratitude can have more impact than general ones. For instance, compare the following:

- *General:* "I really appreciated what you said yesterday. Thanks!"
- *Specific:* "Thank you for your message yesterday. I needed reassurance, and I felt comforted by your support."

The second appreciation is more satisfying for both people, because it brings feelings and needs into awareness. The result is greater understanding and deeper connection between giver and receiver. It can be broken down into three parts:

1. behavior ("your message")
2. need ("I needed reassurance.")
3. outcome ("I felt comforted.")

The more specific, the more powerful the connection. This is a three-part appreciation.[39] See Figure 14.1.

Encouraging also takes the form of directing participants' attention internally and externally so they notice self-talk and habitual thinking. For example, you can make your own habits explicit to the group in a playful way; for example, "I'm noticing how I want the group to like me. I want approval. Am I the only one?" Revealing your humanity through self-disclosure sends the message that it's normal to have voices of doubt and fear.

---

**In the three-part appreciation, you:**

1. State what the other person did that enriched your life: "Thank you for your message yesterday."
2. Name the need that was fulfilled: "I needed reassurance."
3. Express the positive feelings that resulted: "I felt comforted by your support."

---

Figure 14.1 The Three-Part Appreciation

You can bring attention to the rich texture of human experience. The meditation walk in Lauren's story had this effect. Participants shifted their attention away from the negativity bias (the internal critic) to sensing the body. This opened a creative channel that might have otherwise remained closed. As Lauren walked, she began to feel more at home in her body. She sensed herself in the moment, just being and feeling alive. In her words, "[what] might have easily withered in the numbness I had been feeling, found fertile soil in my heart, which had been coaxed into opening."

## THE SKILL OF QUESTIONING

Inquiry is at the core of all spiritual and scientific exploration. As a leader, you are inviting people to get curious, become interested, and care about their experiences and relationships with others. Instead of jumping to a quick answer or giving advice to a participant, the leader can use questioning to direct attention in many ways. When you're present, you're more likely to pause and use a question to move an individual or the group forward.

> " *Great questioning, great enlightenment; little questioning, little enlightenment; no questioning, no enlightenment.* "
>
> —Dōgen

Questions can be empowering or disempowering. *Empowering questions* focus individual and group attention on what's possible and working. They foster group purpose, stimulate reflection, and expand on what we have in common. *Disempowering questions* focus on what's not working, ascribe blame, identify what's wrong, and elaborate on what should have happened but didn't. Because they are about giving advice, they energetically disconnect rather than connect. They can trigger our default, habitual thinking and lead us down a rabbit hole of negativity. Sometimes a speaker's tone of voice can make the difference between an empowering and a disempowering question.

Facilitators craft questions to direct attention and focus energy in five directions (see Figure 14.2).

- *Future:* to imagine possibilities, set trajectories, and inspire action.
- *Past:* to appreciate and honor past contributions.
- *Purpose:* to answer the question, Why are we here?
- *Foundation:* to identify the values we care about.
- *Present:* to access internal states and present-moment awareness.

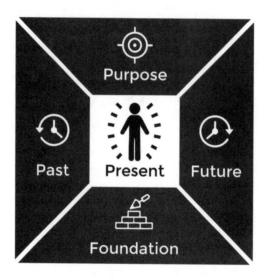

Figure 14.2 The Five Directional Questions

## Future Questions

Groups need to be able to focus on the future to unearth possibilities, discover new capacities, create a sense of momentum, and identify trends or emergent capabilities. Future thinking frees up energy to discover new ways of being. It stimulates imagination and energy to solve problems in the present.

The energy of future questions can feel like excitement, enthusiasm, brainstorming, and creating possibilities. You might hear your participants say,

- "Maybe we could . . ."
- "Wouldn't it be great if . . . ?"
- "Wow, what fun that could be!"
- "How about this?"
- "Let's consider this."

To drive this kind of engagement, you need empowering future questions:

- What are your hopes, dreams, and aspirations?
- Assuming no time or money limitations, what's the potential here?
- How do you want to feel when this is done?
- What wants to emerge?
- Looking back five years from now, how might this look?

Disempowering questions, on the other hand, create a shrinking future. They might look like this:

- Are you sure you are capable of doing that?
- Why would you want to do that?
- Will that really work?
- You really think you'll feel that way?
- Do you think you can predict the future?
- How is this not a waste of time?

## Past Questions

Groups need to honor the contribution of the past, assess impact, identify causes and how we got here, appreciate a sense of common experience, value differences, and develop an identity.

Past-question energy can be quiet, measured, heated, appreciative, sad, thoughtful, reflective, remorseful, or somber.

Empowering past questions include:

- How would we objectively characterize what has happened, without blame?
- What have we learned from what happened?
- How has this formed who we are today?
- What has formed you and your life? What were the pivotal moments?
- As a group, what can we let go of right now?

Default, habitual thinking is sticky. It's easy to lapse into blame and self-flagellation, and spiral into negativity. Past questions that trigger the default mode are:

- Why didn't you take action?
- Are you going to be able to fix it?
- What were you thinking?
- Why did you do that?
- Did you really think that would work?
- This is the third time I've had to go over this. Why aren't you listening?

## Purpose Questions

Leaders and groups need a sense of purpose, a reason for being together, a bigger story to tell—a compelling *why*. Purpose discussions help to unite groups and teams. Creating a common purpose helps us break free of the past and, like future energy, fosters possibility thinking.

The energy of purpose questions can look like deep listening, reflective postures, note-taking, and spontaneous conversations about models, concepts, and meaning.

Empowering purpose questions include:

- What is our purpose in doing this?
- How does this contribute to a greater good?
- What might this mean if we are successful?
- What is motivating this effort?
- What is the bigger conversation we want to have?

Disempowering purpose questions have the opposite effect. They shut down the group and create stagnation, disengagement, indifference, and apathy.

Purpose questions that disempower include:

- Is this really important?
- Aren't we still working at cross-purposes?
- Is this really a big enough reason to be doing this?
- Don't you think we ought to . . . ?
- How is it that you haven't come to agreement yet?
- Wouldn't it be better if we . . . ?

## Foundation Questions

Leaders and groups need to have a sense of what grounds them (shared values) and what brings them together. Foundation discussions help groups get a sense of what unites them at a fundamental level, a sense of oneness and shared humanity, an appreciation of what is, and a sense of me and we ("Mwe," as Dan Siegel calls it). Foundation questions are compassionate, empathic, and connecting.

The energy of foundation questions can look like quiet conversation, participants leaning in, participants being touched (and perhaps some tears), aha moments, hugs, and eye gazing.

Empowering foundation questions include:

- What unites us?
- What do we share?
- How do we foster deeper connection and appreciation?
- What are our strengths and gifts?
- What must be shared?

Disempowering foundation questions highlight differences in a way that breaks down unity. They isolate and create a sense of disconnection and shame. Some disempowering foundation questions include:

- What makes you think we have anything in common?
- What makes you think we care about the same things?
- Do you see anything that unites us?
- Don't you think we are too different to do this thing?
- What do you people know about this subject, anyway?

## Present-Moment Questions

Accessing internal states by pausing, breathing, regrouping, and shifting attention is how we gain self-awareness. Present-moment discussions help people unplug the default mode, widening awareness to open new ways of thinking.

The energy of present-moment questions can manifest as a relaxed and alert posture, eyes looking downward, deep and measured breathing, and an expanded awareness of the environment.

Empowering present-moment questions include:

- What are you sensing right now?
- Where is your focus?
- What do you feel, and where do you feel it?
- How might you shift your focus?
- Where do you feel the breath in your body?
- Can you tell me more?

Disempowering present-moment questions can activate a self-conscious reaction rather than self-awareness. Consider these examples of disempowering present-moment questions:

- What's taking you so long?
- Hey, isn't everybody done?
- Can we move on already?
- You aren't distracted by your inner voices, are you?
- Why did you say that?

## Questions That Get to Underlying Needs

As you facilitate, you might sense an underlying need. Asking questions can help invite a group or participant to look within to find what's needed, rather than relying on the leader or other group members to meet the need.

Figure 14.3 shows how questions can be used in this way. Notice how they invite reflection, reveal underlying needs, and lead to greater self-awareness.

| GOAL | QUESTIONS TO ASK |
|------|------------------|
| **Invite Participation** | ■ How many of you feel … ?<br>■ Would you be willing to … ?<br>■ How might we … ? |
| **Encourage Self-Reflection** | ■ What's working for you right now? What's working for the group right now?<br>■ What's green and growing?<br>■ What's resonating for you right now? |
| **Support and Encourage** | ■ What do you need right now?<br>■ How can you ask for what you need?<br>■ What might help you feel safer right now? |
| **Provide Support After Emotional Release** | ■ How are you going to care for yourself right after this session?<br>■ Do you need to rest, walk outdoors, check in with somebody, eat lunch … ?<br>■ What do you need to wrap this up for now and feel a sense of closure? |
| **Decrease Overwhelm** | ■ What can you say no to? What can you stop doing to make room inside?<br>■ How can you take care of yourself right now?<br>■ What physical action would be most helpful right now? |
| **Invite Self-Discovery** | ■ What do you notice? Tell me more. What else?<br>■ What is your intention?<br>■ What are you excited about?<br>■ Where do you experience a sense of mastery in your life? |
| **Invoke Wisdom or Clarity** | ■ What does your heart say? What is your body telling you?<br>■ What are you committed to?<br>■ What does this experience mean for you? |
| **Encourage Breakthrough** | ■ What's standing in your way?<br>■ What's the impact if things remain the same?<br>■ Who would you be without that thought or belief?<br>■ What are you willing to change or let go of? |
| **Elicit Action** | ■ What's next for you?<br>■ What inspires you? What's one step you can take in that direction?<br>■ If you knew you'd succeed, what would you do?<br>■ What is one action step that, if taken now, would excite you? |
| **Identify Vision, Mission, and Purpose** | ■ What impact do you want to have?<br>■ What do you want for your life?<br>■ How can you create a larger vision for yourself?<br>■ How might we draw a bigger circle? |

Figure 14.3 Examples of Empowering Questions

## ASKING EVOCATIVE QUESTIONS

Asking evocative questions stimulates interest and invites participation on multiple levels. They also help create a *living context*—a space for participants to check in with their whole self (mind, heart, body, and spirit) and tap into wisdom that is deeper than thinking alone. Notice the difference between these two examples.

### Example 1: You'd like to invite the group to make agreements.

- *Less Evocative:* "What agreements would you like this group to make?"
- *More Evocative:* "We're about to go on a journey of discovery together. We'll be exploring feelings, beliefs, and values. What would help you to feel safe, motivated, and effective in this group? Think about what's worked for you in the past. An example of a group agreement is confidentiality. What are some agreements that would help you feel supported? Who'd like to start by proposing an agreement?"

### Example #2: You'd like to invite participants to join a subgroup.

- *Less Evocative:* "What subgroup would you like to join?"
- *More Evocative:* "Wisdom comes from understanding your needs. Which of these topics resonates with you right now? What need is calling to you? Let yourself be guided from within. Take a moment to feel. Which subgroup do you feel called to?"

When you craft questions, sense what's needed in the moment. What do they need? What will help them connect more deeply? Mind? Heart? Body? Spirit?

---

**Practicing the Skill of Questioning**

The next time you feel the urge to give advice, try asking a question instead.

- Be fully present and just listen. Breathe and notice what's happening in yourself and with the other person.
- Ask, "What's happening for you?" Use reflective listening if the other person is having difficulty voicing her thoughts.
- Ask, "Is there more?" to give the other person time to complete her thought.

Figure 14.4 Practicing the Skill of Questioning

## IN SUMMARY

Skillful questioning keeps the energy of curiosity and discovery alive in your groups. Encouraging cultivates a nurturing environment in which people see the good in each other and celebrate how they are enriched by everybody's unique contribution.

We've used the metaphor of a workshop as being like a journey across an unknown sea. On any sea voyage, weather changes, and storms can come up. Turbulence arises. In the next chapter, you'll see how to address upsets, obstacles, and confusion, using the skills of intervening and clearing.

**Putting it into Practice:**
**Journal Prompts**

- Think of someone to appreciate using the three-part appreciation and practice by writing down what you would say.
- Create a set of evocative instructions for a mind-body experience in your workshop.

Figure 14.5 Putting it into Practice: Journal Prompts

# Barry's Story

## When Things Fall Apart

Chapters 15, 16, and 17 are about how to co-create an intentional community that is strong enough to endure conflict and setbacks, and that meets the basic human needs for safety, satisfaction, and connection. Barry's story considers a workshop leader who faces self-doubt when challenged by conflict within the group. Through various interventions and self-care practices, he manages his own uncertainty, handles difficult behavior, and renews the group's shared values and goals.

Outside the program room, it was a crisp, blue-sky fall day. Inside, however, a storm was brewing for the group that had gathered for a leadership training. As the group facilitator, I was fast becoming aware that I had a problem on my hands.

During the first morning session, Jack asked me if he could digitally record the program to help him remember better. I put Jack's request to the group, and most people said that it would feel intrusive and unsafe if they were being recorded.

"I'm sorry, Jack. The group is saying no to recording."

Jack objected, "But it's for my own use—you're not being fair."

Several people offered solutions, such as making their notes available to him, and I offered to make extra handouts from my own notes for him. Still, Jack was disappointed. I felt we needed to move on, and to validate his feelings, I said, "I understand you're not happy with the outcome, but can you live with it since the group has decided?" After another objection, he consented.

I took Jack aside after the session and asked how he was doing. He said he was fine, but his face and body language said otherwise. I met with my teaching staff, Kate and Peter, and we debriefed the session. We agreed the group got off to a good start and was on course, but Jack's behavior raised some yellow flags.

The next day, when I met Jack at the program room door, I was surprised by his positive remarks: "You're really good! Great group! I'm getting so much already." On one hand, Jack's upbeat mood was a relief since he had been so unhappy the day before. But his see-saw behavior was disconcerting. During the morning session, he would sometimes withdraw and avoid eye contact, and at other times, he would be almost over the top with enthusiasm.

Sure enough, later in the session he expressed anger at the group for voting against him. "You're not willing to help me. You say you're 'in service of others,' but you're not willing to serve me." He asserted that others should be willing to stretch into their own discomfort and bend a little.

He clearly wasn't letting this go, and I felt the need to intervene. During a short break, I asked him if he would be willing to meet me privately for 20 minutes during our lunch break.

My intention for the meeting was to help him recognize his behavior and its impact on him and the group. Jack and I met in a private lounge. "So, Jack," I began. "Can you tell me more about your intention for being in the group? What brings you here? What do you hope to get from this program?"

He said that he wanted to lead groups because he had a strong sense that this was his purpose. I asked him to tell me more, and he said that he had been in groups for a long time, and he always admired the way that leaders were able to help him and others.

Then I coached Jack through conscious dialogue, helping him to express his feelings, needs, and requests based on the observation he made about the group saying no to his request. Jack mentioned that some of the group members seemed angry, and others were avoiding him. He said that he felt the pushback from the group, and he just couldn't get over it. He felt hurt and hopeless that the group wouldn't help him. He recounted the ways in which the group was triggering some of his past hurts. Ultimately, he said what he needed was to be understood.

I asked Jack if he'd be willing to do a self-discovery process. With his permission, I turned his attention back to his request to record the program and his feelings about that. I asked him, "Feel what happens in your body when you focus on that hurt and anger." I led him through a guided inquiry in his body, first by welcoming sensations, then feelings and emotions, then images and memories, and finally thoughts and beliefs about what happened when he felt the group's refusal of his request.

At one point, there were tears, and he said that it reminded him of being hurt when he was very young. He made the connection between these memories and his desire to belong while also struggling to trust the group. I asked him to make a positive intention for returning to the next session. Jack said he wanted to show up in the group as caring for and being concerned about the others, just as he wanted the group to care for and be concerned about him. I asked him if he'd be willing to follow the group agreements about how to communicate with each other and to respect the decision of the group. He said yes.

I was encouraged during the next session when Jack showed up as he said he would—caring and concerned. But after that, he returned to his former behavior—retreating, avoiding, and then breaking out in anger. His impact on the group was evident, and I had to pause the group at times to ask him if he would be willing to apologize for remarks that upset group members. Participants began pulling me aside to tell me how much time and energy it was taking for the entire group to process his behavior.

I arranged for another meeting with Jack. I was activated this time. I really needed to clear myself in the privacy of my own room before the meeting. I took some deep breaths, rolled my head around on my shoulders, and let out some deep vocalizations from my belly. I tried to recall what had happened and the whole sequence of behaviors. Although I was still on track with the workshop agenda, the most compelling thing in the room continued to be Jack's behavior.

Then, I tuned in to my body and noticed a sick feeling in my gut. My head was aching, and my jaw and shoulders were tight as if my body was resisting the unfolding drama. I did not want to ride this wave. But I knew I had to self-regulate. My thoughts were racing. *I'm having a panic attack here. I feel paralyzed. I don't know what to do! Stay with it, Barry. You can do this.*

And then it hit me: *Duh! I hate conflict!* I told myself. *Okay, this isn't new. I've felt this way before.* I was aware of how scared I was that I wasn't showing up strong enough as a leader. And I thought, *If I had intervened sooner, I could have headed off some of Jack's difficult behavior.* This critical voice was familiar.

I asked myself, *What do I really need here?* I needed something reliable to hold on to. Some safety for me and the group. I called up the image of my mentor. What would he do in this situation? I smiled. He would be honest, understanding, kind, and firm. I felt the feeling of ease wash over me. Then, I refocused my intention to be present and respectful, first for myself, and then to care for Jack and the group. I had to reestablish a sense of direction and purpose by renewing the group's shared values and goals, and by resetting the boundaries with group agreements. I wanted to include the group in decision making, and I wanted to be transparent about letting the group see my own process, even some of my uncertainty.

Much as before, when Jack and I met, he said he was sorry for his behavior. He said he understood the impact of his actions, and he agreed to follow the group agreements. This time, however, I asked him to sign a written contract to abide by our agreements. He signed the document, agreeing not to mention the recording, not to blame or complain, but instead to use conscious dialogue.

I was hopeful again after he signed the contract, but things didn't change. He made another inappropriate comment. Now I felt the group had reached a tipping point. We had stopped practicing safely. I needed to take action. But before I did, I wanted to be really clear about whether to keep Jack in the group or to let him go for the sake of the group. I called for a 30-minute break and asked Jack if he'd be willing to meet privately.

I reflected on my own role in what was happening, and I let myself feel the sensations of doubt and fear wash over me. I took a deep breath and then another. With each following breath, the feeling of purpose and strength came back to me. Now I was ready to do what needed to be done.

This time, I was calm and clear, and I felt kindness toward Jack. I explained to him that although I had a responsibility to help him stay in the group, I also had a responsibility to the group as a whole. I reminded him of the terms of our contract and that because he had broken it, I would have to ask him to leave the group. I asked him if he would like help finding a group that could better serve his needs. He was sad, but he acknowledged the truth of all I'd said. I offered him the opportunity to say goodbye to individuals in the group at the end of the session, and he said that he'd like to.

We resumed the session without Jack. I informed the group that, as a measure of last resort, and in the best interest of the group, I had asked him to leave. I told them that Jack would be available to say his goodbyes to those who wanted to meet with him after the session.

I encouraged the group to see this as an opportunity to use a real-life challenge as a teachable moment. And then I led a group clearing. I explained how it would work: each of us would have an opportunity to express our feelings and needs, now that Jack was no longer with us. The intention was to acknowledge the loss of a group member and to clear away anything that would keep the group from achieving our stated purpose. I reviewed our group goals, agreements, and shared intention to create a safe place for transformation. Each participant would get a minute to declare their observation, feeling, need, and request.

In the group clearing that followed, I saw that each member of the group had experienced Jack differently. Each one spoke tenderly and authentically and appeared to discover something about themselves in the process. I could feel the energy shifting as we made our way around the circle. By the time we got to the last person, I could sense a lightness in the air. Everyone had been given a chance to get clear.

It was a deep journey for me, practicing staying present in the face of my fear and insecurity. I had wanted Jack to complete the program, and I knew that I had done my best to keep him in the group. It was also a reminder of the resilience of an intentional circle to hold on to challenges and setbacks. As I reflect on that weeklong program, I feel gratitude for Jack, my teaching team, the group, and the work itself.

---

Although this story is derived from real events, each character is a composite drawn from individuals and from imagination. No reference to any real person is intended nor should be inferred.

# Chapter 15

# The Third Key— Attending to Challenges

*As a workshop leader, whatever's not integrated in your life will surely walk through the door, wearing a nametag, disguised as a guest.*

—Aruni Nan Futuronsky

So far, we've explored the first two keys to leading transformational workshops: creating safe space and inviting full participation. We now turn to what may be the most difficult for a workshop leader, the third key: attending to challenges.

Challenges naturally arise in any group. In this chapter, we'll look at feelings and needs, and how unmet needs are the root cause of upsets, obstacles, and confusion. You'll see how participants sometimes try to get their needs met by using default coping strategies. This may show up as behavior that can be a disruptive influence.

As a leader, how do you stay calm in a storm? How do you resolve conflict and restore balance? How do you serve participants in sorting out their feelings, recognizing their true needs, and expressing them honestly in order to stay in relationship?

## NEEDS AND UNMET NEEDS

Needs are at the heart of human motivation. Three basic universal needs are safety, satisfaction, and connection. We manage safety by avoiding perceived harm. We achieve satisfaction by approaching rewards (pleasure, competency, life goals, etc.).

And we experience connection by being with others (being understood, accepted, supported, etc.).[40]

Seeking to meet our universal needs is natural human behavior. When needs are met, there's a sense of well-being and balance; the body and brain are in a resting state (homeostasis). In terms of safety, satisfaction, and connection, we feel peaceful, contented, and loved. When needs are met, there's no deficit condition, no basis for craving, no drive, no urgency. Everything you really need, you already have. There's nothing wrong. You are in *responsive mode*.

When needs are *not* met, there's a sense of agitation or disturbance, a deficit condition. *Something's missing. Something's wrong.* Even in the absence of an actual physiological need, there may still be conditioned habits of craving and striving on account of our default way of being. Instead of safety, satisfaction, and connection, we experience fear, frustration, hurt, or anger. When confronted with uncomfortable or strong emotions, we can be "triggered," going into a *reactive mode*. When we're triggered, the executive functions of the brain, such as decision making and discernment, go temporarily offline. For example, in Barry's story, when Jack lashed out with anger at not getting what he wanted, he was stuck in a reactive mode. He was struggling with frustration and unable to recognize the underlying need for acceptance.

Humans are constantly scanning for threats and seeking opportunities (rewards) by avoiding, approaching, or attaching. Threats and rewards engage the two branches of the autonomic nervous system (ANS): the sympathetic nervous system and the parasympathetic nervous system. When under perceived threat, the sympathetic side reacts to danger—or anything we find unpleasant and want to escape or avoid—by releasing adrenaline and cortisol and activating the fight-or-flight system. Our fear circuitry is like a smoke detector, always on alert for threat, disturbance, or deficit. It influences how we react to unpleasant and unwanted experiences.

In our workshops, we would like people to connect with the group and also the workshop content. We design and lead our workshops with the intention of helping participants meet their own needs by fostering self-awareness. In short, we co-create the conditions for safety, satisfaction, and connection by:

- being clear in our marketing about our intended workshop outcomes
- creating an inviting, compassionate, and holistic environment
- making group agreements
- helping participants set intentions
- providing opportunities for safe interactions

- practicing mindfully and fostering self-awareness

In an optimal learning environment, the brain and body shift into a state that Kelly McGonigal calls the *challenge response*, which gives you energy under pressure and helps you perform better. The heart rate rises, adrenaline spikes, muscles tense, the brain gets more fuel, and you experience the effects of feel-good chemicals. It differs from a classic fight-or-flight response in an important way: instead of fearful, you feel focused.[41]

## Welcoming Feelings as Messengers

Feelings and emotions are messengers, or feedback mechanisms, that give us information about our internal and external experiences.[ix] When we judge some emotions as *good* and others as *bad*, we become caught in an endless loop of either denying the expression of some emotions or overcompensating by dramatically expressing other emotions. Either way, these reactions make us unable to effectively handle daily conflicts and end up with the burden of emotional baggage (unresolved issues). For example, when Jack continually lashed out with anger (a feeling) from not getting what he wanted (a need), he was stuck in a reactive mode and was unable to cope with his frustration.

When you're triggered, the nervous system is in reactive mode. It's not personal; it's a somatic contraction. In our workshops, we often say that everyone is entitled to their first reaction. But before the reaction gets the better of us, we can take a step back. Pause, breathe, and deepen, noticing the emotion and hopefully recognizing the deeper unmet need. Is it safety? Satisfaction? Connection? When Barry realized he was in panic mode, he called to mind his mentor and role model, who became his anchor in the storm. He began to self-regulate, breathing more deeply, and using positive self-talk: "You can do this, Barry." He formed an intention to be present, and was able to make a plan and take action.

Jack showed up to the workshop with underlying needs that he wasn't aware of and feelings he was unable to manage. He wanted to record the sessions, and he made it known. But when Jack's request was denied, he reacted with anger and resentment. And although he was able to keep his emotions under the surface for periods of time, they kept showing up in his behavior. The more he pushed on the group, the more

---

[ix] Throughout this book, we use the terms *emotions, feelings, feeling states, inner sensations,* and *experiences* interchangeably. Modern neuroscience confirms that whatever registers in the brain from an experience is assigned some valence—positive, negative, or neutral—called a feeling tone. Secondary emotions such as joy, anger, fear, and delight arise from this feeling tone. See Kornfield, J. (2008). *The wise heart: A guide to the universal teachings of Buddhist psychology.* Random House.

they retreated from him. As Marshall Rosenberg said, "Anger is the tragic expression of an unmet need."

## EFFECTIVE VERSUS INEFFECTIVE STRATEGIES

We all use strategies to meet our needs. When we're activated, we tend to employ less effective strategies for getting our needs met, sometimes with disruptive consequences. Jack's anger was not bad or good; it was an emotion that he wasn't able to own. He displaced his anger by projecting it out on the group.

A more skillful and effective strategy to get needs met is to make your needs known to yourself first. By learning to pay attention to the body's signals and using sensations as signposts, we can come to see tension, fear, anger, and grief as valuable information rather than as threats. *Interoception*—our ability to feel internal states—is the foundation for self-regulation.

Feelings tell us about and connect us to our needs. They also alert us to take appropriate action. For example, if we feel frustrated, we seek help. Likewise, a fluttering stomach or shaky muscles might tell us we're nervous. Instead of being afraid to listen to the body, we can learn to observe sensations, recognize the feelings, and understand the needs. Then we can make a request or take an action toward meeting the need. Unless we clearly feel sensations, we will have difficulty identifying emotions.

Conscious dialogue—observation, feeling, need, request (see Chapter 11)—gives you the opportunity to identify your feelings and make your needs known so you can evaluate and express yourself in ways that engender growth and promote mutual understanding.[42] But in the heat of the moment, it can be difficult to use conscious dialogue, even if you know the protocol. This is where you as the leader can step in and coach the participant to state their observations, feelings, needs, and requests.

For example, if your participant is angry and frustrated and seems unable to get beyond those feelings, you might ask her these questions:

1. **Observation:** "Susan, I notice that you seem different today. Is there something bothering you? Would you help me understand what's happening for you?"

2. **Feeling:** "How do you feel about that?"

3. **Need:** "What do you need right now?"

4. **Request:** "How can I or the group help you?"

5. **Thank you:** "Thank you for helping us understand."

Conscious dialogue might be all that's needed to connect with a person and redirect them from a reactive state to a more open, responsive state. Barry used conscious dialogue with Jack, which revealed that underneath his wanting to record the sessions was a need to be understood and to receive care and concern from the group. Barry appealed to Jack's intention for being at the workshop and pointed out how Jack's behavior might be getting in the way of attaining that goal. This resonated with Jack, and he agreed to change his behavior. But as we saw in the story, Jack was still activated, and there was more to come. We'll return to Barry and Jack in the next chapter.

---

### Examples of Real Feelings Versus "Non-feelings"

Masking blame, judgment, evaluation, or criticism as a feeling can get in the way of clear communication and getting your needs met. Expressing these "non-feelings" can easily be misinterpreted by the other person and trigger a defensive reaction in them. Notice in the examples below the difference between non-feelings and real feelings and how expressing real feelings can lead to clearer communication:

**"I feel let down."**
- The statement might be heard as "You let me down."
- The real feeling could be stated in this way: "I feel *hurt*."

**"I feel that I was violated."**
- The statement might be heard as "You violated me."
- The real feeling could be stated in this way: "I feel *helpless*."

**"I feel neglected."**
- The statement might be heard as "You neglected me."
- The real feeling could be stated in this way: "I feel *sad*."

**"I feel like I was pressured."**
- The statement might be heard as "You pressured me."
- The real feeling could be stated in this way: "I feel *embarrassed*."

Figure 15.1 Examples of Real Feelings Versus "Non-feelings"

## Difficult Behaviors: The Baby Crying is Not the Real Problem

Activation can show up as disruptive and even destructive behavior. If a participant is feeling lonely or disconnected and has a need to be heard, he might talk too much or have sidebar conversations. If a participant is overwhelmed and has a need for safety, she might slowly disengage by not participating, by arriving late, or by leaving early. And if a participant is feeling foolish or embarrassed and needs to feel competent, he might belittle others or sabotage the group in some way. We've loosely classified these behaviors as yellow-, orange-, and red-flag behaviors.

*Yellow-flag behaviors* are attention seeking:

- making repeated requests
- talking too much
- long-winded storytelling

*Orange-flag behaviors* show disengagement:

- folded arms
- perpetual distraction
- sidebar conversations
- facing away from the group
- leaving early or arriving late
- no participation or total silence

*Red-flag behaviors* show acting out or aggression:

- expressing dissatisfaction openly and provocatively in the group
- making inappropriate or disruptive comments
- leaving the room in obvious disgust
- making harsh remarks or verbal attacks
- physical violence

These behaviors (yellow, orange, and red) are ineffective strategies for getting needs met. The baby crying is not the real problem. The real problem is the unmet need. Scanning the room for these behaviors can help you know when to intervene. Discovering the unmet need and de-escalating the situation can head off problems before they become unmanageable. We'll look at the skills of intervening and clearing in the next chapter.

Some difficult behavior may arise from mandatory attendance. Sometimes participants are required to attend a workshop for a variety of reasons. In these cases, buy-in can be challenging, and participants may start off with yellow- or orange-flag behaviors simply because they don't want to be there. You can increase cooperation, buy-in, and motivation by:

- acknowledging the elephant in the room, perhaps with humor (e.g., "Who was dragged here against their will?" or "Who would rather be somewhere else right now?")

- showing yourself as human (e.g., "I get it. I've been through mandatory trainings more times than I can count. We're going to do our best to make this worth your time.")

- connecting to their intrinsic motivation (e.g., "Would becoming more skillful at your job help you meet your goals in life? We're going to show you how to do that over the next two hours.")

- encouraging an open mind (e.g., "Even though you might rather be somewhere else, perhaps there's something here for you.")

- creating an inclusive environment in a light-spirited way (e.g., "We've done extensive research and found there are three types of people who come to this training: those who want to be here, those who don't want to be here, and those who don't care. Raise your hand if one of these describes you.")

Group members may be naturally cautious or reluctant to participate for any number of reasons. The more you can create safety and inclusiveness early on in your workshop, the more buy-in you'll get, and the easier it will be to head off difficulties that might arise.

### In the Tiger's Mouth: When You're Triggered

When a participant gets triggered, it can trigger you in return. As Aruni reminded us at the beginning of the chapter, "whatever's not integrated in your life will surely walk through the door, wearing a nametag, disguised as a guest." Difficult feelings and disruptive behaviors can activate you and uncover your own unresolved issues. If you're able to stay present, you can choose not to react and not to feed the participant's reaction.

How can you stay present and aware when you're activated? You step back, pause, breathe, and deepen before speaking or acting. When you take a slow, conscious breath, you calm the reactive state and restore the responsive mode. New possibilities emerge, and intervening is more likely to be successful.

#### IN SUMMARY

Difficult behavior will show up. Don't assume that all conflict must be stifled or resolved immediately and that big feelings must be avoided at all costs. Sometimes, instead of trying to *solve*, let things *evolve*. Disruptive behavior may be exactly what's needed in the moment to bring out what really needs to emerge in the group. Rough seas are part of the journey. By being open to everything that arises, you can stay attuned to yourself and to the group process.

The leading edge of facilitating transformational groups is to transform challenge into opportunity. In the next chapter, we'll explore two skills—intervening and clearing. Skillfully attending to challenges will help the group to grow and mature.

**Putting it into Practice:**
**Journal Prompts**

- Have you experienced uncomfortable situations in workshops you have led or have attended? Do you recall what you felt in your body?

- When you're activated, which emotion(s) do you tend to feel most strongly? Can you identify any underlying unmet needs?

- Do you remember a leader who handled a difficult situation skillfully? How did they do it?

Figure 15.2 Putting it into Practice: Journal Prompts

Chapter 16

# The Skills of Intervening and Clearing

*There are no classes in life for beginners. Right away you are always asked to deal with what is most difficult.*

—Rainer Maria Rilke

We've examined creating safe space and inviting full participation, and in this chapter, we continue exploring how to address upsets, obstacles, and confusion. Intervening and clearing may be the most challenging skills for workshop leaders to master, because most of us are uncomfortable with the feelings that are stirred up around conflict. The role of leaders is to step in and use legitimate power to uphold the values and agreements of the group.

If there's disruptive behavior, an argument between participants, or someone expressing dissatisfaction with your leadership, intervening and clearing are skillful ways to guide the group to the next level of mutual understanding and trust.

## THE SKILL OF INTERVENING: WHAT'S AT RISK?

Intervening means managing difficult behavior by defusing energy and redirecting attention toward wholeness and positivity. You intervene to protect group safety, promote effectiveness, and foster awareness.

As a leader, you guard the group agreements—the contracts that define the boundaries of accepted behavior. A group with firm boundaries can safely handle any conflict. Group safety is at risk when agreements are broken and when people are disrespectful or even violent. When safety is at risk, intervene by stopping the group, if necessary, or calling for a break.

Group effectiveness can be derailed by tangents, distractions, and disagreements. Intervening to promote effectiveness can take the form of problem solving, keeping the group on course, or energizing the group by standing, stretching, or taking a break. In Barry's story, we saw how Jack's behavior was taking time and attention away from the group goals.

Intervening to foster awareness might mean caring for a member who needs attention, reinforcing objectives, modeling behavior, or pointing to patterns that are not useful.

How do you know when to intervene?

1. **Recognize.** Notice what's happening in the room. Is it dysfunctional? You can "shuttle" your attention between yourself and the other(s) to try to discern what's going on beneath the surface. Pause, breathe, and deepen.

2. **Name it.** What's at risk? Is it safety? Effectiveness? Workshop outcomes? Awareness?

3. **Discern.** Decide what to address and what not to address. Ask yourself what really matters.

4. **Act or Bracket.** Intervene with reflective listening, encouraging, or questioning. Alternatively, postpone action (bracketing). If the disruption triggers you, and you can't self-regulate in the moment, make an appointment with yourself to get clear and reset privately (more on how to do this later).

## How to Intervene: Clear Seeing and Steady Presence

Our approach is nonviolent. When we confront someone about the impact of their behavior on the group, we focus attention on the behavior, not the person. Interventions depend on the type of group, its values and goals, the behavior in question, and where the group is on the journey. You may have to intervene more often early on in the culture-setting stage. As a group matures, participants will often take responsibility for upsets, making requests, and settling difficulties on their own. If you're leading a personal growth workshop, intense emotions can be expected and can act as a catalyst for growth. You might intervene to deepen and explore what's underneath through questions, reflection, or movement.

Reflecting, encouraging, and questioning can work alone as "soft" interventions. Sometimes you can intervene by amending the agreements and reestablishing the group with updated working guidelines. (See Appendix C for examples of group agreements.) Listen to what's happening below the surface. For example, if a participant is passive and seems to be giving up, you might affirm her for something she said or did. If a participant isolates, you might invite him to speak up and then affirm him for what he contributed. And if someone is aggressive, you might invite her to share a skill or an idea with the group. If there's a pattern of dysfunctional behavior, you might remind her of the group agreements. If that doesn't work, a deeper intervention may be necessary.

How you might intervene depends on the kind of disruption, but some key principles are helpful:

- **Foster Awareness.** First, attend to yourself—pause, breathe, and deepen. Then, seek to awaken awareness in the other. ("There's a lot of energy here. Why don't we both pause for a moment and take a deep breath?")

- **Collect Information.** If a participant looks disinterested or withdrawn, don't assume that you know what's going on. Sometimes it's just a headache, normal emotions, or a bad day. ("Help me understand what's happening for you.")

- **Stay in Relationship.** The intention to connect and stay in relationship grounds the intervention in compassion. ("I'm guessing you're unhappy right now, but I'm confident that we can work this out together.")

- **Label the Behavior, Not the Person.** When disruptive behavior shows up, it's tempting to label the person—he's a troublemaker; she's too needy; he's disruptive. Instead, label the behavior—his *behavior* is distracting others; her *questions* are sidetracking the agenda; his *sidebar conversations* are disruptive. ("Emily, I appreciate your questions, and I want to address them, but looking at them now would sidetrack us. Would you be willing to put your questions into the pantry for later?")

- **Be Sensitive.** Intervening in the circle can be embarrassing for the person who's the object of the intervention. It also may be counterproductive unless your intervention can serve the group process. Approach people privately in most cases. ("John, do you mind if we touch base quickly during the break?")

- **Be Specific.** Name the behavior. ("Sally and Steve, I noticed you were having a sidebar when Julie was talking. Our agreement is to respect the speaker by having no cross talk.")

- **Seek Alternatives.** Offer a do-over or a more skillful way of handling the situation. ("Would you be willing to reframe what you just said using conscious dialogue?")

- **See the Good.** Assume positive intent and see the good in whatever comes up. ("Great! I heard a lot of passion in that statement. Can you transform that energy into a positive request?")

- **Use Humor.** Used appropriately, humor can lighten the air and broaden the perspective. ("Oof! There's a lot of fire here. Somebody might get burned. How can we put some water on this, cool it off a little, and stay in relationship?")

Interventions maintain the integrity of the circle. Challenges are part of the creative tension in a transformational workshop. The group will be watching keenly how the leader handles contention to see how safe it is to disagree with the leader or express genuine feelings.

Consider this example: A participant challenged the leader's viewpoint, and the leader reacted harshly, by white-knuckling the microphone and defending himself: "You clearly don't understand what I just said." He made the participant "wrong." A more skillful response from the leader would have been to listen, acknowledge, and perhaps get more information; for example, "Thank you. I understand there may be other ways to interpret this idea." Respecting each voice, even when it may be inconvenient or seem out of place, lets the group know that it's okay to have differences.

By contrast, here's how a leader skillfully responded to a direct challenge: On the second day of a five-day workshop, the leader was confronted by a participant who was confused and annoyed. The participant exclaimed, "I don't know what's happening! Where are we going with this workshop, anyway?"

The leader paused and said, "Let's all take a breath here."

In that moment, she realized, *Oh no! I gave them a verbal overview, but I didn't give them a printed agenda for the week! Maybe that's why he's confused!* She understood the impact of her oversight and owned it. Rather than defending or deflecting, she responded with, "Thank you for speaking up! I realize that I haven't given you a written overview for the workshop. Would that help to show where we are and where we're headed? I'll bring it to the next session."

There is no formula for intervening. Be curious and speak and listen from your heart. Figure 16.1 shows ways of intervening with sample dialogue.

| SITUATION/NEED | WHAT TO SAY |
|---|---|
| To care for members | "Joan, it looks to me like you're having a hard time. Is there something you need right now? How might the group help you?" |
| To get the group unstuck | "It feels to me like we're stuck right now. Would it work for the group to do a structured round so each of us can make a request or suggestion to get past this block?" |
| To redirect instead of saying no | "That's a great idea. Can we put that suggestion in the pantry for now to take it up later?" |
| To address unhelpful patterns emerging | "John, you said you are shy. What would it be like to state that you've been shy *in the past* and that now you are becoming aware of ways to participate more fully?" |
| To handle disrespectful behavior | "Our agreement is to speak with respect. I appreciate your passion, and I wonder how you can say that in a way that focuses on your need and the behavior that bothers you, rather than the person." |
| To model behavior | "I just caught myself getting upset. Notice that nobody else did this to me. I got myself upset by interpreting an event in a way that made me a victim. I'm reminding myself that I'm in control of how I manage my feelings." |

Figure 16.1 Examples of Verbal Interventions

## What if Your Early Intervention Doesn't Work?

Here are some ways to catch dysfunctional behavior before it reaches red-flag status. Watch for power struggles, rebellion, or despair. Notice people who break agreements, appear to be obsessing, or are unable to maintain boundaries. Be aware of whether they are overwhelmed, unable to focus, withdrawn, or unwilling to interact with staff or group members.

If someone makes harsh remarks or verbal attacks, cut off the attack by physically standing between the attacker and the other if possible. If there's a physical attack, immediately stop the session, and let your participants know when to return. In extreme cases, you may need to invite the participant to leave the workshop and refund their money (we'll discuss this situation next).

If *you're* the target of an attack, call a break and check in privately with the person. If there's a group sponsor, consult with him or her. It's one of the hardest things to do, but try not to take challenges personally.

### Climbing the Ladder of Intervention: Protecting the Circle

Remember, the aim is to stay in relationship while resolving the issue, and in extreme cases, you may need to climb the Ladder of Intervention (see Figure 16.2). It's up to the leader to create clarity, deflect attacks, draw a line in the sand, and point the way forward—ultimately to defend the agreements and protect the circle.[x] The following is an example of moving up the rungs. As you read, think back on Barry's story and notice where he used this process. We've presented the rungs as being linear, but in reality, each situation is unique. The basic principle is to be kind. Intervening isn't just about what you do, but about how you do it.

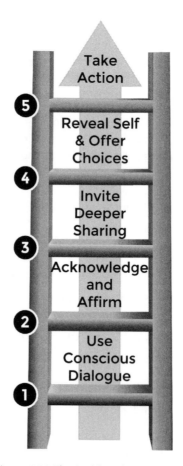

Figure 16.2 The Ladder of Intervention

---

[x] In wisdom traditions, leaders are said to wield the "Sword of Discernment."

### Rung 1: Use Conscious Dialogue

Try to facilitate a conscious dialogue (observation, feeling, need, request). This gives the participant a chance for self-awareness and self-expression. This may be all that's needed to create connection. But if conscious dialogue is causing disconnection, then drop it.

### Rung 2: Acknowledge and Affirm

If conscious dialogue doesn't resolve the issue, acknowledge and thank the person. ("Thank you, [name], for coming forward. I appreciate your concern about [issue].")

### Rung 3: Invite Deeper Sharing

Collect more information if necessary. Only ask if you're not sure what the request, comment, or dispute really is. ("Tell me more about [issue]. Help me understand [issue].")

### Rung 4: Reveal Self and Offer Choices

Reveal what's happening for you and offer to address the issue later. If that doesn't resolve the conflict, offer a private conversation.

- **Reveal Self.** "Here's what's happening for me. From my perspective, it seems as though [reveal self]. I'm here to help you meet your needs as best I can. I also have a promise to serve each person here, as well as our group goals."

- **Offer a Choice.** "Would it be okay with you if we put this issue in the pantry for now and handle it in the next session? I'm concerned that we have just enough time to finish the task in front of us before ending this session."

- **Offer a Private Conversation.** "Would you be willing to meet with me privately to speak about this after the session?"

### Rung 5: Take Action

If this is a person with a pattern of disruptive behavior, and you've tried to use conscious dialogue and offered choices, yet they are unwilling to meet with you privately, then bring the group session to a stop. Ask the group to return in 30 minutes. You have to determine how to resolve this situation. If it can't be resolved, you may need to ask the person to leave the group.

Here's what it might look like: "It looks to me like this workshop isn't meeting your needs. I'm sorry about that. Since you're not satisfied with the choices I've offered you, I have to ask you to leave the group. I'm willing to give you a refund for the workshop, and if you meet with me right after the session, we'll make arrangements to do that." (Offer a refund only if you feel it is appropriate and only if you have the authority to do so.)

---

**Practice Climbing the Ladder**

Practice climbing the Ladder of Intervention with a friend or colleague who is willing to play the role of a participant with difficult behavior. Here's how:

1. Come up with a scenario where your partner is challenging you with difficult behavior. Ask your partner to not back down and to persist at being disruptive.

2. Begin climbing the ladder. Work through each rung.

3. Notice what it feels like when you ask the participant to leave at the final rung.

4. De-role and then debrief the experience with your partner.

---

Figure 16.3 Practice Climbing the Ladder

If the person wants to stay in the group and is willing to abide by the group agreements, create a working contract (sometimes known as a behavior contract), verbally or in writing (see Appendix C for an example). Specify the conditions by which the participant can return to the group. Clearly state your concern, define appropriate behavior, and agree to a plan. You can ask questions such as:

- What might you do next?
- What resources do you need to act differently?
- What will you do that will change the outcome next time?

Once agreement is reached, solidify it verbally or in writing:

- "Now we agree that the next time this happens, you will [agreement]. Did I get that right? Is there more? Are we agreed?"

Have a written record of what occurred so that you can refer to it later if necessary. Document the behavior, important facts, and the outcome. If a working contract was made, include it in your written record. Try to include the testimony of one or two witnesses to establish the facts. Keep one copy for yourself and provide another to the venue supervisor. If you need to refer to it later, you will be glad you took the time to document what happened while it was still fresh in your mind.

If a crisis occurs in your group, put safety first. Bring the group to a stop if there is illness, injury, or violence. If you need privacy, ask everyone to leave the room, or take the individual needing intervention out of the room. If the injury is severe, or if the person is unresponsive, call 911 and contact the venue supervisor. If you don't know what's happening with the individual, contact a medical professional.

If you're able to continue facilitating the individual, speak with her privately to express concern and to understand her needs. Act within the scope of your practice, and know when to seek outside support. Make a written incident report. Document the important facts and outcomes of the crisis. Keep a copy and submit a copy to the venue.

## THE SKILL OF CLEARING: FINDING NEW GROUND

*Clearing* is a way to bring the truth to light. When trust and creativity are at risk, speaking the useful truth helps to identify and release inauthentic behavior in the form of withheld communication, unexpressed blocks, and hurt feelings. How you function in a group today depends a lot on how you functioned in your first workshop group—your family. Conflict in a workshop can trigger unfinished business from our past—often from our families—interfering with how we relate today. If you had what D. W. Winnicott called "good-enough parents," you felt a sense of basic "okay-ness."[43] Being okay with yourself gives you a sense of resilience that helps you bounce back from a challenge.

By observing with curiosity and kindness, we can examine and acknowledge hurt feelings and break free from habits, such as feeling right by making someone else wrong. Reactive patterns play themselves out in the form of pettiness, jealousy, guilt, shame, or anger. Acknowledging negative feelings may not sit well with an idealized image of ourselves as kind, tolerant, and generous. Skillful clearing helps to get past these barriers and restore a sense of safety, openness, and honesty.

But how do you know when a clearing is needed? Your own body awareness is a barometer to track the states of both your participants and yourself. You can discern when a clearing is necessary by looking for signs:

- in yourself (vague uneasiness, tension, discomfort, anger, shame, resignation, hopelessness)

- in a participant (frustration, irritability, finger-pointing, withdrawal, reluctance to participate fully, avoiding eye contact, apathy)

- in the group (no joy, inability to reach agreement or move on, conflict between participants or subgroups)

Clearing can be a top-down or bottom-up process. Top-down clearing is cognitive based and begins in the mind; for example, through conscious dialogue, reestablishing agreements, and reaffirming intentions. Embodied practices like breathing, moving, tapping, guided body-awareness, and shaking are examples of bottom-up clearing.

## How to Clear Yourself

When you are activated, pause, breathe, and deepen. Reconnect with your nonactivated self. If you think you need to clear yourself before continuing, call for a break. Although calling for a break is a simple solution, you might not think to do it because you're not fully present when triggered. Physical movement, such as taking a brisk walk, might be all that's needed. If you need to express yourself, find a private place away from the group. If you have a co-leader or assistant, you may want to invite them to witness or support you. If alone, ask yourself, *What do I need to get clear?* Watch the feelings arise. Breathe slowly. Do what's appropriate to self-regulate: coach yourself, think of your anchor, or pray. Let yourself be angry. Cry, vent, or pound on a pillow if you need to. When you feel like there's nothing else left to express, come back to your breath and your intentions for yourself and for the group.

Barry made sure to clear himself before meeting with Jack. Taking time to do this helped Barry get perspective. He saw that his own insecurities were wrapped up in the situation, which would have clouded his ability to be present during his conversation with Jack.

## How to Clear One or Two Participants

Use conscious dialogue as the basis for clearing participants individually or together. To clear an individual, first ask whether the individual is willing to have a conversation in private, then help her express herself through conscious dialogue (see Chapter 11). You may need to coach her to express her observations, feelings, and needs, and to make a request.

You can also use conscious dialogue to clear two individuals in conflict. First, ask them if they're willing to use conscious dialogue with each other. Let them know they'll each have a chance to speak while the other listens. Suggest that they each make an intention to resolve their issue and to stay in relationship.

1. Coach the first person through the steps of observation, feeling, need, and request.

2. Ask the second person what she heard.

3. Ask the first person if there's anything else she'd like to say.

4. Repeat Steps 1–3 for the second person.

5. Ask if there's anything more.

6. Thank them both.

While Barry checked in with Jack a few times prior to their meeting, it wasn't until Barry coached Jack through a conscious dialogue and a guided body-awareness process that he was able to identify unmet needs from his past experiences.

## Clearing the Group

In our transformational learning cycle (safety, experience, integration), we recognize that unexpected and unplanned experiences also require integration for closure, making it possible to move forward.

When you become aware that the group needs clearing, stop the group session and propose a clearing. You can engage the group in deciding whether the whole group needs to be involved and whether the clearing should happen in the moment or be scheduled for a later time.

Start the clearing by stating the vision and purpose of the group. Review the group agreements. Each person says what they need to say to get clear. You can model this by saying, "Something's not working here. To me, [issue] seems to be in the way of our purpose." State your factual observation, and then state your feelings, needs, and requests. Each group member then does the same.

What do you do with the requests? Record and honor them. The group may come to consensus on their own, in which case the requests are resolved. If not, requests can be taken up in a group discussion or in a second round. The clearing is complete (for yourself, an individual, or the group) when there is nothing left to say—the storm has passed. You feel empty. Effective clearings create a sense of appreciation and a willingness to continue on the journey together.

After a big upset, group clearings help the group to move forward. In Barry's group, clearing helped participants appreciate what the experience meant to them. Here's what several group members said in Barry's group clearing:

> (Gail) I'm new at this, and I'm grateful to see how the circle-share works
> in action. I had a breakthrough. In an earlier session, I had the oppor-
> tunity to speak directly to Jack, with the group as a witness. I learned that
> I was able to speak to him from my heart in front of a group, that I could
> feel safe to do so, and that my words could affect another human being.
> I'd like for us as a group to move on.

**(Jessie)** I'm disappointed that Jack left the group. I think if he had been allowed to complete the workshop, it might have served us better by letting the group get stronger in the face of this really tough stuff. It would have been a test for me, and perhaps others. It might have given me more resolve in my work and sharpened my skills in dealing with difficult behavior. But since it turned out this way, I am okay because this is the way it is. But I'd like closure with Jack, and I'm glad he'll be available at the end of this session.

**(Diane)** I was aware of how tense I got and how soon I was able to calm down during the times when I felt chaos coming into the room. I remembered how I was years ago, before my recovery. This situation would have been really hard for me. But overall, now I realize how much empathy I felt for Jack. I really felt my own need for love and acceptance, as I imagine he must have felt. Right now, I feel the need to simply feel held by the group.

**(Debra)** In my life, my need is for affirmation, which I did not get growing up. I can really feel the emotional charge that gets triggered so easily in me. I am beginning to see that the way I act is just perpetuating my needing others to give me what I can only give myself. But this charge also feels a little like my great need to do my own work. I am so hungry to be working at my depth and capacity. This circle may never be complete, but I am resolved to find my place and do this work.

**(Joyce)** I want every circle to hold. I was waiting for Barry's lead in how to handle it. But when Barry didn't call Jack out strongly enough for me, I finally stepped forward. I felt strong enough to speak up and to take greater ownership of my place in the circle. It was powerful to speak my truth even when I felt scared to do so. I felt the circle hold—and it was awesome to witness it. I'm grateful for the opportunity to learn how to use the circle's power with new light and clarity, and right now I'd like to see us move on in compassion and truth.

## Clearing a Disagreement

Disagreements aren't necessarily disruptive, but if they're not dealt with effectively, they can lead to confusion and hard feelings. Most disagreements happen for one of three reasons: a lack of shared information, value differences, or an underlying inability or unwillingness.[44]

When there's a lack of shared information, it's because people did not hear each other well enough, heard but misunderstood, or did not receive vital information. To resolve any of these issues, begin by identifying and sharing the missing information. This is the classic "Oh, I missed the memo."

Second, disagreements occur when people hold different values or have different background experiences. Here, both parties understand each other's position but don't agree on the desired outcome. For example, people from opposing political parties understand the other's platform but don't agree on the principles. What do you do? Seek agreement through compromise by identifying the needs and benefits each is looking for.

Third, participants may be unwilling or unable to agree because of an underlying issue. Most frequently this is due to an historical dispute or incident, or an illness or psychological condition. In this case, you may not be able to seek a resolution within the group. You may need conflict resolution or a therapeutic intervention. Handle this type of obstacle by pausing the group and speaking with the unwilling or ill participant on the side.

Let's return to Barry's story. There was a disagreement between Jack and the majority of the group on whether to let Jack record the session. This disagreement was based on different values. At the surface level, Jack valued getting the information he needed. His method of getting his needs met (recording the sessions) clashed with the group values of confidentiality and safety. The disagreement was brought to a simple majority vote, and Jack didn't like the outcome. Barry and others proposed alternate ways of meeting Jack's needs, such as providing notes, but those alternatives were unacceptable to Jack. As Barry explored Jack's needs further, it became clear that underlying needs were contributing to Jack's activation, such as the need to be understood and to be cared for. So, although the story began with what appeared to be a simple disagreement, it evolved into something more complex because of underlying issues and differences.

## GROUP DECISION MAKING

After you have cleared the group, you may need to decide how to proceed. Involve the group in this decision or call for a break while you consider the options for next steps.

If your group needs to come to an agreement, decide what protocol to use. Choose from one of these decision-making processes and explain to the group how it will work:

- **Propose Choices.** Present the choices. Ask for a show of hands or a hidden ballot, and have the majority determine the outcome.

- **Propose a Decision.** Propose a decision and ask the group, "Who can live with this and support it?" Ask for a show of hands. Everyone needs to abide by the statement.

Sometimes it may not be practical to try to reach a group consensus. As the group leader, you have the authority to make a decision. You may need to decide for the group to ground the group or defuse an escalating situation. It may be as simple as calling the group to a stop. Consider the difference between these two options:

**Option 1: Engaging the Group in Decision Making.** "I'm sensing that we might need a break in order to regroup. Is that okay with everyone?"

**Option 2: The Leader Decides for the Group.** "I'm sensing that we might need a break in order to regroup. Let's meet back here in 15 minutes. Do whatever you need to do in the next 15 minutes to take care of yourself."

Option 1 opens the door for further discussion, which may not be practical. In Option 2, the leader makes the decision. While both options are valid, Option 2 moves quickly beyond the energy of the problem so that participants can turn their attention to how they will use the break to take care of themselves.

## IN SUMMARY

Conflict and discord are challenging. The moment you need to use the skills of intervening and clearing, you yourself might be activated. These are moments of potential growth. Difficult behavior is humbling and shows us that every person in the group can be our greatest teacher.

Sensing what's at the heart of an issue and being flexible in your approach requires skill and experience. Your group wants you to succeed and hold the rim of the circle. If you show up as a kind and clear steward of the group values, your integrity will show through. You will earn their trust, and ultimately, you and your group can weather any storm.

**Putting it into Practice:**
**Journal Prompts**

- Have you experienced a situation in your group where you needed to intervene? What happened for you?

- Every encounter is an opportunity for growth. Think of a recent challenging situation that you handled well and one that you thought you could have handled better. What was the difference?

- How do you clear yourself after an upset?

Figure 16.4 Putting it into Practice: Journal Prompts

# Chapter 17

# Group Dynamics

*If you want to travel fast, go alone.*
*If you want to travel far, go together.*

—African proverb

One of the great mysteries of life is the relationship between the individual and group. Kurt Lewin coined the term *group dynamics*, referring to the forces that shape the patterns of interaction between group members. Lewin saw that roles and behaviors that people take on affect other members and the group as a whole.[45]

We are all members of many groups—family, work, sports, social, ethnic, cultural, national, and species groups. We are swimming in unexamined relationships that are driving us as individuals and as group members. This chapter explores factors influencing relationships within a workshop over time. Understanding these dynamics can help us to improve performance, communication, and cohesiveness.

## SEVEN KEYS TO GROUP WISDOM

Functional groups contribute to meeting our needs for safety, satisfaction, and connection. On the other hand, needs go unmet where group dynamics are poor. This happens, for example, where there is lack of direction, unclear priorities, fear of being judged, domination or withholding, or anything that disrupts the flow of information and energy in the group. By contrast, transformational groups depend on honest inquiry, leading to individuals feeling empowered, strengthened, and inspired through collective wisdom.

What really matters when fostering and maintaining healthy group dynamics? Figure 17.1 is a checklist.

---

**Checklist for Healthy Group Dynamics**

☐ **Set A Purpose.** All members commit to a common higher focus.

☐ **Create Safe Space.** Make group agreements and name the values underlying them.

☐ **Listen Deeply.** Honor all voices.

☐ **Attend to What's Happening Between Group Members.** Be aware of the field of energy—the relational field—created as the group identity forms.

☐ **Be Open to Not Knowing.** Be willing to suspend assumptions, even strongly held ideas. Be open to surfacing hidden agendas that influence the group.

☐ **Participate Authentically.** Give permission to reveal rather than conceal, express rather than repress. Give options and stay connected.

☐ **Communicate Consciously.** Speak your "useful truth" with passion and discipline. Take responsibility for your feelings, actions, and words.

---

Figure 17.1 Checklist for Healthy Group Dynamics

## THE FOUR SEASONS: PHASES OF A GROUP

We are inherently social beings, and our nervous system unconsciously mediates social engagement, trust, and intimacy. For example, the vagus nerve is constantly picking up signals from the body, assessing the safety of a situation or mood of someone we're interacting with, and communicating that information to the brain.[46]

Social environments change as individuals interact with each other, becoming more nuanced over time. *Group mood* is the feeling state of the group, and it can show up in individual participants as trust or trepidation, fear or love, acceptance or resistance, engagement or boredom.

Each group journey has a life of growth and development. This natural life cycle unfolds through four organic phases, like the seasons of a year. Each season has its time, and the role of the leader is that of a gardener. You tend to the group through the seasons, sensing and managing the group energy as it matures.

Figure 17.2 is a synopsis of the seasons of a group and the moods that can arise in each season.[47]

| | DESCRIPTION | POSSIBLE GROUP MOODS |
|---|---|---|
| **SPRING** Planting | Getting started | Tentative, eager, energetic, hopeful, fearful, curious |
| **SUMMER** Growing | Transitioning toward trust | Resistant, distracted, fatigued, helpful, accepting, excited |
| **FALL** Harvesting | Getting down to business | Cooperative, engaged, autonomous, reflective, appreciative |
| **WINTER** Nourishing | Wrapping up and moving on | Satisfied, full, sad, hopeful |

Figure 17.2 The Seasons and Their Moods

## Spring: Planting Seeds

Groups typically start out upbeat as participants first gather and meet. Risk taking is relatively low, and exploration is tentative. At first, participants sometimes hang back and observe how the group functions before they commit to joining and belonging. *Is this a group that I want to belong to? Do I trust the leader? Who's in my tribe? Who's not in my tribe?* Basically, they are considering how safe the group feels.

Your role during spring is to create a caring and safe space by establishing the culture. Welcome individuals and the group as a whole, and begin to establish a safe group structure, including agreements, roles, responsibilities, and an agenda. In this phase, you invite a shared vision and a group purpose. You encourage participants to disclose concerns and to do what they need to get present. You model being okay with "start-up" energy—the anxiety, the unknowns, the doubt.

## Summer: Growing (Pains)

With any journey, there is an expansion where a field of possibilities opens up. But this expansiveness naturally has less structure and can be unsettling. Participants move beyond their comfort zone. Disagreements, conflict, and strong emotions can arise as participants explore their edges. They can reach a crisis of engagement where commitment to the group brings up issues of trust. Power and control struggles arise.

Somewhere in the middle, things may appear to "fall apart." Participants might feel anxiety and resistance as they perceive acceptance or rejection from the leader and other participants. *This isn't working for me! I'm not happy. I don't belong. I should never have come. I don't like the leader!* Participants are practicing self-expression, being self-directed, and how to resolve conflict. See Figure 17.3.

If you're conflict avoidant, summer can feel very uncomfortable, especially if the group triggers your own issues. Encourage and stabilize the group with your presence in the face of challenge. Though it may be tempting to buy into the drama of disputes, trust the group process and shore up the culture of cooperation established by the group agreements. Use all your tools and skills to resolve conflict and nurture wholeness, well-being, and creativity. Model how to normalize and deal with resistance positively. Accept diversity, align with group goals, and stay in relationship.

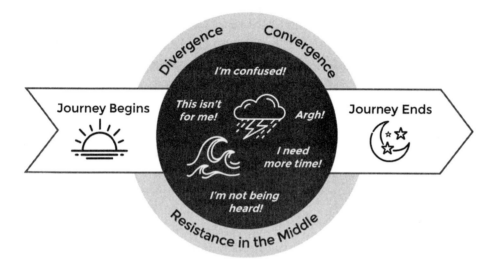

Figure 17.3 Things Appear to Fall Apart in the Middle

## Fall: Harvesting

In the fall, participants are arriving at a place of trust, cohesion, and communication. They are willing to be coached. They feel supported to take greater risks, and they begin to claim new territory. Leadership functions may be shared by the members as they take more responsibility for resolving conflict and threatening issues. *I think I'm getting what I need here. You're not so bad after all. Wow! I didn't know that about myself.* Interactions outside the group are smoother. Members are more hopeful and willing to do what it takes to get what they came for.

Fall can be exhilarating because you'll see participants gaining insight, working well together, showing up as empathic and compassionate, and sharing positive feedback. You might be tempted to energetically or mentally check out because the group is running so smoothly. However, continue to move the process forward by exploring deeper, asking for what's wanted and needed, and modeling what it looks like to take further risks.

## Winter: Nourishing

As members prepare for closure, they may feel sad or fearful of separation from the group. During winter, participants are likely to express both hopes and concerns for each other. They may feel a sense of accomplishment and also be anxious about completion and follow-up. They are reflecting upon and evaluating their experience and planning how to act on it. They may be doubtful about whether they will be able to take what they learned and bring it back to their daily life.

In winter, help members clarify the meaning of their experience and assist them in transitioning out of the group. Deal with unfinished business and integrate and reinforce new insights. Help participants make commitments for their next steps, and support their ongoing growth. Encourage participants to network with each other, and provide additional resources for ongoing learning.

Whether your group has been together for a half day or half year, design a closing ritual that symbolically and emotionally transitions participants beyond the group. Ideas for closing rituals include:

- A structured round, offering each person a chance to express their thoughts and feelings to the group. You can let participants say whatever they like to get closure, or you can lead with a question (e.g., "What are you taking away, and what are you leaving behind?").

- A party to celebrate the success of the group and to give participants a chance to thank and say goodbye to each other.

- A chance for everyone to state their intentions and action steps for moving forward.

- A ritual to symbolize the growth that's taken place.

As the group completes its life cycle, you may experience a wintery mix of grief and relief. Honor your own feelings and celebrate what grew in you and what you'll carry forward. You'll find the same seasons are mirrored in your own internal journey. Your groups will teach you what you need to learn for your own growth.

### TWO GROUP DYNAMICS CASE STUDIES

Jim served in the Peace Corps in India. Later, he became a program administrator and oversaw training the volunteers who were placed in Western Samoa. The Peace Corps had become aware that many volunteers were leaving their countries of service a quarter to halfway through their commitment. Using the Culture Shock Model of cultural adaptation[48], Jim and his team categorized the volunteers' attitudes into four seasons:

1. Honeymoon (1–3 months)

2. Irritability (3–8 months)

3. Adjustment (8–14 months)

4. Full adaption (14–24 months)

Those who dropped out did so four to eight months into the two-year program. The Peace Corps recognized from this pattern that volunteers needed additional support during the irritability phase. They instituted a policy of in-service training to help volunteers make the adjustment to feeling comfortable in a new culture.[xi]

The new training program succeeded so well that, after two years in the country, the Peace Corps Samoan volunteer group had no attrition. This was the first no-attrition volunteer group in Peace Corps history. By recognizing the natural life cycle of the volunteer program, Jim and his team were able to provide the right supports at the right times. What resulted was a much more fulfilling experience for the volunteers as well as greater effectiveness of the service program.

In another case, Ken was a director of a month-long massage training at Kripalu. During this four-week immersion program, participants did yoga classes twice a day, in addition to learning massage. They were challenged physically, emotionally, and mentally by the intensity of it. By the third week of the training, it was not uncommon for trainees to have strong emotions and interpersonal disputes. The directors were prepared for this phase. They expected to intervene more, and they provided encouragement and extra support for self-care.

## WORKING SKILLFULLY WITH AWARENESS AND ENERGY

Like the weather, the group mood will change over time. But unlike the weather, you can do something about your group's mood: You can monitor it and take steps to shift it.

---

[xi] In the case of Western Samoa–bound volunteers, the Peace Corps and the University of Hawaii also created a customized three-month training program designed to minimize the impact of culture shock. They set up the volunteer training program in the Hawaiian village of Nanakuli, which was the site of a large Samoan population on western Oahu. The volunteers were immersed for 11 weeks in Samoan language, volunteered in local schools, and lived for three weeks with Samoan families.

How do you monitor group mood? You have a natural barometer of group mood: your body. Stay connected to your body, and you will sense what's happening in the room. You can also ask the group how they're feeling. One quick way to do this is the *internal weather forecast* (see Figure 17.4). It's a low-risk, light-touch tool to help participants become aware of their inner landscape using a playful metaphor.

**The Internal Weather Forecast**

1.  The leader starts by naming his or her emotional mood in the moment (e.g., sunny and bright, foggy and heavy, cloudy with a chance of rain).

2.  Each participant expresses her internal mood in the same way.

Figure 17.4 The Internal Weather Forecast

The internal weather forecast fosters insight into one's own experience and empathy for others. You can use it at any stage of the group process, but it's most useful when you have several options available and want to determine which direction to take based on the energetic and emotional pulse of the group.

We want our participants to be relaxed, alert, steady, and comfortable. If they're dysregulated, they're not primed for learning. Help your participants access the optimal state for learning where energy and awareness are balanced.

How do you shift the mood of the group? Yoga uses the terms *prana* and *chitta* to describe two ends of a spectrum. On one end is *prana*, or "energy"; on the other is *chitta*, or "awareness." Sometimes you may notice that the group is weighted toward one end of the spectrum. Mind-body experiences can be used to address an imbalance by either enhancing focus (*chitta*) or raising energy (*prana*).

Use energy-raising practices to mobilize vitality, and use energy-lowering practices to diminish obstacles. There is too much energy (*prana*) if participants are feeling overwhelmed, anxious, indecisive, light-headed, unfocused, or fearful. Grounding activities help to reduce energy and enhance awareness. On the other hand, if participants are feeling numb, tired, or bored, embodied activities will help them get out of their heads and into their bodies. Figure 17.5 summarizes this difference.

Some of these activities can be done in the moment as you sense the group's mood. For example, if you notice heads nodding and eyes drooping, you can invite your participants to stand up and stretch. Or if you sense extremely high levels of energy and want to calm the group down, invite participants to sit down, close their eyes, and practice deep, slow breathing.

| WORKING WITH AWARENESS/CONSCIOUSNESS (*chitta*) | WORKING WITH ENERGY (*prana*) |
|---|---|
| Increase awareness when participants are:<br><br>■ overwhelmed, anxious<br>■ indecisive, light-headed<br>■ unable to focus<br>■ frustrated<br>■ fearful about their experience | Increase energy when participants are:<br><br>■ unable to feel<br>■ trapped in cynicism<br>■ not in touch with intuition<br>■ unmoved by beauty<br>■ insensitive to subtleties<br>■ lost in endless speculation |
| **Suggestions:** Use grounding activities—walking, feeling feet on the ground, feeling the weight of the body, breathing deeply, or drinking water. Do mental activities requiring intense concentration. Do focusing and strengthening/standing yoga postures. | **Suggestions:** Get physically active—move, dance, sing, shake, chant, or do yoga or vigorous exercise. Reduce mental stimulation (talking, reading). Get out of the head and into the body; slow down and bring awareness to sensation, self-massage, or do guided imagery focusing on feeling. |

Figure 17.5 Working Skillfully With Awareness and Energy

Consider how you bridge and transition from one experience to another. The transition is just as important as the experience. For example, to awaken and harmonize your group in the morning or after lunch, use energizing experiences—moving in unison, chanting, breathing, or yoga postures.

The mood of the group impacts the level of openness, vulnerability, active participation, and connectedness. Mind-body experiences are an effective way to shift and/or meet the mood in a way that keeps participants relaxed and alert, steady, and comfortable.

## IN SUMMARY

In skillful groups, the participant's individual identity and creativity emerge within the context of the group and not separate from the whole. Groups are often smarter than the smartest people in them, so chasing the expert is not as wise as creating wise groups.

Over the course of the book, we've explored our holistic view, the twin roles of teaching and facilitating, and the three keys of creating safe space, inviting full participation, and attending to challenges. We've outlined these essential leadership skills: listening, reflecting, encouraging, questioning, intervening, and clearing. The most important skill as an embodied leader is your presence.

In the final chapter, we'll explore ways to maintain, sustain, and improve your work, as well as how leading workshops can fit into a larger portfolio of services that you can offer.

---

**Putting it into Practice:**
**Journal Prompts**

- Which of the four seasons challenges you most?
- Name one or two facilitation tools or practices that you can use for your most challenging season.
- Which phase of the group process do you think is the most critical? Why?

---

Figure 17.6 Putting it into Practice: Journal Prompts

# Robin's Story

# From Recovering Shy Person to Workshop Leader

Chapter 18 is about how you can make workshops a bigger part of your work in the world, how you can continue to improve, and how you can sustain your energy and motivation through self-care. Robin's story shows us how one workshop leader overcomes her fear and debilitating social anxiety. She learns to walk by faith, taking small, brave steps to achieve her dream of creating and delivering workshops.

*I*'ve suffered from social anxiety for years. I cried from fear and shame any time I had to speak out loud. My journey from debilitating shyness to workshop leader is still mind-boggling to me. I started at square one with no public speaking or workshop experience. I didn't know how I was going to achieve my goal of creating and delivering workshops. It was just a vague dream.

I love people! I love helping them live happy, healthy lives. I love being surrounded by other healers, yogis, and inspiring achievers. But speaking out loud? That was quite another thing.

I can vividly recall what it was like for me when I was asked to introduce myself in a workshop:

*Everyone seems so relaxed and open. I should be feeling excited, looking forward to a wonderful opening session of this weekend workshop. But my heart is pounding. My blood pressure is rising. Panic is setting in as my turn to introduce myself gets closer and closer. Blood pounds in my head. I try to coach myself. Use the tools. Take a deep breath. I'll be okay. I can do this. And then, when my turn comes, verbal vomit. I'm overcome by shame.*

This was true until recently. Deciding to take workshop-leadership training was my turning point, and becoming certified as a transformational workshop leader has been the most empowering journey I've ever embarked on. I was hoping to simply be inspired by being in the company of experienced workshop leaders. But what I found was so much more.

Through the leadership training and personal coaching from one of the leaders, I started to have faith in my authentic voice in groups. I learned how to self-regulate by breathing, relaxing, and watching without judging. I reconnected to myself in anxious moments with my new mantra: *Everything I need is already on board.* I learned how to sit with my discomforts and name them while acknowledging my gifts. As it turns out, there were many of both!

I found I have a passion for mentoring. And you know what? I'm good at it. People like and respond to me in powerful ways. Although I dreamed of this, I never thought it possible. I've been leading healing circles now for over a year, and I developed and led my first transformational workshop—stepping into the fire and offering what I created, nurtured, planned, and showed up for. I learned that once I did it, I could do it again.

I'm thrilled by how far I've come, and as part of my certification process, I reflected on my victories in leading that first workshop:

- Recognizing the value of pausing for presence helped me and the group.

- Having a helper/assistant was invaluable in handling the unexpected so that I could attend to the program and the group.

- In the heat of the moment, I was able to flow without skipping a beat when there were outside interruptions or when a participant came late.

- Sensing the mood of the group in the moment, I offered a guided relaxation as an unplanned option.

- Remembering to pause, breathe, and deepen when I got triggered kept me present and focused.

- My timing was perfect. I promised a 90-minute workshop, and that's what I delivered.

- Holding the space for the participants while at the same time seeing the bigger picture, I saw the mystery of spirit at play.

- I showed up for myself authentically and with compassion and integrity.

- I had fun!

I've also learned that part of being a transformational workshop leader is engaging in honest self-reflection and being willing to do it differently next time. After reflecting and reviewing the participant evaluations, these are some of the things I'd like to do differently next time:

- establish better eye contact when sharing my personal stories

- get better at summarizing at the end of the workshop and reviewing what we learned

- create a stronger connection between the mind-body experiences and the purpose of the workshop

When I attend workshops now and get to share, I say calmly and truly, "Hi. I'm Robin. I'm a recovering shy person." Oddly, I'm soothed by sharing this truth. And it seems to help others come forward with their own vulnerabilities. My heart beats slower. My eyes get teary. All is well.

I've come so far, and I'm so excited by the road ahead. I'm now able to use mind-body practices to help others find clarity, purpose, and healing in their own way. I recently sent a postcard to my workshop coach that says it all: "Stay tuned. Anything is possible!"

---

This story was written by Robin Mathiesen and edited by the authors. Robin is a yoga-Ayurveda specialist and massage therapist and makes her home in Brattleboro, Vermont. You can reach her at sepiessa1@gmail.com.

# Chapter 18

# Conclusions

*When the flower opens, the bees will come.*

—Kabir

*W*orkshops, retreats, and trainings are greenhouses for healing, growing, and awakening. In this book, we've explored our model for how to co-create the conditions for transformation in a group setting. As an embodied leader, you form an intentional community by showing people new ways of being together and by engaging the whole person with mind-body experiences. In this sanctuary, a field of possibilities arises where group wisdom can emerge.

The heart of your work is who you are and your vision for what you want to see the world become. Your workshops are an expression of you. It's not a career; it's a calling. What you bring to your groups is your own journey, your personal transformation, and your presence. Robin was willing to take those first few brave steps despite debilitating fear, opening the way so she could find her gifts and fulfill her dream.

Many people feel lost in the forest of their lives. As the leader, you remind them that they are not lost. You help them find their true north, their inner compass. Your service is to create a space where people can discover that they already have everything they really need: insight and empathy.

Being a leader is a balancing act. Your twin roles are teacher and facilitator. You co-create a caring and safe space, invite full participation, and intervene when necessary to clear upsets, obstacles, and confusion. Within the workshop, everything is unfolding in a field of information and energy. You're listening for truth, reflecting the integrity that's already there, asking questions that reveal inner guidance, and encouraging participants to presence themselves.

As with any other skill, the more you do it, the better you get at it. With practice comes fluency. One way of getting better at something is to try things out and get compassionate feedback. It's invaluable to get post-workshop evaluations from your participants, and if you team-teach, your colleagues can give you feedback. Debrief on your own or with your team, identifying what worked well and what could have gone better, so that you can improve the next workshop. As Robin did, start with what went well, savoring the good.

---

**Tips for Continual Improvement**

- Compile your handouts into a workbook or manual so that you're not juggling individual handouts.
- Give your pre-workshop survey online so that you can easily reuse it each time.
- Keep a file of experiences, ideas, and quotes that you can go to when designing mind-body experiences.
- Make notes in your agenda during the workshop, and review them after the workshop for lessons learned.

---

Figure 18.1 Tips for Continual Improvement

If you're in this field, you care about people and want to make a difference. How can you serve without getting depleted? Consider one leader's experience:

> When I first started leading workshops, I couldn't possibly imagine ever being disillusioned or growing tired of it. I was so enamored that I thought I had it made. I'm not sure when my own practice began to suffer, but I gradually became aware that it was more about not disappointing my participants than about meeting my own needs. I was tired, and my mood began to flatline. In my urge to please, I gave so much to my workshops that I had very little left for me. I was giving all my energy away.

Remember to nourish yourself with practices that restore you. Know when to take a break. Before a workshop, unclutter your mind so you're not coming in too full.

Burnout can happen more quickly when you're teaching solo. It's hard to do everything by yourself. There are benefits to teaching with a partner or a team. If you plan to co-teach or team-teach, find someone who shares your vision and complements your style. A partner will bring her own life story and skill set to the workshop, and the interplay between the leaders can add texture and depth to the group dynamic. Good chemistry with your team is essential. When the staff bonds, the group will "get it" and surpass ordinary limits.

Remember, the primary unit of experiential learning is the dyad, or pair sharing. What do you do if you have an odd number of people in your group? As Robin discovered, having an assistant was invaluable. Without an assistant, each time you ask an odd-numbered group to pair-share, you have to be both leader and participant. An assistant frees you up to lead and see the big picture. She can manage logistics, respond to last-minute needs, set up the room, and take care of technology. You don't always need to pay for an assistant. You can offer that role to someone who's taken your workshop and who wants to deepen their own work.

Be clear with your assistant, partner, or team about all roles and responsibilities. Designate the lead teacher, or prime mover, for each session of the workshop, as well as who is in a supporting role and how they will serve the goal of the session. Trust your partners. If your co-leader is the prime mover for a session, don't step on her toes, even if you think you could do it better.

---

### Discussion Points for You and Your Co-Leader

- Does each co-leader understand the time he or she is allotted, and is it okay for the co-leader to give signals if time limits are being pushed?

- Is it okay for the co-leader to speak up and add to what the prime mover is saying? If so, do you need further clarification on how and when this is done?

- Does the co-leader participate in activities with the group members? Is her role to assist?

- Is it okay for the co-leader to take a break and leave the room for the session, or do you want all leaders present and contributing to the energy at all times?

Figure 18.2 Discussion Points for You and Your Co-Leader

---

There are many ways to serve people and fulfill your passion and vision. Workshops can be part of a bigger portfolio. For instance, you can complement your workshops with other services, such as coaching, consulting, writing, and online programs. Coaching one-on-one gives you immediate feedback about how you're meeting needs and what might work experientially in your group work. Consulting with individuals and organizations helps you understand the challenges of groups and teams related to your field. Writing can take many forms (newsletters, blogs, articles, or books) and helps you get clear about your concepts, models, and approaches. Online programs can reach more people with fewer overhead expenses to you.

How do you get people to come to your workshops? Many people struggle with marketing: *I don't have the knowledge or skills to market. I don't have the money to market effectively. I have no idea where to start. I feel "icky" when I promote myself or my work.*

The key to marketing is to connect with people and build relationships. Be authentic and true. If they trust and like you, they will be more likely to come to your workshop. Marketing is not manipulation. It's about communicating the value that you offer to the people who will benefit. Be clear about what your workshop is and what it isn't. Explain what participants will experience in the workshop and what they will take away.

What does it take to stay true to your calling and put yourself out there? Richard Miller says it pays off to stay aligned with your intentions. "Listening to and remaining in harmony with the inner voice has stood me in good stead. Then, I knocked on a lot of doors with incredible patience and persistence, never knowing where or when fruit would bear. I just had faith."[49]

If you're just starting out, practice honing your craft at local libraries, community centers, adult education programs, yoga studios, and spiritual organizations. These venues are often looking for programs that will enrich the people in their communities and further their mission.

If you're pitching your workshop to a larger retreat center, they will want to know your teaching experience, your track record of being able to draw participants, and your marketing platform (mailing list and/or social media following).

As you develop a marketing plan, be in conversation with your community. Look at how other people are teaching what you teach. Align your words and images with the *why* of what you're offering. We've included marketing and contracting resources in Appendix C.

We hope this book serves you by helping you bring your passion into the world. In pursuit of your dreams, remember what's true for you. Get in touch with your gift and what's calling you. As David Whyte says, "To have a firm persuasion in our work—to feel that what we are doing is right for ourselves and good for the world at the exact same time—is one of the greatest triumphs of human existence." When you're following your path, you naturally take the right action. This sets up a field of energy that supports you. Follow the call and the way will open up.

# Acknowledgments

*T*his book would not have been possible without the entire Kripalu community. From the first train-the-trainer program in the 1990s (Secrets of Powerful Experiential Workshops) to the current series (Designing and Leading Transformational Workshops, Facilitating Transformational Workshops, and Creating Transformational Workshops), Kripalu has been a supportive and creative environment for developing curricula and fostering leaders in the craft of mind-body teaching.

We would like to recognize the directors of the original Secrets workshop—Alison Shore Gaines, Rasmani Deb Orth, Atma Joanne Levitt, Megha Nancy Buttenheim, and others. Their early work gathered and developed foundational teaching practices that have since become readily available to others. In 1998, Ken began directing the Secrets program under the supervision of Rasmani Deb Orth. Later, as a Kripalu scholar-in-residence, Ken revised and expanded the training materials with the support of Stephen Cope, currently a Kripalu scholar emeritus. Our thanks also go to Maureen O'Reilly, Adrea Mach, and Eileen Daily for helping to develop early versions of the workshop manual.

Our gratitude goes to Kripalu's CEO, Barbara Vacarr; the senior leadership team; the board of directors; and current and former senior teachers at Kripalu, including Thomas Amelio, Susie Arnett, Maya Breuer, Yoganand Michael Carroll, Stephen Cope, Diana Damelio, Vidya Carolyn Delluomo, Danna and Richard Faulds, Kate and Joel Feldman, Sudhir Jonathan Foust, Aruni Nan Futuronsky, Shantipriya Marcia Goldberg, Devarshi Steven Hartman, Sita Deborah Howard, Grace Jull, Rebecca Kronlage, Sudha Carolyn Lundeen, Richard Michaels, Richard Miller, Bhavani

Lorraine Nelson, Todd Norian, Rudy Pierce, Arti Roots Ross, Don and Amba Stapleton, and Ila and Dinabandhu Sarley. They are committed to creating an awakened, compassionate, and connected world and helping people realize their full potential as they learn to apply the principles of yoga on and off the mat.

We are grateful to the individuals who offered personal stories in this book—Erica Conway, Hisla Bates, Beth Charbonneau, Meira Alper, Vivian Geffen, Katie Jay, Lauren Behrman, Robin Mathiesen, and those who chose to remain anonymous. Their honesty and willingness to share their own journey is an inspiration to us.

We want to acknowledge Lisa Nelson and Angela Wilson for their expertise in reviewing and editing Appendix A (Research and Theory Behind Mind-Body Teaching) and to Meira Alper, Lisa Love, and Aron Steward for their contributions to Appendix B (A View Toward Trauma-Informed Workshops).

Thank you to our beta readers for reviewing early manuscripts of the book: Meira Alper, Lisa Anderson, Amanda Carpenter, Erica Conway, Jen Harry, Paul Heumiller, Kathy Leblanc, and Lisa Love. Their dedication to and passion for their calling is awesome!

We are also indebted to our launch team—a group of graduates from our programs who committed to helping us get this into the hands of readers.

As a team, we deeply appreciate each other as friends and colleagues, and for the unique contributions that we all bring to our work together. In 2004, Lesli Lang joined Ken to co-lead the training programs and enhance the teaching curriculum. Jim White joined the teaching team in 2010, and Liz Korabek-Emerson in 2014. They bring to the work their backgrounds in mind-body science (Jim) and mindfulness (Liz). David Ronka joined the team in 2015 and led a six-year process of integrating and synthesizing our models and theory of action, revising the program curriculum, and producing this book.

Finally, each of us wishes to thank our partners and families who support us personally in our calling.

Ken Nelson, David Ronka, Lesli Lang, Liz Korabek-Emerson, and Jim White
www.life-changingworkshops.com

# About the Authors

**Ken Nelson, PhD,** is dedicated to helping people heal, grow, and awaken with mind-body practices and the wisdom traditions. He has offered transformational workshops worldwide since 1975. He directs a leadership training program serving presenters who want to offer dynamic, holistic, and interactive workshops, retreats, and trainings. Ken enjoys mentoring leaders and consulting with health and wellness organizations. He is known for teaching accessible, beginner-friendly yoga, qigong, meditation, and bodywork. Ken is a cross-disciplinary innovator, originating programs such as Slow Yoga & Qigong, Thai-Shiatsu Bodywork, and Healthy Aging: The Wisdom Years. His CD, *Yin Yoga*, and DVD, *Qigong & Taiji for Healing & Vitality*, are Kripalu best sellers. Ken is a former Fulbright lecturer, and a longtime Kripalu faculty member and scholar-in-residence. He holds a doctorate in interdisciplinary studies from Tulane University. (www.powerfulworkshops.com)

**David Ronka, EdM**, is passionate about helping those who feel called to bring their work to the world via workshops and retreats. He does this through coaching, training, writing, and consulting. Drawing from his diverse experience as teacher, management consultant, life coach, civil engineer, Naval officer, musician, and artist, David helps workshop leaders create logical learning structures that help creativity, spontaneity, and personality thrive. He is the author of *The Flipside of Fear* and holds a master's degree from Harvard in teaching and learning. (www.davidronka.com and www.learningexperiential.com)

**Lesli Lang, BA**, is a truth seeker and brings to her work a lifelong exploration of esoteric knowledge, meditation, yoga, and the expressive and healing arts. She is committed to supporting people in their quest for authenticity, creative freedom, and full self-expression. Drawing on her experience as a creative producer in New York City and in business theater and multimedia communications, Lesli is able to keep the big picture in mind while attending to the details. She grew up in Zimbabwe and has a Bachelor of Arts from Rhodes University, South Africa.

**Liz Korabek-Emerson, MFA**, is a certified mindfulness teacher, wellness coach, theater artist, and owner of Korabek Training. She is dedicated to creating opportunities for people to connect to their inherent wisdom, confidence, and compassion, helping them to become more resilient in their workplaces, families, and communities. She holds a Master of Fine Arts in theater from Ohio University and brings over 30 years of theater experience to creating mindfulness-based programs that are insightful and empowering. She is also on the faculty of New Hampshire Technical Institute's Mindful Communications program and is co-creator of the Fiercely Human Workshops for businesses. (www.korabektraining.com)

**Jim White, MA**, is an organization development consultant, leadership trainer, and neuroscience enthusiast who is passionate about translating behavioral-science breakthroughs into actionable practices for individuals, groups, and teams. He has provided technical assistance and workshops in 22 countries, served as director of training for the Peace Corps, assisted NASA in the integration of somatic practices into their staff development programs, and teaches principles of neuro-leadership at the University of Maryland, Baltimore County. He has taught ballroom dancing and, in his leisure, herds two cats. He holds a master's degree from the Maryland University of Integrative Health in transformational leadership and social change.

# Research and Theory
# Behind Mind-Body Teaching:
# A Brief Overview

*M* ind-body practices are receiving increased scientific interest, and research in neuroscience and psychology, in particular, is starting to point to how mind-body practices work in individuals and groups. For a bit of perspective, it was in the late 1960s that Herbert Benson coined the phrase "relaxation response" to describe physiological changes that occur with meditation. But public acceptance of the mind-body connection came many years before science acknowledged it. It wasn't until 1994 that complementary medicine had finally come far enough for Herbert Benson to found the Mind/Body Medical Institute at Harvard University. Today, mind-body practices provide the self-care aspect of a three-legged model of medicine, which also includes surgery and pharmacology.[50]

We've divided this survey of the research behind mind-body practices into two sections: how the research informs what's happening within our *individual workshop participants* and how it informs what's happening in terms of the *group formation and process*. Mind-body science is still in its infancy, so our approach is necessarily a modest exploration. However, we believe that research is beginning to suggest that mind-body integration and relational integration are at least partially responsible for the profound changes we see in transformational workshops.

---

[50] Brower V. (2006). Mind-body research moves towards the mainstream. *EMBO Reports*, *7*(4), 358–361. doi:10.1038/sj.embor.7400671

## INDIVIDUAL PARTICIPANTS: MIND-BODY INTEGRATION

All human learning begins with and is shaped by our experiences. Our brains are wired to change and grow through life experience. This is what science calls *experience-dependent neuroplasticity*—the capacity of mental activity to change neural structure.[51] Far from being static or fixed, the brain is a dynamic organ that is constantly wiring and rewiring itself and creating new neural pathways, like water gently reshaping the landscape. Learning from experience is encoded into the brain's neural circuitry by the twin mechanisms of conditioning and neuroplasticity. *Conditioning* is how the brain learns and stabilizes patterns of response through repeated experience. *Neuroplasticity* is the brain's ability to transform itself physically, alter learned responses, and connect them in new ways.[52]

As we wrote earlier, for better or worse, experience drives the changes. Another way of saying this is that what you practice grows stronger. With practice, "passing states become lasting traits."[53] But brain-based studies demonstrate that just having positive experiences is not enough. We need to engage actively and to participate consciously in weaving them into our emotional memory in order to reshape old, unhelpful behavior and to free the mind—"pulling weeds and growing flowers," in the words of author and psychologist Rick Hanson.[54]

Conditioning and neuroplasticity therefore work together to change patterns of behavior, as attention is deliberately directed by the individual. By placing your attention where you want it, keeping it there, and redirecting it away from negative preoccupations such as self-criticism and mental agitation, you can literally change your brain, your mind, and your life for the better through *self-directed neuroplasticity*.[55]

This capacity to actually change the brain through self-directed changes in attention was demonstrated by neuroscientist Sara Lazar in her study of 16 novices participating in an eight-week mindfulness meditation course. Study participants practiced

---

[51] Fu, M., & Zuo, Y. (2011). Experience-dependent structural plasticity in the cortex. *Trends in Neurosciences, 34*(4), 177–187. doi:10.1016/j.tins.2011.02.001

[52] See, for example, Graham, L. (2013). *Bouncing back: Rewiring your brain for maximum resilience and well-being.* New World Library.

[53] Hanson, R., & Hanson, F. (2018). *Resilient: How to grow an unshakable core of calm, strength, and happiness.* Harmony.

[54] Hanson, R. (2013). *Hardwiring happiness: The new brain science of contentment, calm and confidence.* Harmony.

[55] Cramer, S. C., Sur, M., Dobkin, B. H., O'Brien, C., Sanger, T. D., Trojanowski, J. Q., . . . Vinogradov, S. (2011). Harnessing neuroplasticity for clinical applications. *Brain: A Journal of Neurology, 134*(6), 1591–1609. doi:10.1093/brain/awr039

for an average of 27 minutes per day and reported decreased feelings of stress as a result. Lazar measured the brain cell volume of these subjects and found an increase in gray matter in the hippocampus and frontal cortex (areas associated with emotion regulation and self-referential processing), as well as a significant decrease in size of the amygdala (an area associated with anxiety) at the end of the course. Lazar, in a follow-up study, showed that the feelings of reduced stress endured over time, suggesting long-term changes in traits and not just passing states.[56]

The possibility of reinventing ourselves by awakening the brain's attention processors is having profound effects. Norman Doidge, in *The Brain That Changes Itself* and *The Brain's Way of Healing*, offered case studies of people who were able to heal themselves by changing the ways their bodies and brains processed sensations and movement through interventions using sensory inputs (or energy), including light, sound, electricity, vibration, movement, and thought itself. Most of the techniques Doidge illustrated use both energy and thought. Energy paired with the mind is familiar to people who practice traditional Eastern medicine and is also found in the Eastern traditional practices of yoga, tai chi, qigong, meditation, and chanting.

Understanding that the brain can change its own structure and function through thinking, learning, and acting has revolutionized learning enhancement in many fields and disciplines. Doidge calls the practitioners, scientists, and teachers of this new science of changing brains "neuroplasticians." He states that "The neuroplastic revolution has implications for, among other things, our understanding of how love, sex, grief, relationships, learning, addictions, culture, technology, and psychotherapies change our brains."[57]

Transformational workshops can play a role in this rewiring process by providing participants with opportunities to consciously think, learn, and act. For example, as leaders we can help our participants direct their attention to noticing how moving and breathing affects how they think and feel, and conversely, how they think and feel affects how they move and breathe.

Directing attention inward, or *interoception,* is a mechanism for self-directed neuroplasticity. Interoception leads to *embodiment*—being fully present in your body. When embodied, we sense the body's signals and can self-regulate to restore balance.

---

[56] Hölzel, B. K., Carmody, J., Vangel, M., Congleton, C., Yerramsetti, S. M., Gard, T., & Lazar, S. W. (2011). Mindfulness practice leads to increases in regional brain gray matter density. *Psychiatry Research, 191*(1), 36–43. doi:10.1016/j.pscychresns.2010.08.006

[57] Doidge, N. (2008). *The brain that changes itself: Personal triumphs from the frontiers of brain science.* Penguin. See also Graham, L. (2013). *Bouncing back: Rewiring your brain for maximum resilience and well-being.* New World Library.

For example, our sensation of thirst motivates us to drink water. As yoga therapist, clinical psychologist, and author of *Yoga for Emotional Balance* Bo Forbes says, "many illnesses—anxiety, depression, gut disorders, eating disorders, and more" can be thought of as "diseases of disembodiment."[58] In addition, it is helpful to be aware that the body responds to cues that the mind may be unaware of. Therefore, while scanning the body for the subtle cues of sensation, it's important to honor the wisdom of the body's natural responses rather than attempting to override or ignore what the body is telling us.

Interoception is one mechanism behind *self-regulation*, which is important in counteracting the stress response, also known as *fight-or-flight*. The fight-or-flight response evolved as a survival mechanism, enabling us to react quickly to life-threatening situations, but we can't heal well or learn well when the nervous system is overly aroused. Self-regulation is mediated by the autonomic nervous system (ANS), which has two branches—the sympathetic system and the parasympathetic system. While the arousing sympathetic side of the ANS is the accelerator, the calming parasympathetic side is the brakes. The parasympathetic system has been called the "rest-and-digest" or "calm-and-connect" system because it dampens the fear response (fight-or-flight). Self-regulation is enhanced when we become aware, through interoception, of sympathetic hyperarousal and when we consciously engage the parasympathetic nervous system to restore balance.[59]

Although chronic sympathetic hyperarousal has adverse effects under perceived danger of threat, the sympathetic system also governs activated responses of engagement, heightened awareness, relaxed alertness, and excitement. These milder aspects of the sympathetic system's response continuum are conducive to optimal learning environments.[60] Through self-regulation, you can learn to downshift from "bad stress" to "good stress" (which is also called *eustress*).

Here, mind-body practices can help. Researchers are looking for frameworks to study the neural mechanisms of change that mind-body practices have in our ability

---

[58] Forbes, B. (2015). Interoception: Mindfulness in the body, *LA Yoga*. http://boforbes.com/ wp-content/uploads/2015/08/MayLAYoga_Page56.pdf. See also Zatti, A., & Zarbo, C. (2015). Embodied and exbodied mind in clinical psychology. A proposal for a psycho-social interpretation of mental disorders. *Frontiers in psychology*, 6, 236. doi:10.3389/ fpsyg.2015.00236

[59] Harvard Medical School. (2018). Understanding the stress response: Chronic activation of this survival mechanism impairs health. *Harvard Health Publishing*. https://www. health.harvard.edu/staying-healthy/understanding-the-stress-response

[60] See also McGonigal, K. (2016). *The upside of stress: Why stress is good for you, and how to get good at it.* Avery.

to self-regulate. Current research suggests that mind-body practices cultivate our capacity for self-regulation using both top-down and bottom-up processing. *Top-down processing* emphasizes cognition and refers to the use of focused attention, concentration, mental energy, and self-reflection to consciously evaluate our thoughts or behaviors. *Bottom-up processing* emphasizes embodiment, or the input of bodily sensations into our experience. Practices such as mindful movement and breathing exercises aid in self-regulation by promoting balance between the parasympathetic and sympathetic branches of the ANS.[61]

In particular, breathing patterns impact mood, emotion control, stress, attention, and body awareness by calming or arousing the nervous system. For millennia, Eastern traditions have used breathing practices for concentration, vitality, longevity, and as a spiritual practice. Meditation, yoga, tai chi, qigong, and other stress-reducing practices teach that focusing on the breath can have positive effects on the body and mind.

Recent research supports a link between breathing patterns and thoughts, feelings, and behaviors. For instance, Zaccaro et al. suggest that various breathing strategies may be a useful tool to help people to manage their thoughts, moods, and experiences.[62] Your breathing slows and deepens naturally when you are at rest, feel calm and safe, or engage in a pleasant endeavor. Slow breathing engages the parasympathetic nervous system, which produces a relaxing effect. In fact, simply paying attention to the breath diverts and slows down thinking and eases stress and negative emotions by activating the executive functions of the brain.[63] Conversely, your breathing speeds up and becomes shallower when you are frightened, in pain, tense, or uncomfortable. This stimulates the sympathetic nervous system to respond to the challenge with heightened awareness and in anticipation of a fight-or-flight reaction to stress.

Russo, Santarelli, and O'Rourke have shown that slow breathing at approximately six to 10 breaths per minute appears to be optimal in enhancing stress resilience.

---

[61] Gard, T., Noggle, J. J., Park, C. L., Vago, D. R., & Wilson, A. (2014). Potential self-regulatory mechanisms of yoga for psychological health. *Frontiers in Human Neuroscience*, (8) https://doi.org/10.3389/fnhum.2014.00770

[62] Zaccaro, A., Piarulli, A., Laurino, M., Garbella, E., Menicucci, D., Neri, B., & Gemignani, A. (2018). How breath-control can change your life: A systematic review on psycho-physiological correlates of slow breathing. *Frontiers in Human Neuroscience*, *12*, 353. doi:10.3389/fnhum.2018.00353

[63] André, C. (2019, January 15). Proper breathing brings better health. *Scientific American*. https://www.scientificamerican.com/article/proper-breathing-brings-better-health/

Further research is needed to determine the ideal ratios of inhalation and exhalation.[64]

Individuals processing mind-body experiences often become more aware of their default modes of thinking, or default mode network (DMN), which affect mood, emotions, and behavior. The DMN is active during passive rest and mind wandering, which usually involves thinking about others, thinking about oneself, regretting the past, or worrying about the future. We often see this default mode show up as internal voices or stories in the mind related to identity. Negative events tend to have a greater psychological impact than positive experiences of the same magnitude, which is called the *negativity bias*. As leaders, we can help our participants become aware of this tendency and encourage self-kindness and compassion.

Mindfulness and meditation provide workshop participants with practices for becoming more aware of their DMN and habitual ways of thinking. Mindfulness training appears to help individuals divert thoughts from self-chatter and the obsessive preoccupation with thoughts about *me*. Mindfulness appears to enhance the ability to shift from the *narrative mode* (negative thoughts relating to past experiences or future worries) to the *experiential mode* (present-moment bodily sensations and sense experiences) and other levels of experience.[65]

To summarize, current research suggests that the brain adapts by changing itself through neuroplasticity; that interoception leads to self-regulation, which allows us to manage our own behavior, emotions, and thoughts, in accordance with the demands of the situation; and that mindful attention helps us limit internal chatter and become more embodied.

What, then, is an overall framework that includes these underlying mechanisms for self-transformation? Harvard researcher David Vago put forth a neurobiological model that seeks to explain this. He describes transformation as a reduction in suffering through an increased awareness of the conditions that cause (and remove) distortions and biases of the mind. Vago's model, S-ART, is named after its three key ingredients: self-awareness, self-regulation, and self-transcendence. S-ART is described as "a way of systematic mental training that develops meta-awareness (self-awareness), an ability to effectively modulate one's behavior (self-regulation), and a

---

[64] Russo, M. A., Santarelli, D. M., & O'Rourke, D. (2017). The physiological effects of slow breathing in the healthy human. *Breathe*, *13*(4), 298–309. doi:10.1183/20734735. 009817

[65] Farb, N. A., Segal, Z. V., Mayberg, H., Bean, J., McKeon, D., Fatima, Z., & Anderson, A. K. (2007). Attending to the present: mindfulness meditation reveals distinct neural modes of self-reference. *Social cognitive and affective neuroscience*, *2*(4), 313–322. https://doi.org/10.1093/scan/nsm030

positive relationship between self and other that transcends self-focused needs and increases prosocial characteristics (self-transcendence)."[66]

We believe that S-ART is a useful model that informs our view that the key to transformation is self-awareness. This means that as we direct participants' attention to their internal processes (interoception), they become more aware of their reactive patterns (default mode network), including their negativity bias. When we use mind-body experiences and practices, we are intentionally and holistically engaging the individual, cultivating self-awareness, and in so doing, bypassing habitual patterns and focusing on what is wanted rather than what is automatic.

When we become more aware, we have choices for how we think and act by employing the supporting mechanisms of intention and motivation.[67] In her book *The Willpower Instinct*, researcher Kelly McGonigal outlines a theory of willpower that centers on three powers: *I will*, *I won't*, and *I want*. The third power, *I want*, is much more powerful than *I will* and *I won't*. People often overlook the importance of connecting to what they really want in making behavior changes. According to McGonigal, recognizing when you're making a choice—and coming back to what you want—is the basis for continued transformation.[68] In transformational workshops, we activate this *I want* power by encouraging our participants to connect with their motivation and intentions for learning and growing.

However, being mindful of what we want doesn't always come naturally. Our minds wander. Researchers used experience sampling to interrupt people at unpredictable intervals to catch people in the act of feeling good or feeling bad in everyday life. The researchers asked the individuals what they were doing or thinking at that moment. About half the time, the attention of the mind was in the future or the past—worrying, projecting, planning, and fantasizing about the future, or ruminating, regretting, and reliving past experiences.[69]

---

[66] Vago, D. R., & Silbersweig, D. A. (2012). Self-awareness, self-regulation, and self-transcendence (S-ART): A framework for understanding the neurobiological mechanisms of mindfulness. *Frontiers in Human Neuroscience*. doi:https://doi.org/ 10.3389/fnhum.2012.00296

[67] Vago, D. R., & Silbersweig, D. A. (2012). Self-awareness, self-regulation, and self-transcendence (S-ART): A framework for understanding the neurobiological mechanisms of mindfulness. *Frontiers in Human Neuroscience*. doi:https://doi.org/ 10.3389/fnhum.2012.00296

[68] McGonigal, K. (2013). *The willpower instinct: How self-control works, why it matters, and what you can do to get more of it*. Avery.

[69] Killingsworth, M. A., & Gilbert, D. T. (2010). A wandering mind is an unhappy mind. *Science*, *330*(6006), 932. doi:DOI: 10.1126/science.1192439

Finally, storytelling sits at the heart of our team's largest unifying theory of transformation. Our brains remember stories better than they do other types of information, and the story of identity—the story of *me, my,* or *mine*—is the most powerful and enduring story we can tell ourselves and others. Ultimately, healing and learning is about our stories. In fact, *narrative medicine* is increasingly being used as a psychosocial practice for people to feel heard and understood, to build empathy, to recognize hopes, and to confront fears.[70]

Dr. Lewis Mehl-Madrona has used story as a healing modality in both clinical settings and in groups. He started asking himself this question, What is it really that healers do to help people heal? He discovered that constant immersion in stories that reinforce the notion that healing is possible actually helps people get better. In sum, hearing the right stories under the right conditions is healing. By telling and listening, we can "re-author" a new story in a collaborative setting through the power of being witnessed.[71]

In a transformational workshop, we help our participants form a coherent story that says they already have everything they really need to live fully and on purpose, and that they can heal, grow, learn, and transform.

## GROUP FORMATION AND PROCESS: RELATIONAL INTEGRATION

In terms of the group process, research in self-regulation, co-regulation, polyvagal theory, attachment theory, emotional contagion, interpersonal neurobiology, and quantum theory are beginning to shed light on how we can form functional groups and more skillfully manage their dynamics. Groups are vitally important in developing a sense of self, and functional groups have the potential to contribute to meeting our primary needs for safety, satisfaction, and connection.[72]

From the beginning of human history, fundamental needs naturally motivated humans to become good group members. The group was the source of safety, food, community, and purpose, and banishment from the group was as good as death. Self-regulation, in addition to helping us manage our internal world, helps us alter or

---

[70] Muneeb, A., Jawaid, H., Khalid, N., & Mian, A. (2017). The art of healing through narrative medicine in clinical practice: A reflection. *The Permanente Journal, 21,* 17–013. doi:10.7812/TPP/17-013 https://www.ncbi.nlm.nih.gov/pmc/articles/ PMC5638639/

[71] Mehl-Madrona, L. (2007). *Narrative medicine: The use of history and story in the healing process.* Bear & Company.

[72] Siegel, D. J. (2012). *Pocket guide to interpersonal neurobiology: An integrative handbook of the mind.* Norton.

inhibit behaviors that might put us at risk of exclusion from the group. In a review of recent social neuroscience research, Todd Heatherton cites the psychological components required for self-regulation in groups: we need to be aware of our behavior as it relates to social norms. We need to predict how others will respond to our behavior, which includes how we detect threats in complex social situations, and we need to be able to resolve discrepancies.[73] As leaders, we help our participants self-regulate so that they can co-regulate with others. Co-regulation is self-regulation in relationship—monitoring and managing your behavior while interacting with others.

*Polyvagal theory* (PVT), developed by Stephen Porges, provides insights into co-regulation and how inherently social we are as humans in the way our ANS unconsciously mediates social engagement, trust, and intimacy. PVT helps us recognize the hierarchical nature of the ANS in a more sophisticated understanding of the biology of safety and danger. PVT suggests that our most recently evolved defense against stress is our prosocial engagement system, followed by the fight-or-flight system and our most primitive dorsal vagal, the freeze-faint system. The vagus nerve (the longest cranial nerve in the body, connecting the gut, heart, and brain) mediates a subtle interplay between the visceral experiences of our own bodies and the voices and faces of the people around us. With insights from PVT, leaders can understand how vital it is to know that tone of voice, gestures, and eye contact are being interpreted unconsciously by participants. Porges calls "the subconscious detection of safety or danger in the environment" *neuroception*, which helps determine whether we feel safe or threatened in a given situation.[74]

As transformational leaders, we are seeking ways to help individuals approach and connect to a group rather than to avoid, isolate, or resist the material, the activities, the learning, and others. *Attachment theory* further describes how this happens by stressing the importance of early experiences with parents in child development.[75] It suggests that the child-parent relationship forms an "attachment style," and when the child becomes an adult, he or she then is (consciously or unconsciously) predisposed toward feeling relatively secure, avoidant, or anxious when with a group.

---

[73] Heatherton T. F. (2011). Neuroscience of self and self-regulation. *Annual review of psychology, 62*, 363–390. doi:10.1146/annurev.psych.121208.131616

[74] Porges, S. (2011). *The polyvagal theory: Neurophysiological foundations of emotions, attachment, communication, and self-regulation.* Norton.

[75] Cassidy, J., Jones, J. D., & Shaver, P. R. (2013). Contributions of attachment theory and research: A framework for future research, translation, and policy. *Development and Psychopathology, 25*(4 Pt 2), 1415–1434. doi:10.1017/S0954579413000692

Attachment theory posits that our attachment style is heavily influenced by the mother-child relationship. When a mother soothes her child and meets its needs, the child learns to regulate its own emotions, first through co-regulation with the mother and then through self-regulation. Through physical and emotional interactions, especially through the energy and information of facial expressions, sounds, words, and the eyes, the mother's mind attunes to the mind of the baby in what psychologists call *mental state resonance*. Mother and child are in "a mutual co-regulation of resonating states."[76] To the extent that this early connection with the mother was successful in meeting the baby's needs, the grown adult is more able to meet, join, and belong with others.

As leaders, we are responsible for understanding our own predispositions and for valuing the predispositions of each individual. In doing so, we are creating and maintaining an environment with a low-threat and high-reward experience to maximize the potential for learning, growth, and transformation.

Group formation and relational integration can also be understood through the lens of *mirror neurons*.[77] Mirror neurons are part of our complex systems of interconnection and can begin to explain one source of empathy, which helps us to feel what others are feeling and respond appropriately and with compassion. Daniel Goleman, known for his groundbreaking work on emotional and social intelligence, likens mirror neurons to a kind of "neural Wi-Fi network." He explains that this neural Wi-Fi observes what's happening in others—movements, emotions, intentions—and activates the same areas of the brain that are active in the other.[78]

Mirror neurons may help explain the phenomenon of *emotional contagion*.[79] Research suggests that people tend to "catch" others' emotions; that is, one person's emotions and related behaviors directly trigger similar emotions and behaviors in other people through mimicry and synchrony. As leaders, we need to be aware that we are the most "contagious" person in the group. Our own ability (or inability)

---

[76] Siegel, D. J. (2012). *The developing mind: How relationships and the brain interact to shape who we are* (2nd ed.) Guilford Press.

[77] Ferrari, P. F., & Rizzolatti, G. (2014). Mirror neuron research: The past and the future. *Philosophical Transactions of the Royal Society of London, 369*(1644). doi:10.1098/ rstb.2013.0169

[78] Goleman, D., & Boyatzis, R. (2008). Social intelligence and the biology of leadership. *Harvard Business Review, 86*(9), 74–136.

[79] Hatfield, E., Cacioppo, J. T., & Rapson, R. L. (1994). *Emotional contagion: Studies in emotional and social interaction.* Cambridge University Press.

to self-regulate in the midst of challenging or triggering situations will be passed along to our participants.

It's useful at this point to come back to polyvagal theory. PVT is being used by clinicians and trainers to better understand how individual nervous systems reach out for contact and co-regulation, in part through mirror neurons. As we scan and relate to our environment, the nervous system encounters incidents of resonance and misattunement, which are experienced as either connection or protection.[80] In other words, our participants are constantly (and unconsciously) receiving signals about safety and danger from the gut, heart, and brain that translate into a sense of connection or the need for protection.

Mind-body practices may in fact help to improve our sense of connection. Brain studies reveal that when we become absorbed in the story and experience of another, our brains begin to sync with theirs, and we begin to experience a sense of oneness or deep connection to the other. Mindful attention is key in this experience of heightened attunement.[81] Porges suggests that the PVT can help us understand the basic physiological processes that lead to social engagement or disengagement. Porges studied mind-body rituals and practices, such as meditation, listening, singing, chanting, prayer, conscious breathing, mindful postures, art, play, and gratitude. He suggests that these methods have the capacity to establish cues of emotional safety while inhibiting, or down-regulating, our stress and defensive systems by recruiting our ventral-vagal prosocial, altruistic, and compassionate behaviors. Porges explains that these rituals and practices affect the neural regulation of visceral organs (even before their cognitive top-down effects), and he emphasizes the importance of the context of safety and connection to others.[82]

*Interpersonal Neurobiology* (IPNB) is the interface of human relationships and basic biological processes and provides a unifying way to look at group dynamics and mind-body experiences. IPNB is rooted in attachment theory and refers to the

---

[80] See, for example, Dana, D. (2018). *The polyvagal theory in therapy: Engaging the rhythm of regulation.* Norton.

[81] Fredrickson, B. (2013). *Love 2.0: How our supreme emotion affects everything we think, do, feel and become.* Penguin. See also Creswell, J. D., Irwin M. R., Burklund L. J., Lieberman M. D., Arevalo J. M., Ma J., Breen E. C., & Cole S. W. (2012). Mindfulness-based stress reduction training reduces loneliness and pro-inflammatory gene expression in older adults: A small randomized controlled trial. *Brain Behavior Immunity, 26*(7), 1095–1101. https://doi.org/10.1016/j.bbi.2012.07.006

[82] Porges, S. W. (2017). Vagal pathways: Portals to compassion. In M. Seppala, E. Simon-Thomas, S. L. Brown, M. C. Worline, C. D. Cameron, & J. R. Doty (Eds.), *Oxford handbook of compassion science* (pp. 189–202). Oxford University Press.

notion that the mind is both embodied and relational. As a practical working model, it describes human development and functioning as being a product of the interaction between the body, mind, and relationships. What results is a healthy mind, integrated brain, and empathic relationships.[83]

Also called relational neuroscience, IPNB describes how the brain and mind develop and function within the interplay between genetic factors and social contexts. Dan Siegel's work, as well as advances in brain imaging, show us how interpersonal (relational) experience forms the brain's neural network, which in turn mediates our experience of relationships and the concept of self.[84] Author Stephen Cope sums it up this way: "We know that 'tuning in' to another mind, another self, another brain, is absolutely essential to the development of the self. The self is, in fact, almost entirely a social and interpersonal creation."[85]

Finally, *quantum field theory* suggests that relationships, not particles, make up the most minute levels of life. This field of relationships contains infinite potential, and what emerges in our time-space reality does so in response to the environment. Quantum field theory suggests paying attention to holism, rather than individual parts, focusing more on the interaction of relationships. The *field* in quantum field theory represents both the reality and the metaphor for the aggregate affective state (wave) created within and between our participants and ourselves (particles). This interconnected web is fostered by possibility thinking and imagination, supported by safety and inclusion, nurtured in an atmosphere of positivity, and fueled by experimentation and discovery.[86]

In our model for transformational workshops, *group wisdom* is the ultimate effect of coming together as a group. We refer to this as the *field effect*, which is the emergence of collective wisdom through shared knowledge and group synergy. The combined power of a group working together is greater than the total power of many individuals working separately. This energy of relationship is what we are cultivating in the shared relational space of a transformational workshop. This shared relational space could also be called a field of interpersonal neurobiology. In his book *The Power of Collective Wisdom and the Trap of Collective Folly*, author and sociologist Alan Briskin proposes

---

[83] Siegel, D. J. (2012). *Pocket guide to interpersonal neurobiology: An integrative handbook of the mind.* Norton.

[84] Siegel, D. J. (2012). *Pocket guide to interpersonal neurobiology: An integrative handbook of the mind.* Norton.

[85] Cope, S. (2019). *Deep human connection: Why we need it more than anything else.* Hay House.

[86] See, for example, Wheatley, M. J. (2006). *Leadership and the new science: Discovering order in a chaotic world* (Revised ed.). Berrett-Koehler Publishers.

a set of contributors to group wisdom: listening, suspending certainty, seeing whole systems, seeking diverse perspectives, respecting the discernment of others and the group, welcoming all that is arising, and trusting in the transcendent.[87] As transformational leaders, we seek to model and cultivate these practices and perspectives.

This survey merely touches the surface of how these fields of research and inquiry apply to transformation and adult learning. The science is quickly evolving, and new findings and applications are frequently being published. We're excited by the breakthroughs that are yet to come, and they will no doubt provide us with yet more tools, practices, and approaches for transformational learning.

---

This overview was reviewed and edited by Lisa Nelson, MD, family physician and director of medical education for Kripalu Center for Yoga & Health.

---

[87] Briskin, A., Erickson, S., Callanan, T., and Ott. J. (2009). *The power of collective wisdom and the trap of collective folly.* Berrett-Koehler Publishers.

# A View Toward Trauma-Informed Workshops

*I*t is important for workshop leaders to understand the nature and prevalence of trauma and its implications on workshop facilitation and design. Trauma is a subjective experience. It exists on a continuum and takes many shapes and forms. It is prudent to assume that many (if not most) people leading and participating in workshops have experienced some type of trauma or period of chronic stress in their lifetime. Some participants may be coping with severe post-traumatic stress disorder (PTSD) and complex relational trauma. This appendix provides a basic introduction for workshop leaders to the nature of trauma, its potential effects, and how to address it in a workshop setting.

Simply stated, trauma occurs whenever someone is exposed to a physical or psychological stressor that triggers a fight-or-flight or freeze-faint reaction, and at least temporarily overwhelms his or her ability to cope with or process what has happened. Common stressors that can result in trauma include medical procedures, accidents, relational abuse, extreme conflict, sexual or physical assault, war, natural disasters, neglect, and loss. How each person reacts and interprets these stressors depends on multiple factors, such as upbringing, cultural norms, and personal characteristics.[88]

---

[88] Follette, V. M., Briere, J., Rozelle, D., Hopper, J. W., & Rome, D.I. (Eds.) (2015). *Mindfulness-oriented interventions for trauma: Integrating contemplative practices.* Guilford Press.

Trauma can result from a one-time occurrence or long-term stressful situations and can seriously impair a person's ability to function with resilience and ease.

Having a history of trauma can cause the nervous system to react as if there is an immediate threat even when there is none. When this happens, the nervous system gets "hijacked" by a stress reaction, and as a result, thoughts, feelings, behaviors, and actions arise to manage the sensations and feelings that come up. The default coping strategies of one person in a workshop setting can affect the energy of the whole group and may be a disruptive influence, depending on the behavior.

Underneath coping strategies is a fundamental need to feel safe. As a workshop leader, you can minimize unintentional triggering or upsets by having group agreements in place to foster a safe and caring container for your participants. You don't necessarily need to be a trained trauma professional unless you are leading a workshop that addresses traumatic experience specifically. However, establish in your own mind the scope of your practice; that is, your comfort level and competence. What is your level of comfort and competence with trauma and big feelings? At a minimum, you need to be able to create a safe space, soothe people in distress, know your own limits, advocate for the group boundaries, and know when you need additional support.[89]

As a workshop leader, you are responsible for being sensitive to the needs of your participants and their capacity for various types of mind-body experiences. Anything can activate a participant in a workshop setting, but some things have more potential for triggering than others. Intimacy, for example, is a universal need. However, participants can only be intimate to the extent that they feel safe being vulnerable. Being seen intimately, as in eye-gazing or in revealing something personal, could be experienced as a mildly uncomfortable stretch for one person and a terrifying or shaming experience for another.

Another example is healthy touch, which is fundamental to well-being. However, because many people have a history of physical and emotional boundary violations, workshop leaders can bring awareness and sensitivity to activities where paired or group touch is involved, such as massage, partner yoga, hand holding, hugging, group sculptures, and contact improv.

The following are examples of experiences that are more likely to activate someone with a history of trauma:

---

[89] Steward, A. (2019, December). Supportive assessment and response to mental health needs [Workshop session]. *Kripalu Center for Yoga & Health*, Lenox, MA.

- sudden loud noises

- physical touch

- extreme physical activity or exercise

- hitting objects (for example, punching a pillow with fists or a bataka bat)

- loud music

- yelling or screaming

- activities in pure darkness or extreme temperatures

- physical restraint

- intense coaching

- intensive scheduling (for example, long days, prolonged sitting, standing or staying in one position, inadequate time for bathroom breaks)

In addition to these potentially triggering activities, it's never appropriate to use a participant's experience during a workshop as a teaching moment without their consent, or to call out a person's behavior in a group setting. Within our educational workshop model, it's not appropriate to deliberately expose a participant to the source of their anxiety or trauma (as in exposure-based therapies) in an attempt to heal them unless you are a trained professional.

When overwhelmed, people's ability to receive and integrate information is compromised, and in workshops, this impacts the effectiveness and benefits of mind-body experiences. To prevent overwhelm or nervous system dysregulation, you can design your workshop to balance time between instructional learning and experiential learning. You can help participants self-regulate and ground themselves by including time for quiet self-reflection, meditation, and connecting with others, especially after intense activities.

Because of the subjective nature of personal experience, always give participants the choice to opt out of a mind-body experience without judgment. In fact, the choice to opt out can even be celebrated as a way of caring for oneself and setting healthy personal boundaries.

How can you support a participant who's having a stress reaction? Your calm presence can be a resource. Simply being there and consciously breathing (and thus regulating your own response to the person's distress) may be enough. As you connect with the person, see them as whole and capable, not someone you need to fix or rescue. You can recognize the distress and validate the feelings. Use a warm, reassuring tone, and make a simple observation such as, "I can see this is hard for you.

Thank you for holding that." You can follow such observations with a gentle inquiry: "What might offer you some relief right now?" By exploring options, you are giving the person choice and agency. "I've seen people get better when breathing slowly. Do you want to breathe slowly with me, or do you think breathing slowly won't help?" "Do you want me to come closer or move farther away?" "We have a room where you can be alone, or do you want someone with you?" "Can I participate in a grounding practice with you?"[90]

If the participant is able to manage the stress reaction on their own, they will let you know and take time for self-care. Some people process better alone. Other people process better in a group or with one other person. If they wish to have another person for support, ask to see if they want you or an assistant to be with them. If they need more support, and you have an assistant or co-facilitator, decide who will accompany the individual to a quiet space outside the group. If you're leading the workshop alone, consider calling for a break. If the stress reaction is severe, immediately call for a break and seek professional medical help.

When a participant is unable to self-regulate, consider offering what you can give in the present moment:

- Give indications that you wish to support the participant to be calm and safe (e.g., "This is hard right now. And it can get better," "I'm here for you," "How can I help?" or "Can you tell me what you need?").

- Offer a grounding object for the participant to hold (e.g., a smooth stone in the palm of the hand or a soft blanket).

- Guide the participant's attention to the senses (e.g., "Feel your feet," "Feel your hands," "Notice your breathing," or "What part of your body is calm in this moment?").

- Guide the participant's attention outward (e.g., "What objects do you see in the room?" "What colors and shapes do you see?" or "What do you see out the window?").

- If appropriate and if you have permission, offer reassuring touch (e.g., offering to hold a hand in a firm, compassionate way).

Depending on the content and purpose of your workshop, it may prove helpful to inquire (as part of your pre-workshop survey, for example) whether your participants

---

[90] Steward, A. (2019, December). Supportive assessment and response to mental health needs [Workshop session]. *Kripalu Center for Yoga & Health*, Lenox, MA.

struggle with severe trauma or post-traumatic stress. You may wish to follow up with anyone who answered yes to find out what their vulnerabilities are and what strategies or resources they find most helpful. You also may be able to determine whether their needs might exceed your scope of practice. If that's the case, consider bringing a qualified assistant to the workshop or helping them make an informed choice whether to attend.

As leaders, we must question our own biases and ideas of making people healthy or seeking to improve them. Our model is not therapeutic or medical. It is based on self-inquiry. We invite individuals to be self-directed and to take responsibility for their own experience, within the bounds of the group agreements, and to choose to opt out of mind-body experiences if needed.

It is your responsibility to always follow established ethical guidelines as a leader. If you notice that participants are regularly becoming activated in your workshops, you might consider seeking counsel from other presenters with more trauma experience, to review how you are establishing and maintaining safety in the group. There's no formula for working with trauma in the workshop environment. Calm and soothe yourself first, slow down, use a low tone of voice, and listen deeply. Be present. Above all, be kind and compassionate.

## Sources for Further Study

For a further exploration of the somatic/experiential approach to the treatment of trauma relevant for experiential mind-body workshop leaders, consider the following:

Levine, P., & Frederick, A. (1997). *Waking the tiger: Healing trauma*. North Atlantic Books.

Miller, R. C. (2015). *The iRest program for healing PTSD: A proven-effective approach to using yoga nidra meditation and deep relaxation techniques to overcome trauma*. New Harbinger Publications.

Van der Kolk, B. A. (2014). *The body keeps the score: Brain, mind, and body in the healing of trauma*. Penguin.

# Appendix C

# Additional Resources

Appendix C contains additional resources that you can use to help design and refine your workshops.

These are also available for free download at www.life-changingworkshops.com.

- Checklist: Designing and Leading Your Workshop in Four Phases (Chapter 3)
- Worksheet: Transformational Learning Cycle (Chapter 5)
- Example: Pre-Workshop Survey (Chapter 7)
- Example: Exit Tickets (Chapter 7)
- Example: Evaluation Form (Chapter 7)
- Template: Workshop Agenda (Chapter 7)
- Worksheet: Messaging Your Workshop (Chapter 8)
- Example: Group Agreements (Chapter 11,16)
- Protocol: What to Do in a Crisis (Chapter 16)
- Example: Working (Behavior) Contract (Chapter 16)
- Checklist: Marketing Tips and Tools (Chapter 18)
- Checklist: Negotiating a Workshop Contract: 20 Questions (Chapter 18)
- Checklist: Logistics, Materials, and Support (Chapter 18)

## CHECKLIST: DESIGNING AND LEADING YOUR WORKSHOP IN FOUR PHASES

### I. Visioning

☐ Identify a topic for your workshop that connects with your mission.

☐ Identify your group (your participants).

☐ Describe your group (size, competence, age, gender, marital status, social/spiritual/cultural beliefs).

☐ Articulate what you think your participants need.

☐ Create a mind map of your workshop as a way of brainstorming ideas.

☐ Organize your ideas in terms of best ideas, goals and outcomes, takeaways, and promises.

### II. Designing

☐ Write your marketing copy, including title, tagline, and short blurb. (You can use the Heart-Centered Mind Map in the Appendix for this.)

☐ Design mind-body experiences that help your participants achieve the promised outcomes.

- Always consider your intention: Why are you asking them to do what it is that you're asking them to do?

- How is each mind-body experience multisensory?

- How do you include the body to help people to stay connected to their wholeness? (Consider singing, dancing, stretching, and breathing.)

- How are you using music and ritual?

- Always do each experience for yourself!

- High-value experiences let participants discover answers, encourage involvement and ownership, and create opportunities for self-revealing, opening, and giving and receiving love and acceptance.

☐ Develop a transformational learning cycle for each mind-body experience (safety, experience, integration). You can use the Transformational Learning Cycle Worksheet (see Appendix resources) for this.

- Begin each experience with clear instructions (safety).

- End each experience with enough time for integration.

  ▪ Relaxation allows energy to integrate at a cellular level.

  ▪ Sharing makes conscious what has happened (within dyads, small groups, and the whole group).

  ▪ Journaling enables reflection on paper.

  ▪ Recapping reminds participants what you did and why.

  ▪ Tools can make conscious how they can use what they are learning.

☐ Sequence the transformational learning cycles so they build to your final workshop outcomes.

- Layer the experiences, beginning with simple risk taking to inviting deeper levels of risk.
- Transitions between experiences are as important as the experiences themselves.
- What is the balance of structure versus spontaneity?
- How will you change the tempo for variety (e.g., from intense to playful)?
- How does each experience contribute to the overall workshop goals?

☐ Organize your learning sequence into a session agenda. (Identify timing, key talking points, materials, technology needs, etc.)

☐ Develop resources and handouts.

☐ Consider whether you want to offer continuing education units or credits with your workshop, and submit the required paperwork.

## III. Delivering

### Pre-Workshop

☐ Advertise/market your workshop online, to adult education programs, on community boards, at local places of worship, in coffee shops, at the local library, in relevant print publications, and with networks.

☐ Negotiate the contract (see Appendix resources).

☐ Reserve the workshop space.

☐ Provide pre-readings to the participants, if relevant.

☐ Print out all handouts.

☐ Gather all materials and supplies.

### Day of the Workshop

☐ Eat a good meal before the workshop.

☐ Mindfully prepare yourself. (Remind yourself that you can trust the transformational workshop process.)

☐ Create the right ambiance in the room for your workshop using lighting, music, and visual aids.

☐ Set out all materials, supplies, and handouts so they are ready to use.

### During the Workshop

☐ Introduce yourself.

☐ Give a welcome and overview of what the workshop is and isn't.

☐ Establish group agreements, confidentiality, and schedule.

☐ Address psycho-emotional and spiritual supports.

- Acknowledge fear and newness ("the unknown").
- Acknowledge what is present.
- Acknowledge resistance as a natural part of the process.
- Acknowledge enthusiasm, willingness, openness, acceptance, commitment, calling.
- Teach to the spectrum, and include all the voices.

☐ Consider having the group warm up to help them relax, get to know each other, and get fully present (e.g., dance, movement, yoga, personal interaction, milling about, sharing, shoulder massage, partner yoga).

☐ Identify your core teaching points (two or three points that are essential to the workshop). Refer back to these core teachings throughout your workshop.

☐ Deliver your content/experiences using the transformational learning cycle of safety, experience, and integration.

☐ Make sure to "land the plane" by leaving enough time at the end of each transformational learning cycle for integration.

☐ Include a time for closure/centering at the end of the workshop for:

- a closing ritual to center the group energy
- special awareness for safety following deeper programs
- arranging support groups and making SMART individual and group commitments
- evaluations, feedback, and reflections
- announcements about resources, handouts, and future workshops and events

## IV. Following Up

☐ Encourage your participants to:

- follow through by posting their commitments
- check in with their support group/networking
- support themselves by keeping commitments and honoring their journeys

☐ Write your own pros and cons list.

☐ Review feedback/evaluations.

☐ Modify the workshop design, resources, and/or marketing materials if needed.

☐ Stay in relationship with your group via emails, newsletters, and future programs.

# WORKSHEET: TRANSFORMATIONAL LEARNING CYCLE

## WORKSHEET: The Transformational Learning Cycle

**SAFETY 20%**

How will I cultivate physical and emotional safety? What kind of context and purpose do I offer? Are my instructions clear and understandable? Will I demonstrate or model? How will I manage the group's energy for this experience? How much time do I need for each part?

**EXPERIENCE 50%**

### SPIRIT: Ritual

*Examples: Sacred Space, Opening/Closing Invocation, Repeated Practices, Chanting*

### BODY: Embodiment

*Examples: Deep breathing, Massage, Dance, Body Scan, Mindful Movement*

### MIND: Attention Training

*Examples: Meditation, Mindfulness, Guided Imagery, Journaling*

### HEART: Inspiration

*Examples: Poetry, Music, Singing, Drumming, Drawing, Prayer*

**INTEGRATION 30%**

How will I facilitate individual and/or group processing? How will I help my participants make meaning and claim their experience? How will I help clarify what happened: facts, feelings/thoughts, insights, patterns, and action? How will I use journaling, dyads, triads, and/or large group processing?

**EXAMPLE: PRE-WORKSHOP SURVEY**

# Pre-Workshop Survey

*Please take a few moments to reflect on these questions prior to our time together. This will not only help us get to know you but also help prepare you for the workshop.*

1.  Name: _____     Email:_____

2.  How did you hear about this workshop?

3.  What aspects of this workshop most interest you?

4.  What do you hope to gain from this workshop?

5.  What is your background in the topic of this workshop?

6.  Is there anything you'd like us to be aware of in regard to your participation in this workshop?

### EXAMPLE: EXIT TICKETS

You can pre-print exit tickets or use blank index cards.

---

## Exit Ticket

What's one thing you're excited about?


What's one question you still have?

---

## Plus/Delta

| 1 Plus | 1 Delta |
|--------|---------|
|        |         |

**Verbal Instructions for the Plus/Delta:** "Please take a moment before you leave to note one positive thing (Plus) and one challenge (Delta) from this session."

**EXAMPLE: EVALUATION FORM**

# Workshop Evaluation

Please take a few moments to evaluate the workshop you have just completed. Please be as specific as possible.

1.  How did you hear about this workshop?

2.  Please rate your overall experience in this workshop:

    ☐ Excellent ☐ Above Average ☐ Average ☐ Poor

3.  What part of the workshop was most valuable to you?

4.  What areas of improvement would you identify for the workshop presenter and/or the workshop content?

5.  Would you be willing to provide a testimonial based on your experience? If so, please write below. Include your name if you're willing to be identified.

## TEMPLATE: WORKSHOP AGENDA

**WORKSHOP TITLE** _____

**SESSION TITLE** _____

**DATE** _____

| Time | Who | Experience | Description | Purpose | Materials/Setup |
|------|-----|------------|-------------|---------|-----------------|
|      |     |            |             |         |                 |

# WORKSHEET: MESSAGING YOUR WORKSHOP

## WORKSHEET: Messaging Your Workshop

**Title**
*What's the topic? Make it brief and memorable.*

**Tagline**
*What's a one-liner that would help clarify the topic/title?*

**Participant**
*Who is this workshop for? How would you describe your participants?*

**Who are your participants? What do they expect, want, and need?**

**Nugget**
*What's at the heart of the workshop? Where's the "gold?"*

**Takeaways**
*What are your promises/outcomes? What will the participants get? What are the bullet points?*

**Blurb**
*What's the workshop about? Provide more detail on the topic: your approach, methods, and techniques.*

## EXAMPLE: GROUP AGREEMENTS

**Please Note:** This sample group agreement is designed for intensive group retreats where more accountability and a deeper level of safety is needed.

**Agreements help to keep the group safe in order for everyone to get the most from their experience.** We commit to safety by valuing ourselves, other participants, and the group's purpose. Please agree to support the success of this program by honoring these guidelines in your role as a participant:

- **Take responsibility for your own experience** and be mindful of your health, rest, exercise, diet, and personal needs. Make the most of breaks to take care of yourself. Use personal time to support yourself and your purpose in being here. Bring necessary dietary items.

- **Respect confidentiality and the experiences of others.** Let others have their own experience, and commit to not commenting on or sharing about the experience of others outside of the group without permission.

- **Mindfully follow instructions** for experiences and social interactions. Respect intentional quiet time.

- **Commit to attending each of the sessions**, and alert the staff if you are unable to attend a session. Be present and on time (or early).

- **Participate** as best you can. Use the option to not participate in order to care for your own physical or other needs. If you choose to opt out of an experience, please stay in the room (if you can) and observe the ongoing experiences with respect for others. Please indicate to staff that you are taking the option to not participate.

- **Use conscious communication.** Use "I" statements to speak with responsibility for your own feelings, thoughts, words, and actions. Notice the tendency to blame, complain, or gossip, and commit to taking your questions, requests, issues, and concerns to somebody who can do something about them. Be direct with requests. **Tell the staff what you need to succeed.** Ask yourself, "Are my words true, timely, useful, helpful, and kind?" Be generous with praise.

- **Tolerate differences of opinion and alternate modes of expression.** Promise to stay in relationship despite confusion, doubt, and misunderstandings.

- **Be an explorer.** Be willing to face challenges and opportunities. Pace yourself, but allow yourself to notice when you want to stretch your limits and experience healthy change. Be open to feedback from the leaders. Relax, be yourself, enjoy, and don't take yourself too seriously.

- **Bring loose, comfortable clothing**, layered to be warm when relaxing and light for physical activity.

- **Be considerate of quiet hours and spaces**, especially if you're sharing sleeping quarters with others.

- **Use cell phones only in designated spaces.** Silence your cell phone for each program session. Do not record sessions or take pictures of others without prior consent.

- **If you have medical needs**, let the staff know in advance or at the beginning of the program. *Do not discontinue medication during the program unless you are under a doctor's orders.*

- **Smoking and the use of alcohol and recreational drugs are not permitted on the premises.**

- Because some guests may have allergies, please **use only unscented products**.

- **Couples**, consider working with individuals other than your partner in subgroups (unless this is a program specifically designed for couples).

Prepare to be surprised by a gift of transformation, renewal, growth, joy, comfort, and connection. Let yourself experience the aha moments, tipping points, light bulbs, and tectonic shifts, and share your insights appropriately. If you feel distracted, resistant, uncomfortable, negative, afraid, sad, mad, or a desire to leave, you may be on the verge of a breakthrough or a turning of the tide.

**The role of the staff** is to serve the participants by guiding the group toward meeting the program goals. We are ready to help you to create an extraordinary experience. Staff may not be trained mental health or medical professionals, and **this program is not intended to substitute medical, psychological, or drug-treatment therapy. If you need such attention, seek a licensed professional.** During physical, emotional, mental, and social activities, you may experience headaches, nausea, and physical discomfort.

**You are responsible for monitoring your own welfare and seeking help from staff when needed.**

I have read, I understand, and I agree to these guidelines.


PRINT NAME: _____


SIGNATURE: _____        DATE: _____

## PROTOCOL: WHAT TO DO IN A CRISIS

Caring for individual and group safety is our responsibility as facilitators. Since this is an educational model—not a medical or therapeutic one—it is important to know when the scope of our practice requires us to seek support, make referrals, or request group members receive more support than we can offer in our workshops. A crisis may be an illness, injury, or a group member becoming activated and behaving in a way that is violent, injurious, or unacceptable.

If a crisis happens, you as the facilitator do the following:

**1. Call the group to a stop.**

- If a participant is unresponsive or severely injured, call 911 and contact the venue supervisor.
- Ask all members to take a break, and tell the members when the group will resume.
- Take the person out of the room, or ask permission of the group to use the room privately.

**2. Do an intake interview.**

- Speak with the person privately to express your concern and to help the person feel safe.
- Determine their ability to continue as a group member.
  - "What do you need right now?"
  - "What support do you have here? What support do you have at home?"
  - "Who is a contact person or family member who can support you?"
  - "Do you take any medications? Are you taking them now?"
- If they have an active health condition or are in psychological crisis, call their emergency contact or 911.

**3. If necessary, get support.**

- Say, "We are concerned for you. We believe the best course is to get more support for you."
- If necessary, call the contact person to take the person home.
- If necessary, call for an ambulance or drive the person to a hospital.
- A co-facilitator or experienced assistant can care for the group or the person in crisis so that the group can continue with one of you as facilitator.

**4. If the person wants to stay in the group, reaffirm the group intention.**

- Say, "Our intention is to create a safe space for all of us in order to fulfill the group purpose."

- Make a working contract if necessary, specifying conditions under which the individual can return to the group (see the working contract steps at the end of this resource). If you do not feel safe making a contract, you may have to ask the person to leave the group.

- Here is one way to reaffirm both the group's intention and the person's needs: "There's a lot coming up for you. Your welfare and the group's welfare are important to us. We do not have the resources you need in this program. Because this is an educational model, not a therapeutic one, we must ask you to rely on support from a different source. We are not able to give you the support you deserve. How can we help you to get the support you need?"

**5. Document any injury, illness, criminal activity, or psychological episode.**

- Document in written form what occurred so that you can refer to it later if necessary.

- Document the behavior, all important facts, and the outcome.

- Document what the person promised to do in order to get support for themselves.

- If necessary, call a contact person to help the group member.

- Inform the venue supervisor and give them a copy of your documentation.

**6. Integrate the group and get closure using the group clearing process.**

- You and the group will need to acknowledge the event and support yourselves with a group clearing session. It's important to clear anything activated in you and in the group to feel complete and get closure.

**Working Contract: Steps in Taking Action**

Come to a shared understanding of what occurred and develop a plan of action:

1. Approach the participant privately, or, if still in the group, speak to the agreements.

2. Empathize with the symptoms ("I understand how you might be frustrated right now.").

3. Focus on the underlying cause ("Is there something else happening for you right now?").

4. Get agreement on a way forward:

    - "What might you do next? What resources do you need to act differently? What do you need help with? What will you do that will change the outcome this time? What do you choose to do that will help you face this problem in a way that moves you forward?"

- "Now we agree that the next time this happens in the group, you will [explain your understanding of the terms]. Did I get that right? Is there more? Are we agreed?"

5. You may wish to have a written contract if this behavior has been repeated. Refer to the Working Contract Example.

## EXAMPLE: WORKING (BEHAVIOR) CONTRACT

Agreements help to keep the group safe in order for everyone to get the most from their experience and to fulfill the group's purpose. They are the guidelines for group behavior and interactions. We commit to the principles of honoring all voices and allowing each person to discover for themselves what they need.

Please initial the following agreements.

_____    I agree to support the success of this program by honoring the agreements we have already established within the group.

In addition to the group agreements, I agree to the following:

_____    I will be on time for every session.

_____    I will sit within the circle and not outside of it.

_____    I will use "I" statements and speak only from my own experience.

_____    I will refrain from giving unsolicited advice, and when I notice the urge to do so, I will pause and allow the other person to share, without making comments or offering feedback.

_____    If I am dissatisfied with any aspect of the workshop, I will bring my concern to the leader or a staff member in order to resolve the issue.

I acknowledge and will abide by these agreements in order to be a respectful and valuable member of the group. I understand that failure to abide by these agreements may lead to my being asked to leave the workshop.

**SIGNATURE OF PARTICIPANT:**        **SIGNATURE OF LEADER:**

_____        _____

**DATE:**        **DATE:**

_____        _____

## CHECKLIST: MARKETING TIPS AND TOOLS

**Look for ways to network.** You never know who your next participant or partner will be.

- ☐ Join a business networking group, such as Business Network International.
- ☐ Find people who love your work and who have an interest in you. Find out where they hang out, what organizations they belong to, what they read, etc.
- ☐ People trust their friends. Encourage people who attend your events to tell their friends and to "like" your social media page. These earned impressions are invaluable.
- ☐ Where are your potential clients/participants? Who's already communicating or working with your population?
- ☐ Remember to have packets, flyers, and back-of-the-room sales at your workshops, along with an email collection list.
- ☐ Don't be afraid to seek help in the areas where you feel challenged. You never know where partnering will lead!

**Hone your message.**

- ☐ What are the needs that can be met by your product, service, or workshop? Pay particular attention to an emotional need. Effective marketing speaks to an emotional need.
- ☐ Identify the problem or the dream. What's the itch that you can scratch? Always connect your message to something that your audience is hungry for.
- ☐ Make your copy or pitch short and concise, especially for email campaigns. Write your elevator pitch and then cut it in half.
- ☐ Create a niche statement to help you and your clients/customers understand what's on offer. Here's a script you can follow: "I help [target customer] to [accomplish what?] so they can [outcome they experience]."
- ☐ Digital space is a cold environment. Warm it up with emotion. Address needs. Make your message simple, use seasonal language, create a sense of urgency, personalize, and pose (and answer) questions that are relevant for your audience.
- ☐ Use recommendations, testimonials, past publicity, press sheets, well-written copy and bios, great titles, good photos, and class descriptions.

**Build an email list** using an online service.

- ☐ Create a regular newsletter with a specific call to action.
- ☐ Don't clutter: Use one link as the call to action, with a picture and two to three sentences of text.

☐ Offer content about what your audience wants and what they value. Address their "pain points."

☐ Offer discounts for early workshop registration.

☐ Try not to send newsletters or posts on the first of the month or the couple of days following a holiday weekend. Determine when your clients are most likely to take action.

☐ Make sure to capture email addresses at every one of your events, and add those to your email list.

☐ Maintain your email list by removing undeliverable email addresses.

**Create a website** using a free platform.

☐ Do a web search for "free website builder reviews" to start exploring.

☐ Make sure your website is optimized with words that reflect your business. Search engines will be looking for whether your content matches your keywords. Search engine optimization (SEO) is a science and an art, and there are many resources for how to do this. Beware of companies that send you offers to radically maximize your search engine results. They often use "click-bait" tactics to do so. Your best bet is to do some reading or hire a local technical consultant to help you out.

☐ Make sure your website is mobile friendly. Most website builders will do this automatically.

**Advertise your events** using multiple platforms and methods.

☐ Buy an online ad for people in your geographic location. You can also further specify by gender, age, income, and other demographic factors. You can also specify how much you want to spend ($25–$50 will go a long way).

☐ Do a social media campaign. Choose your target audience (e.g., by area, interest, age, gender). Choose how many days you will run the campaign, how much to spend, and whether you are trying to reach a target audience or the public in general. (Example: A Yoga teacher spent $20 for a five-day campaign to about 1,000 people. 84 people expressed interest and 12 people liked her social media page.)

☐ Carefully consider your headline for workshops and events that you advertise online. Search engines are very literal, so if you really want a poetic title, make sure the behind-the-scenes keywords are literal. Make sure your content is authentically relevant to your title. Ask your friends for their opinion.

☐ Print media (e.g., advertising in publications) tends to be expensive and not very effective.

☐ Putting up posters in local hangouts for your events can be fruitful. Consider creating little tabs on the poster that people can tear off with the time and date of the event and/or your contact information. (You might tear one or two off before posting the poster—this can help create a sense of demand for your services.)

☐ Consider a wide range of venues for delivering your workshop: YMCAs, community centers, libraries, adult education centers, yoga studios, wellness centers, private groups, and virtual learning spaces.

☐ Consider partnering with another organization to sponsor your event.

**Build a strong web presence** by regularly offering authentic content.

☐ Use one or more social media platforms.

☐ If you like to write, start a blog and regularly offer short and valuable posts. You can use a free blogging platform. If you choose to blog, it's best to be regular about it. Posting something every week or every other week builds a virtual relationship with your audience. They come to expect it.

☐ Create a short (no more than three minutes) video of who you are and what you offer, and post it on social media.

☐ Hold a short webinar, offering a taste of the kind of service that you offer. Advertise it on social media. Webinars don't have to be geographically bound.

☐ Get your business listed on recognized review sites, and monitor them for reviews. Encourage your participants to write reviews.

☐ Consider building web-based courses if you want to introduce some sort of virtual element to your work (a blended learning model). Do a web search for "online course builder reviews" to start exploring.

☐ Use free downloadable photos to enhance emails or blog posts. Overlay a quote on a photo for a nice effect.

☐ Use a mobile app to create inspirational marketing messages.

☐ Hire a virtual assistant (starting at about $25 per hour) to manage your social media accounts (updating them with new and relevant posts).

---

Special thanks to Susie Arnett, Alison Crosthwait, Stacy Hammel, and Jimmy Hickey for helping to compile this list.

## CHECKLIST: NEGOTIATING A WORKSHOP CONTRACT WITH 20 QUESTIONS

You can use these questions as you negotiate a contract for your workshop with a host organization or venue.

### Initial Question:

1. How did you hear about me?

### About the Client:

2. Who is my client?
3. To whom am I accountable? (The senior person? The contact person? The whole group?)
4. Who will negotiate the required outcomes with me?

### About the Group:

5. What is the background of the group?
6. What is the age, gender, sexual orientation, and ethnic mix of the group?
7. Do my values and experience match the group's goals and values?
8. Has the group been consulted and agreed to accept me as a facilitator?

### About the Content:

9. What is the request?
10. What are the underlying issues that the workshop needs to address?
11. What outcomes are required?
12. What other agendas do they have? (What else do they want to accomplish?)
13. What does success look like?
14. How will success be evaluated?

### About the Contract and Logistics:

15. How much time is available?
16. Is the time already scheduled? What date?
17. Will written confirmation be provided? By whom? The written confirmation should include group, date, time, venue, agreed outcomes, performance measures, and compensation details.
18. What is the agreed-upon fee or hourly rate and terms of payment?
19. Are CEUs required?
20. How will supplementary services be provided (assistants, printing of handouts, notes, research)?

## CHECKLIST: LOGISTICS, MATERIALS, AND SUPPORT

### Preparing for the Workshop: Nuts and Bolts

Consider the following while preparing for the workshop:

- ☐ What are the needs of the sponsoring agency or host?
- ☐ What are the goals and outcomes expected?
- ☐ Who are the participants, and what do they expect?
- ☐ Will there be other principle attendees, their roles and participation?
- ☐ What support staff are available for assistance?

### Preparing Participants: Welcome Letter with Event Details

Provide a welcome letter that includes information about the following:

- ☐ with suggestions to make participants more comfortable
- ☐ letter from host or sponsoring agency
- ☐ place (address, telephone, email, fax, and map if necessary)
- ☐ arrival time
- ☐ transportation details (bus, train, routes by car)
- ☐ parking
- ☐ weather, season, and/or dress suggestions
- ☐ a schedule of times and places
- ☐ arrangements for meals, restaurants, etc.
- ☐ housing arrangements and any community resources
- ☐ advice for any special needs: journals, required books, photos
- ☐ arrangements for people with special needs
- ☐ agreements and policies (scents, smoking, drug/alcohol use)

### Checklist of Supplies and Materials

Be sure to have all you need prior to the workshop. Your list might include:

- ☐ an overview/agenda with time schedule
- ☐ handouts
- ☐ products or resources for sale
- ☐ other resources for reference (to be available for yourself/guests)
- ☐ props (music, talking stick, blankets, yoga mats, etc.)
- ☐ a flip chart and easel (extra pads if needed) or whiteboard
- ☐ marking pens (flip chart pens or whiteboard markers)
- ☐ consent forms (if using video or audio taping)
- ☐ masking tape or putty for placing flip charts on walls

- ☐ name tags
- ☐ a basket of pens, pencils, marking pens, and/or crayons
- ☐ writing boards if necessary
- ☐ blank paper or 3 x 5 cards
- ☐ refreshments, snacks, beverages, cups, napkins
- ☐ evaluations/personal reflections
- ☐ a mailing list for participants
- ☐ certificates of participation (if relevant)

## Space and Other Arrangements

Make arrangements with the contact person for the following in advance:

- ☐ contact person information (phone number, email, meeting arrangements upon arrival)
- ☐ advance arrangements with contact person for checking room and supplies
- ☐ room information about size, shape, lighting, heating, air-conditioning, and housekeeping
- ☐ arrangements for valuables (safety of personal items)
- ☐ room layout regarding seating, flip charts, technology placement
- ☐ a table for products, resources, evaluations, mailing list, etc.
- ☐ a table for refreshments and snacks
- ☐ maps/location of services (restrooms, water fountains, phones, restaurants, motels)
- ☐ permission to post on wall space
- ☐ technology needs (e.g., audio/visual) and information about who will operate or orient the facilitator to equipment
- ☐ recording arrangements, equipment, and contact person
- ☐ arrangements for people with special needs (audio, seating, sensitivities, etc.)
- ☐ arrangements for phone messages
- ☐ recycling services

# Table of Figures

# Endnotes

Where helpful for clarification, we have added footnotes directly in the text (*i, ii, iii,* etc.). Citations in Appendix A and Appendix B are listed in those sections. All other citations are listed as endnotes here.

---

[1] Pearson, C. S. (1989). *The hero within: Six archetypes we live by* (p. 51). Harper and Row.

[2] *Jata Sutta: The Tangle.* (Thanissaro Bhikkhu, Trans.). 1998. Access to Insight.
http://www.accesstoinsight.org/ tipitaka/sn/sn07/sn07.006.than.html

[3] To find out more about Richard C. Miller and the iRest program, visit www.irest.us.

[4] Siegel, D. (2012). *Pocket guide to interpersonal neurobiology: An integrative handbook of the mind.* Norton.

[5] Wilber, K. (1999). *Integral psychology.* Shambhala.

[6] Mindful Staff. (2017, January 11). Jon Kabat-Zinn: Defining mindfulness.
https://www.mindful.org/jon-kabat-zinn-defining-mindfulness

[7] Davis, D., & Hayes, J., (n.d.). What are the benefits of mindfulness?
http://www.apa.org/monitor/2012/07-08/ce-corner.aspx

[8] Hanson, R. (2016). *Hardwiring happiness: The new brain science of contentment, calm, and confidence.* Harmony Books.

[9] See, for example, Dweck, C. S. (2017). *Mindset: Changing the way you think to fulfill your potential.* London: Robinson.

[10] Susan Cooper first introduced the idea of "twin roles" in leading workshops. See Cooper, S. (1980). *Preparing, designing and leading workshops: A humanistic approach.* Van Nostrand Reinhold.

[11] The transformational learning cycle is adapted from Caine, R. N., Caine, G., McClintic, C., & Klimek, K. J. (2009). *12 brain/mind learning principles in action: Developing executive functions of the human brain* (2nd ed.). Corwin Press. See also Kolb, D. A. (1984). *Experiential learning: Experience as the source of learning and development.* Prentice Hall.

[12] Surowiecki, J. (2004). The *wisdom of crowds: Why the many are smarter than the few and how collective wisdom shapes business, economies, societies, and nations.* Abacus.

[13] Hanson, R., & Hanson, F. (2018). *Resilient: How to grow an unshakeable core of calm, strength, and happiness.* Harmony Books.

[14] Graham, Linda. (2013). *Bouncing back: Rewiring your brain for maximum resilience and well-being.* New World Library.

[15] Caine and Caine refer to the experience as "orchestrated immersion." See Caine, R.N., Caine, G., McClintic, C., & Klimek, K.J. (2009). *12 brain/mind learning principles in action: Developing executive functions of the human brain* (2nd ed.). Corwin Press.

[16] See Hanson, R. (2016). *Hardwiring happiness: The new brain science of contentment, calm, and confidence.* Harmony Books.

[17] Adapted from Khalsa, S.B.S. & Gould, J. (2012). *Your brain on yoga (Harvard Medical School guide).* RosettaBooks. See also Jahnke, R. (2002). *The healing promise of chi.* McGraw Hill. See also Wayne, P. (2013). *Harvard Medical School guide to tai chi: 12 weeks to a healthy body, strong heart, and sharp mind.* Harvard Health Publications.

[18] Russo, M. A., Santarelli, D. M., & O'Rourke, D. (2017). The physiological effects of slow breathing in the healthy human. *Breathe, 13*(4), 298–309. doi:10.1183/20734735.009817.

[19] Brown, Richard P., & Gerbarg, Patricia L. (2012). *The healing power of the breath.* Shambhala. See also Appendix A.

[20] Jensen, Eric. (2005). Movement and learning. In *Teaching with the brain in mind* (2nd Edition). Association for Supervision and Curriculum Development. http://www.ascd.org/publications/books/104013/chapters/ Movement-and-Learning.aspx

[21] This table is based loosely on Bloom's Taxonomy of Educational Objectives, a popular model in the field of education for describing different levels of learning.

[22] Caine, R. N., Caine, G., McClintic, C., & Klimek, K. J. (2009). *12 brain/mind learning principles in action: Developing executive functions of the human brain* (2nd ed.). Corwin Press.

[23] From personal interview between Ken Nelson and Sudhir Jonathan Foust.

[24] See, for example, Jones, J. E., & Pfeiffer, J. W., (Eds.). *The 1980 annual handbook for group facilitators.* Pfeiffer & Co.

[25] Whyte, D. (2002). *Crossing the unknown sea: Work as a pilgrimage of identity.* Riverhead Books.

[26] There are variations of the SMART goals model. It was first articulated by George Doran in Management Review (Nov. 1981) and has been expanded upon by Peter Drucker, Paul Meyer, and others. There are resources in print and on the Internet about SMART goals.

[27] Fisher, H. E. (2017). *Anatomy of love: A natural history of mating, marriage, and why we stray.* Norton.

[28] Harden, J., & Dude, B. (2009). *What makes you tick and what ticks you off: How the basic elements of temperament will lead you to a happier life.* Shadow Stone Publishing.

[29] These lists were adapted from Harden and Dude (2009). Used with permission.

[30] Killingsworth, M. A., & Gilbert, D. T. (2010). A wandering mind is an unhappy mind. *Science, 330*(6006), 932. https://doi.org/10.1126/science.1192439

[31] The metaphor of "riding the wave" comes from the Kripalu tradition.

[32] Mehrabian, A. (1971). *Silent Messages* (1st ed.). Wadsworth.

[33] Adapted from Cooper, S. (1980). *Preparing, designing and leading workshops: A humanistic approach.* Van Nostrand Reinhold.

[34] Adapted from Heron, J. (1999). *The complete facilitator's handbook*. Kogan Page.

[35] Cope, S. (2015). *The great work of your life: A guide for the journey to your true calling*. Bantam.

[36] This model is adapted from the Center for Nonviolent Communication[SM]. Visit www.cnvc.org to learn more.

[37] Rizzolatti, G., & Craighero, L., (2004). The mirror-neuron system. *Annual Review of Neuroscience, 27*:1, 169-192.

[38] Blakeslee, S. (2006, January 10). Cells that read minds. *The New York Times*. https://www.nytimes.com/ 2006/01/10/science/cells-that-read-minds.html.

[39] The three-part appreciation comes from The Center for Nonviolent Communication[SM]. Visit www.cnvc.org to learn more.

[40] Adapted from Rick Hanson's model. See, for example, Hanson, R. (2018). *Resilient: How to grow an unshakable core of calm, strength, and happiness*. Harmony.

[41] McGonigal, K. (2016). *The upside of stress: Why stress is good for you, and how to get good at it*. Avery.

[42] Dan Siegel describes a similar method as "connect and redirect" and also "name it to tame it." See Siegel, Dan. (2011) *The whole-brain child: Revolutionary strategies to nurture your child's developing mind*. Mind Your Brain, Inc. and Tina Payne Bryson Creative Productions, Inc.

[43] Winnicott, D. W. (1973). *The child, the family, and the outside world*. Penguin.

[44] See Wilkinson, M. (2012). *The secrets of facilitation: The SMART guide to getting results with groups* (2nd ed.). Jossey-Bass.

[45] Lewin, K., and G. W. Lewin (Eds.) (1948). *Resolving social conflicts: Selected papers on group dynamics*. Harper & Brothers. See also the Research Center for Group Dynamics. (2019). *History*. Institute for Social Research at the University of Michigan. http://rcgd.isr.umich.edu/history/

[46] Porges, S. (2011). *The polyvagal theory: Neurophysiological foundations of emotions, attachment, communication, and self-regulation*. Norton & Company.

[47] Bruce Tuckman characterized the stages of a group as forming, storming, norming, and performing. His model is often used to describe teams in project-based work. See Tuckman, B. W. (1965). Developmental sequence in small groups. *Psychological Bulletin, 63*, 384–399. https://doi.org/10.1037/h0022100.

[48] Oberg, K. (1960). Cultural shock: Adjustment to new cultural environments. *Practical Anthropology, os-7*(4), 177–182. https://doi.org/10.1177/009182966000700405

[49] From training with Richard Miller, 2013. To find out more about Richard C. Miller and the iRest program, visit www.irest.us.